IMAGES
of America

KANKAKEE
1853–1910

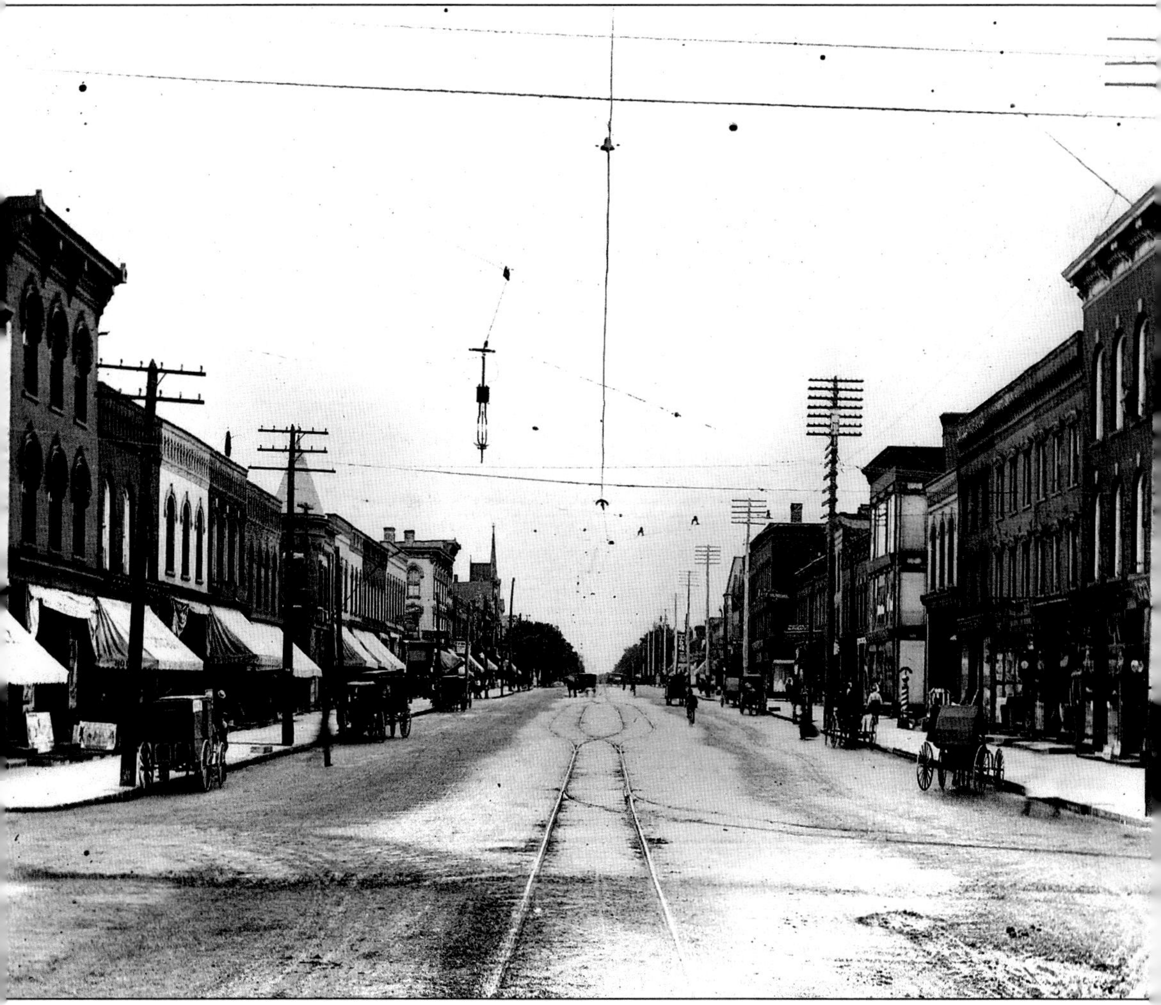

This image shows the City of Kankakee's main street at the beginning of the 20th century. This 1900 photograph was taken from East Avenue looking down Court Street. Horse-drawn vehicles can be seen on either side of the street, yet running down the center of Court Street there are also rails for electric streetcars that had only been in service nine years. These tracks, accompanied by their connecting overhead wires combined with the telephone poles lining both sides of Court Street, well-symbolize the merging of the past with the future that has always characterized Kankakee's steady growth. (Kankakee County Museum Photographic Collection, P2793.)

IMAGES
of America

KANKAKEE
1853–1910

Norman S. Stevens
and The Kankakee County
Historical Society

ARCADIA
PUBLISHING

ISBN 978-0-7385-3338-4

Published by Arcadia Publishing
Charleston, South Carolina

Printed in the United States of America

Library of Congress Catalog Card Number: 2004112532

For all general information contact Arcadia Publishing at:
Telephone 843-853-2070
Fax 843-853-0044
E-mail sales@arcadiapublishing.com
For customer service and orders:
Toll-Free 1-888-313-2665

Visit us on the Internet at www.arcadiapublishing.com

Contents

Acknowledgments

The photographs in this book all come from the photographic collection (totaling over 18,000 images) of the archive section of the Kankakee County Museum, home of the Kankakee County Historical Society since 1906. In 2006, this organization will have been collecting, preserving, and exhibiting materials relating to the history of Kankakee County for a century. I have been the executive director since 2002, and in that capacity have selected and organized the photographs, written the caption text, and, through the cooperation of Arcadia Publishing, made these images available to the public. I would like to thank Jane Van Ostrand (administrative assistant), Loretta Mason, and Robin La Voie (museum assistants) for photocopying caption material from the card file and assisting generally in bookkeeping duties. I would also like to thank Judi Furia (museum volunteer coordinator and research assistant) for answering questions of detail. I would like to sincerely thank them all for the daily deflection of normal office distractions that would have made this process longer than it was. I would also like to thank all the society and museum volunteers, who for over 80 years have been assembling the museum's splendid photographic collection. Finally, I would like to thank my lovely wife Linda Stevens for her patience on those nights I stayed at the museum way longer than usual working on this project. Although mostly I would like to recognize the extraordinary value she adds daily to my life and career.

INTRODUCTION

"We are a great people, damn me if we are not!"

The northeastern portion of Illinois was one of the last areas in "Illinois Country" to be settled by Americans migrating westward. Long inhabited by the Pottawatomi Indian group and visited occasionally by French traders (a few of whom stayed) it was not until the mid-19th century that the population of the area achieved any significant number of permanent inhabitants dedicated to replicating American society in a rediscovered wilderness. It was the advance of the railroad, that symbol of aggressive 19th-century American materialism, which instigated the creation and drove the organization of Kankakee County. By 1852, there was much national discussion of building a transcontinental railroad system to connect eastern markets to territories, such as California, recently acquired during the successful War with Mexico. There was considerable support for Chicago to be the eastern terminus of such a railway system, which meant building feeder lines to the south and east. As a result, in February 1853 the Illinois State Legislature authorized the creation of Kankakee County, subject to a positive vote from the citizens of Will and Iroquois Counties, from which the new county would be drawn. On May 13, 1853, the first meeting of Kankakee County officials was held and the following month the Village of Kankakee Depot, eventually to become the City of Kankakee, was selected as the county seat. Kankakee Depot was chosen because it was near the center of the county, it was directly on the railroad line, and the Illinois Central Railroad donated $5,000 toward building a court house.

In 1853, Franklin Pierce, a lawyer from New Hampshire, was the Democratic president of the United States. The nation's politics were dominated by increasing sectional conflict, which revolved around the rights of individual states, the slavery question, and the extension of the slave system into new territories. Americans even argued over continuing controversies dealing with the very meaning of the Federal Constitution. In economic terms, the Industrial Revolution, "King Cotton," and the Transportation Revolution was forcing a general reevaluation of American society, a transformation of the American scene fueled by movements such as the Second Great Awakening, a profusion of utopian experiments, the Cult of Domesticity, and in the end perhaps best characterized by the dynamic general reforming zeal of the mid-19th century that could produce a concept like abolitionism that would have been unheard of at the Republic's beginning. In 1853, Illinois' newest county clearly demonstrated all of this in microcosm and certainly the growth of the City of Kankakee symbolized the ongoing development of the nation.

The images selected for this book are divided into eight sections, each intended to illustrate particular aspects of the City of Kankakee's development from an antebellum frontier settlement to a stable and vibrant middle-American community at the commencement of the 20th century. Chapter one traces the beginning of Kankakee from its initial association with the railroad and its function as the new county seat, with a look at the area's earliest businesses and street scenes. It concludes with a brief glimpse of Kankakee's participation in the Civil War, the great crisis of the Republic. Kankakee area men served in a number of Illinois formations, but it is the 76th Illinois Volunteers and the 113th Illinois Volunteers that are most closely associated with the city. Chapter two considers business activity in the City of Kankakee from the end of the Civil War through first decade of the 20th century, although it should be noted that this section is impressionistic rather than inclusive. It contains some splendid views of Kankakee streets during this period. Chapter three considers the all important place of the Kankakee River in the community's life, as entertainment and as business, the latter particularly well-illustrated by the once splendid Hotel Riverview. Chapter four contains wonderful images of the Illinois Eastern Hospital for the Insane, which at the end of the 19th century was the second largest such facility in the United States. Chapter five considers the organizations necessary to support a growing community, such as police and fire fighting services, churches, and schools. Chapter six takes the reader on a tour of the most imposing and also of some of the less imposing residences in the City of Kankakee. Chapter seven is a figurative photographic montage of the various types of entertainment engaged in by Kankakee's citizens, including mundane drives through the country and picnics, as well as the more spectacular circuses, tight rope acts, and parades. This chapter illustrates the growing late 19th-century mania with physical fitness that would eventually produced spectator sports like team cycling, racing, baseball, and football. Finally, chapter eight discusses Kankakee's movement into the beginning of the 20th century, starting with area participation in the Spanish-American War and concluding with the coming of modernity represented by the telephone, automobile, and the airplane.

It is hoped that these images taken collectively will comprise a fairly complete view of the first 60 years of the City of Kankakee. They have been selected specifically to be seen in combination. The author bears sole responsibility for any errors of fact or any omission of any elements of Kankakee's story not represented in the photographs chosen for inclusion in this book. At the middle of the 19th century, photography was a new process that was unfamiliar to many and a mystery to most, yet it is photography that has so well-captured the essence of the American tale now for over 150 years. In January 1853, just as Kankakee County was organizing itself on the Illinois prairie, the eminent "Photographic Shadow Artist" Matthew Brady published his "Gallery of Illustrious Americans," which included images of the notables of the day, people like Henry Clay, John Calhoun, and Daniel Webster. In his introduction Brady said, "The magic of photography will help our posterity understand us by searching the faces of those who led us." The images we have left, quietly fading views of what once was, are indeed the best medium, as Mr. Brady observed, for understanding what we were and from where we have come. The images of the City of Kankakee are presented here in that spirit.

One

The Antebellum Era Through the Civil War

"We have a fair prospect of success"

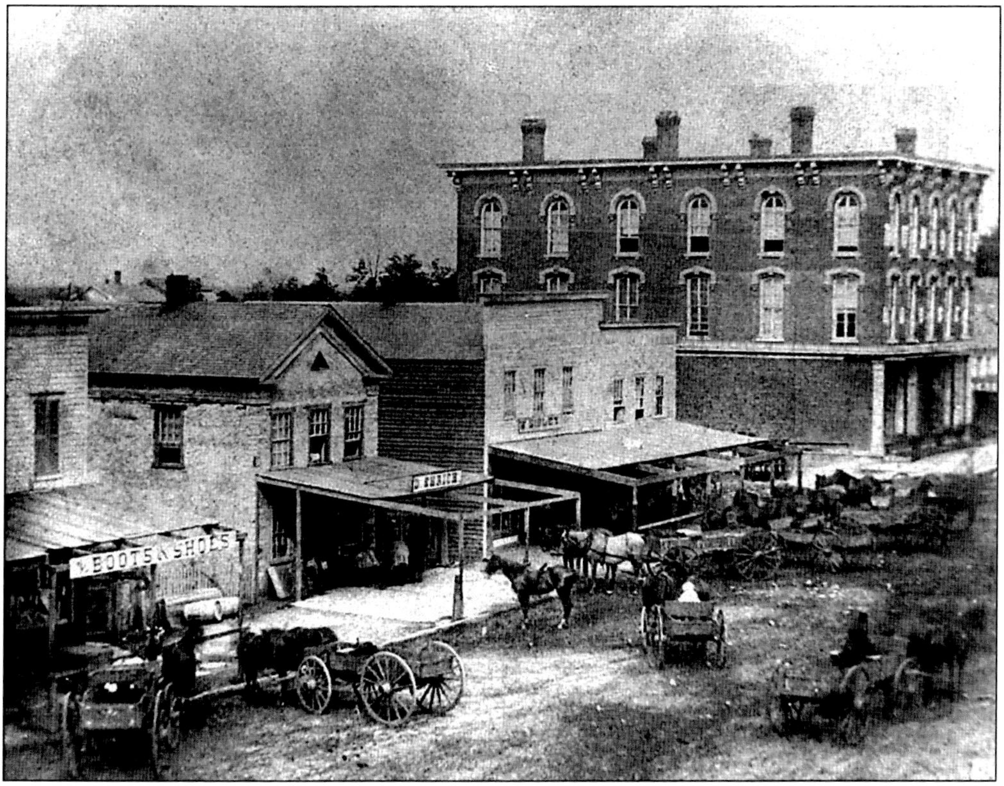

The earliest known photograph of the City of Kankakee, this antebellum image, *c.* 1858, shows Court Street (looking northeast) with the cross street Schuyler Avenue appearing in the right center of the photograph. Patrons are seen arriving at Deidrich Ehrich's Grocery Store and also at William Sibley's General Store, two of the city's first merchants. (Kankakee County Museum Photographic Collection, P0002.)

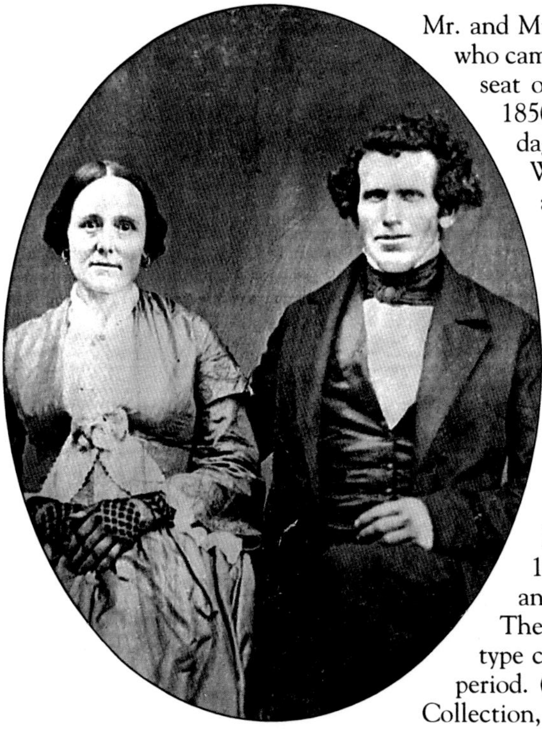

Mr. and Mrs. Burt illustrate the middle class families who came to settle in the City of Kankakee, county seat of the new Kankakee County in the mid-1850s. Their portrait was done by a Kankakee daguerreotype artist, *c.* 1856. Their son, William Christian Burt, would become a hospital administrator in Chicago. (Kankakee County Museum Photographic Collection, P1828.)

Antebellum railroad construction created the City of Kankakee. The first passenger train to arrive at Kankakee Depot, the Illinois Central Railroad's Engine No. 10 is shown here, with two passenger cars and a coal car, in this image made in 1854. The engine is a 4-4-0 "American" style, the type commonly seen on American tracks in this period. (Kankakee County Museum Photographic Collection, P1369.)

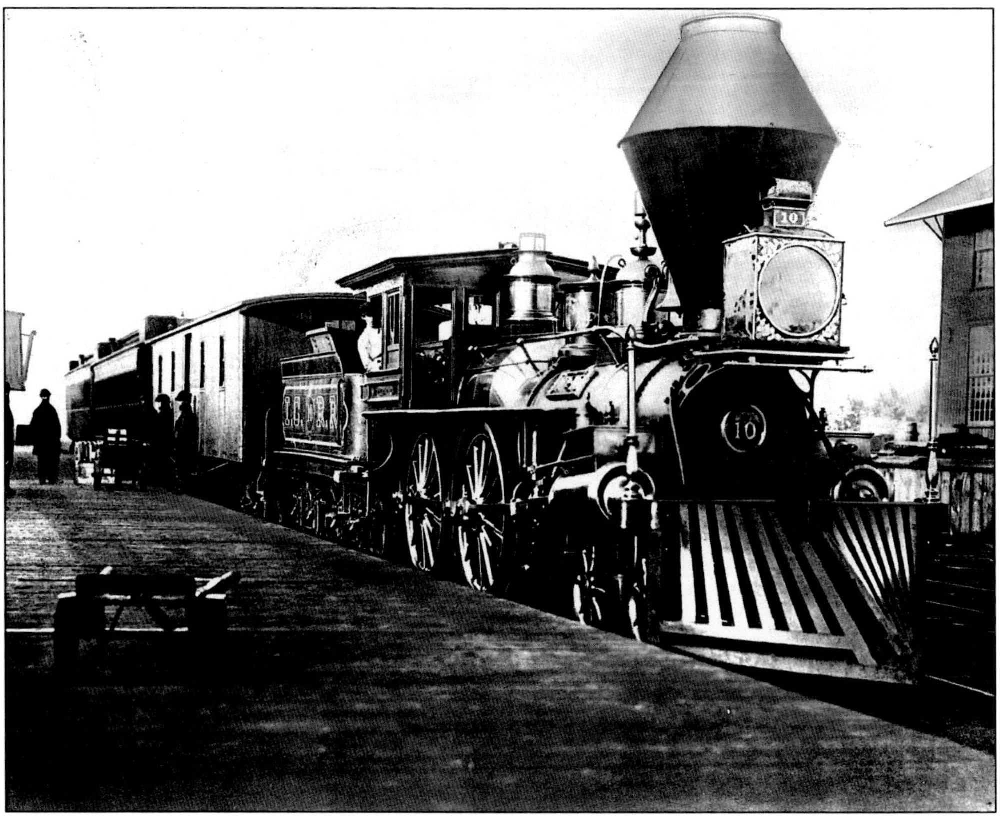

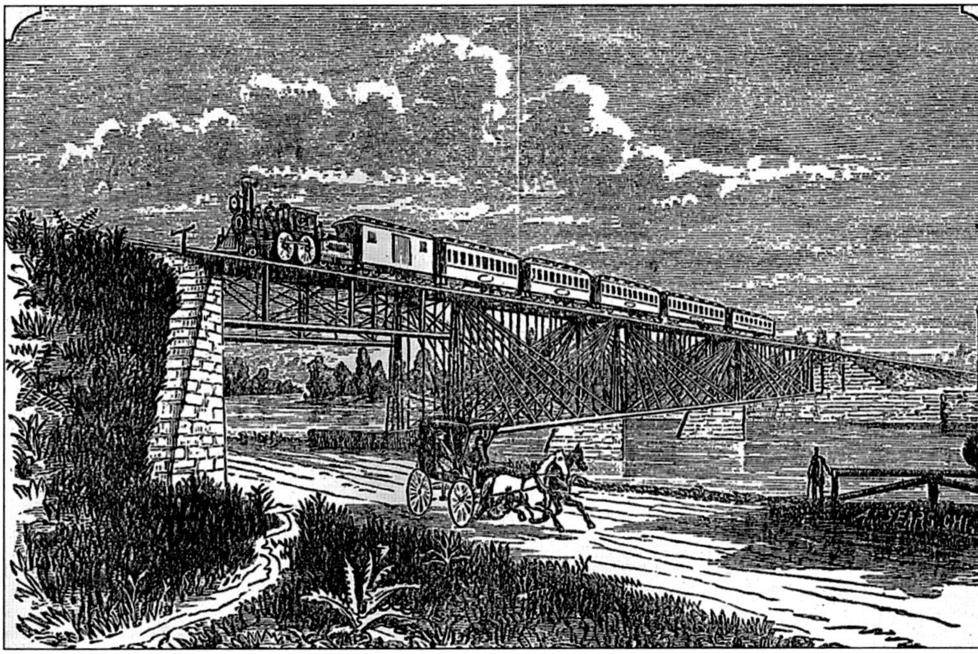

This antebellum etching is taken from a piece of Illinois Central Railroad promotional literature, meant to encourage financial investment and settlement in the Kankakee area. It depicts the Illinois Central's new railroad bridge built over the Kankakee River in 1853. Americans were convinced that railroading represented the nation's future. (Kankakee County Museum Photographic Collection, P3102.)

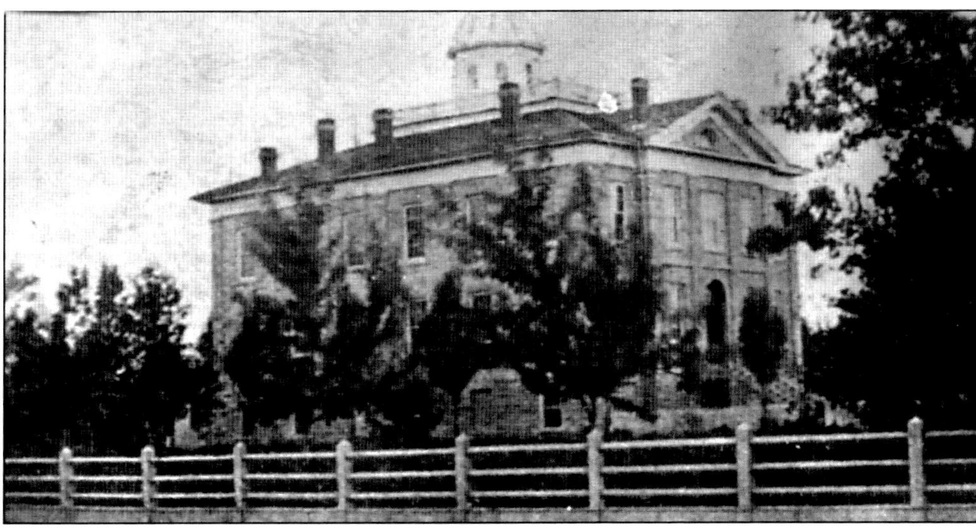

Kankakee Depot (the future City of Kankakee), located directly on the Illinois Central's tracks, was selected by public vote as the county seat in June 1853. Construction began on the Kankakee County Court House in 1854, finished the following year at a cost of $19,182.80. This 1868 image shows the completed court house, which housed its first session of the Kankakee County Circuit Court in September 1855. The court house was destroyed by fire in October 1872 and replaced with a nearly identical structure in 1873. (Kankakee County Museum Photographic Collection, P2722.)

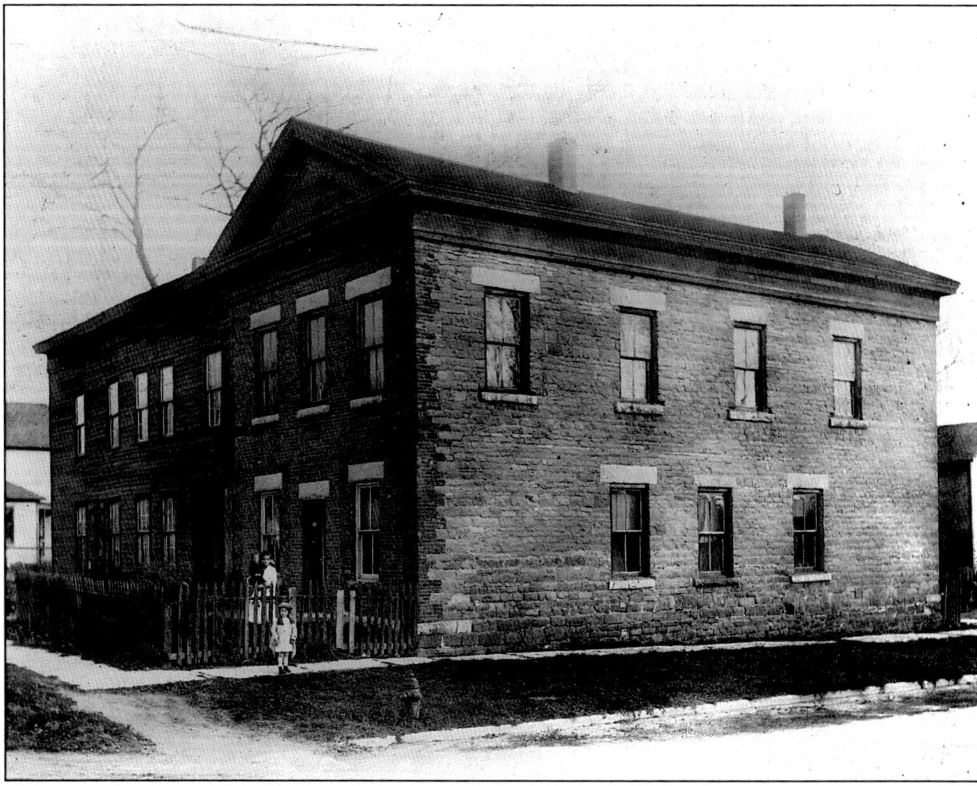

This 1870 photograph shows the Van Meter Hotel, which stood at the corner of Fourth and Oak Streets in the City of Kankakee. Built in 1852 as a hotel on the "American Plan," the Van Meter was used for the first two sessions of the circuit court, while the first Kankakee County Court House was being finished. The Van Meter also housed public offices, a church, school, and public meeting rooms. It was the center of social, political, and business activity in Kankakee until the beginning of the Civil War. (Kankakee County Museum Photographic Collection, P0001.)

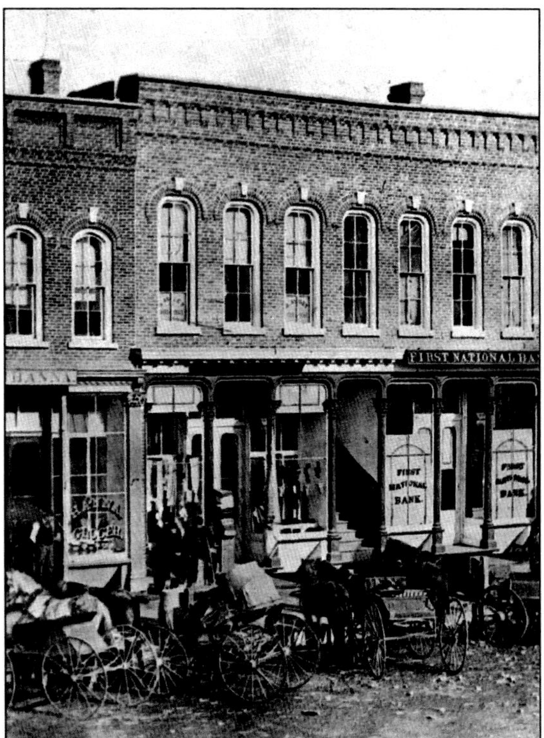

The corner of Kankakee's Court Street and Schuyler Avenue appears in this 1860 image, illustrating the growing business activity of the city. At right is the office of the First National Bank of Kankakee and in the center of the block is Deidrich Ehrich's grocery store, which had been in the same location since 1850. (Kankakee County Museum Photographic Collection, P1362.)

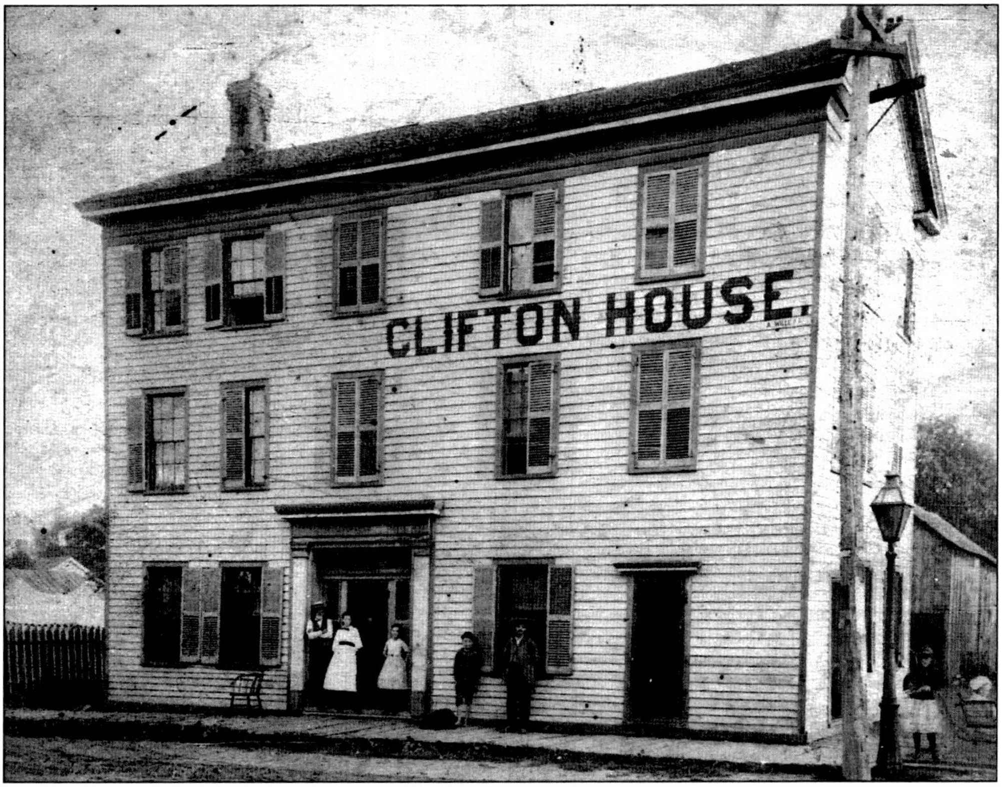

Antebellum Kankakee needed hotels to meet the needs of the railroad and the county seat. This late 19th-century image shows the Clifton House, located at East Station Street and Schuyler Avenue, which was constructed in 1859 as the Grove City House. (Kankakee County Museum Photographic Collection, P0574.)

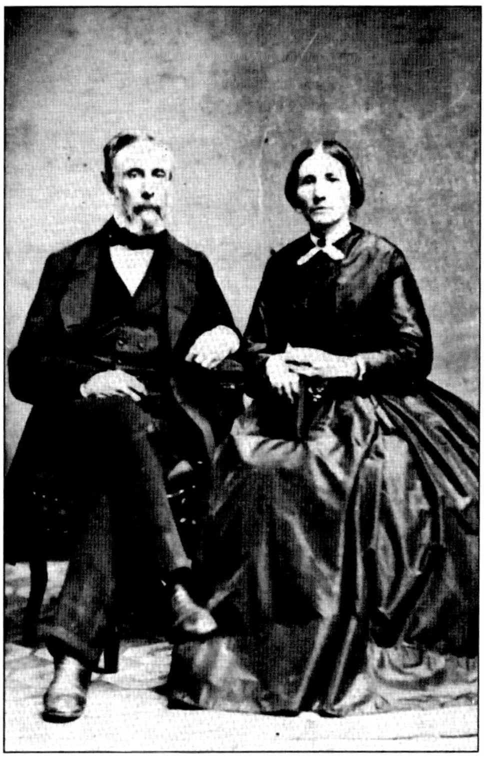

The strong French element in antebellum Kankakee society is represented by this studio portrait, taken in 1860, of Paulin and Solina Roger Pallissard, who relocated to Kankakee from their native France in 1855. They were farmers who would have done their shopping in the City of Kankakee before the Civil War. Their sons Edward and Joseph also established large farms in the St. Anne area of Kankakee County. (Kankakee County Museum Photographic Collection, P0522.)

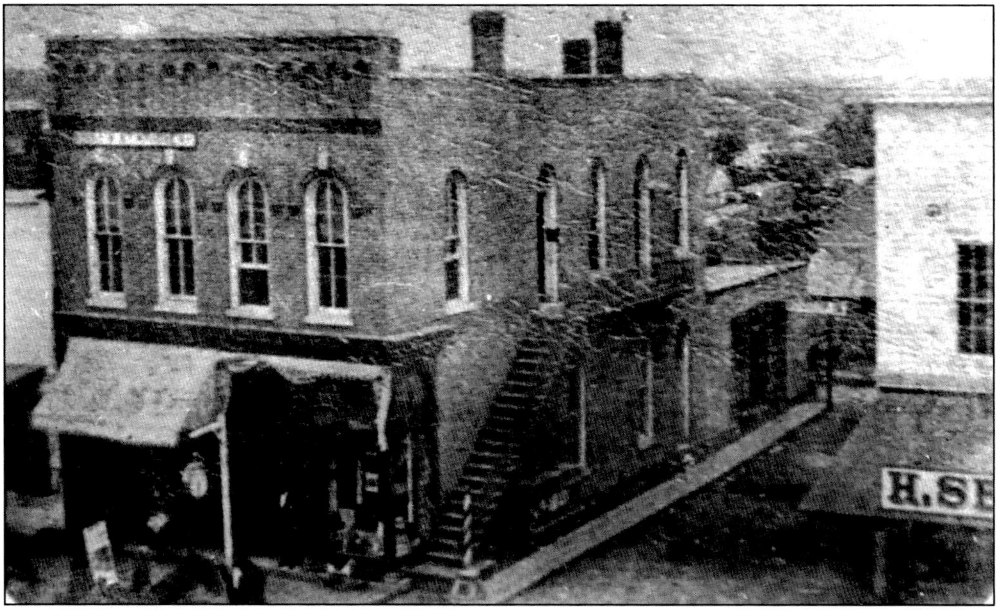

These three images show the City of Kankakee *c.* 1860, with which the Pallissards would have been familiar. East Court Street is seen here. In an era of more limited literacy, merchants employed large symbolic signs, such as the large watch in the lower right marking a jewelry establishment and the barber's pole standing on the corner. (Kankakee County Museum Photographic Collection, P0036.)

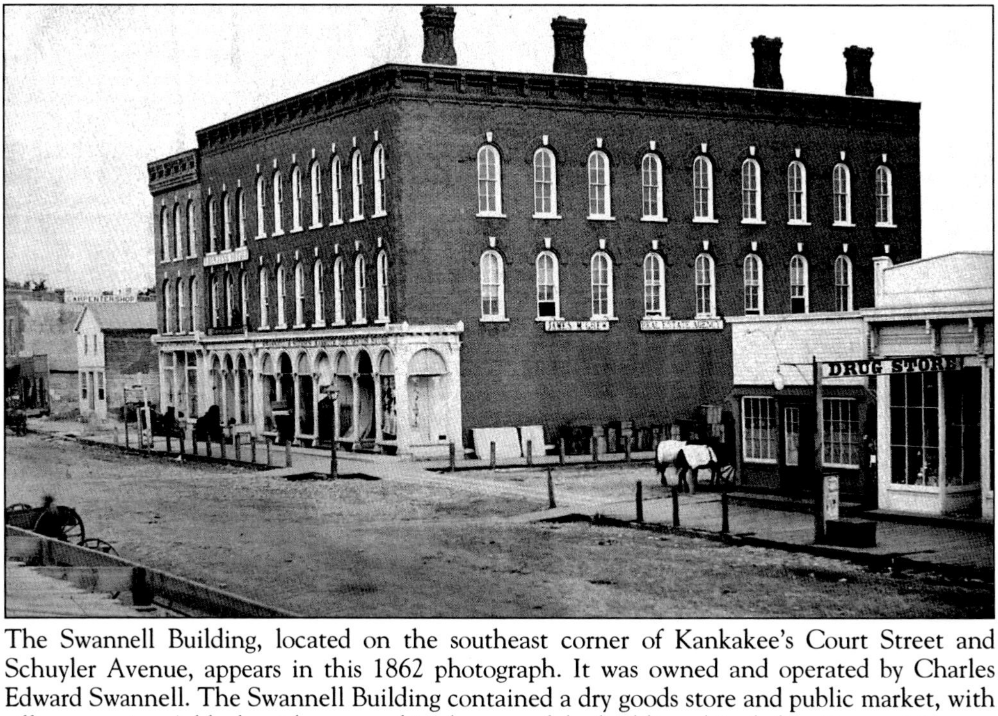

The Swannell Building, located on the southeast corner of Kankakee's Court Street and Schuyler Avenue, appears in this 1862 photograph. It was owned and operated by Charles Edward Swannell. The Swannell Building contained a dry goods store and public market, with offices upstairs. A blacksmith operated in the rear of the building. (Kankakee County Museum Photographic Collection, P2787.)

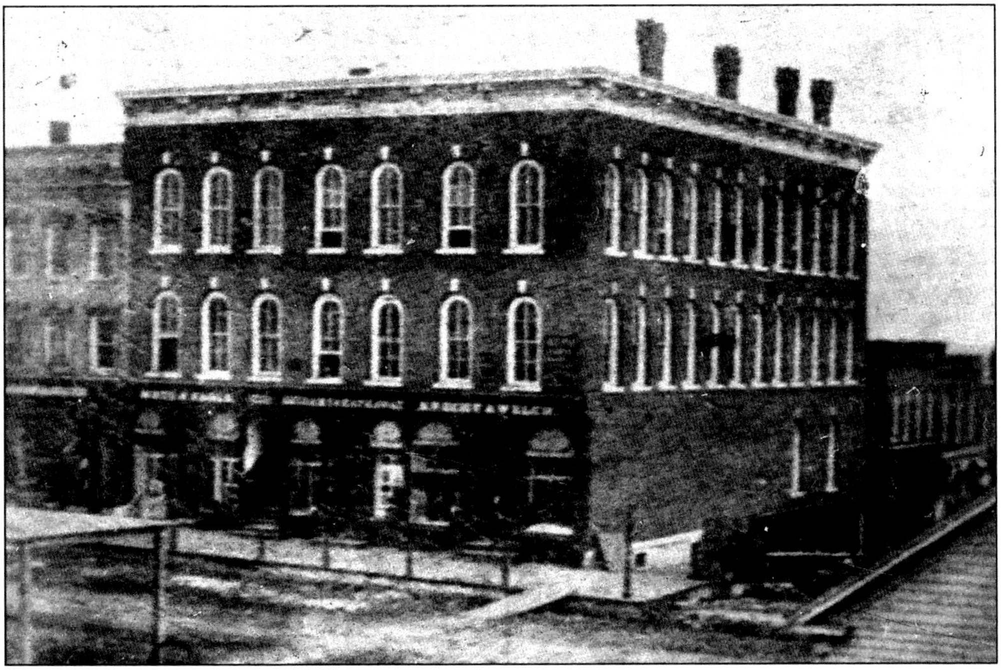

The Knecht Building, located on the southeast corner of Kankakee's East Avenue and Court Street, is shown in this 1868 photograph. It and the Swannell Building were constructed in 1855 by Kankakee contractor Walter Smith. Having established his business in 1854, recent German immigrant John George Knecht operated a men's store in the Knecht Building, offering "proper clothes and gentleman's furnishings." (Kankakee County Museum Photographic Collection, P0038.)

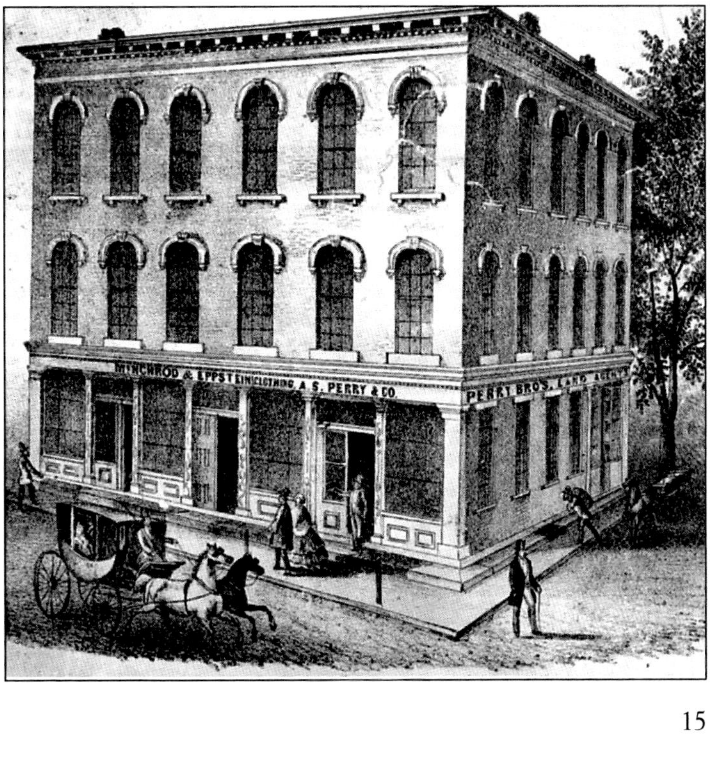

This etching appeared as decoration to the first map of the City of Kankakee, published in 1858, and was intended as a piece of promotional literature. It depicts the Commercial Hotel, which was located on the corner of East Avenue and Station Street. The building was erected in 1858 by local banker Alfred Perry, who had been selling area real estate for the Illinois Central Railroad from Bourbonnais since 1851. (Kankakee County Museum Photographic Collection, P0074.)

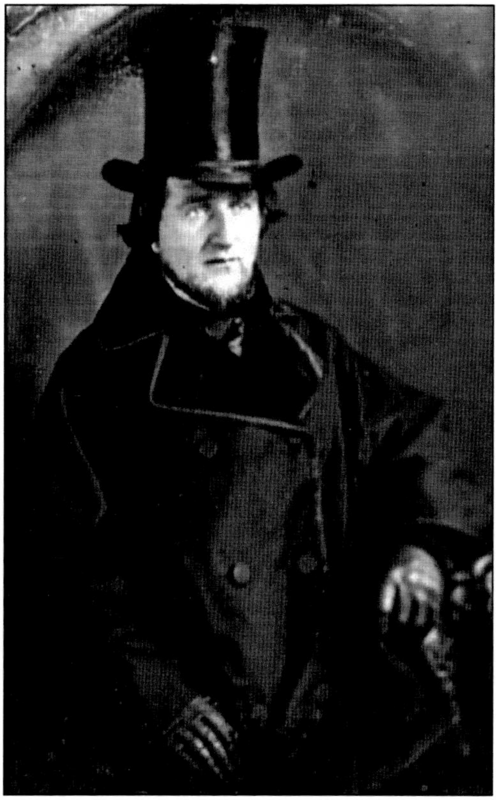

In 1851, determined to improve his family's fortune, John Livingston, shown here in this 1852 image taken in Kankakee, came to Kankakee with his son Charles. They were direct descendents of Robert Livingston, who, as a delegate to the 2nd Continental Congress, was on the committee that drafted the Declaration of Independence. Charles Livingston became a prominent Kankakee newspaperman, owner of the *Kankakee Gazette*. (Kankakee County Museum Photographic Collection, P5519.)

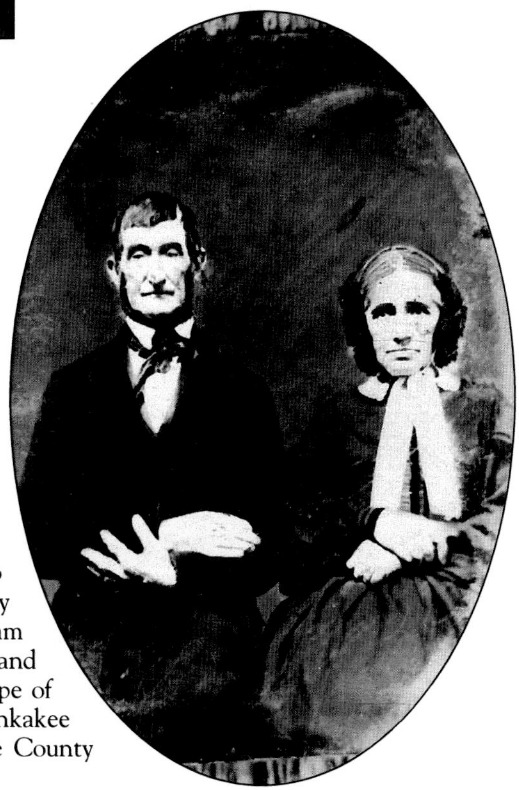

By 1860, the City of Kankakee was a developing community that encouraged the arrival of new citizens. This 1856 image shows William and Elizabeth Rantz, who came to what had become Kankakee County in 1837. They raised 12 children. William Rantz brought the first mechanical thresher and separator to the area. They were the very type of solid farming folk that made the City of Kankakee and Kankakee County a success. (Kankakee County Museum Photographic Collection, P0691.)

The American Civil War was the single most dramatic event of mid-19th-century America. From the beginning, the City of Kankakee contributed men to the Union cause, such as these three comrades of Company B/113th Illinois Volunteers, who posed for this 1862 image. Seated are musicians and brothers, Albert and Franklin Nichols. First Sgt. John Kellogg, later captain of Company B, stands behind them. (Kankakee County Museum Photographic Collection, P1374.)

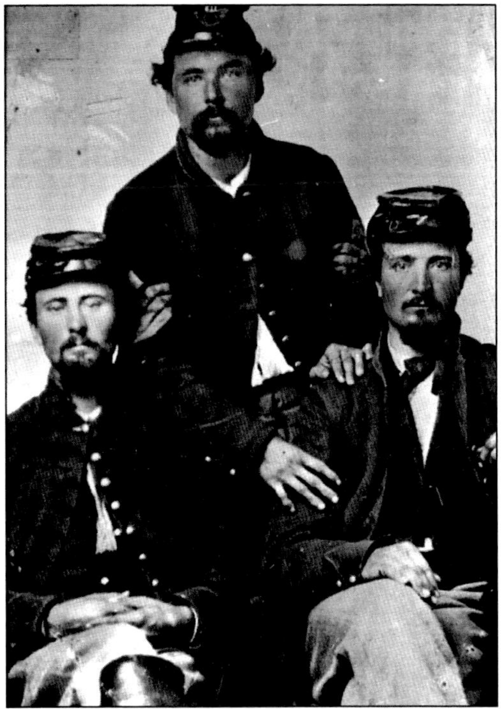

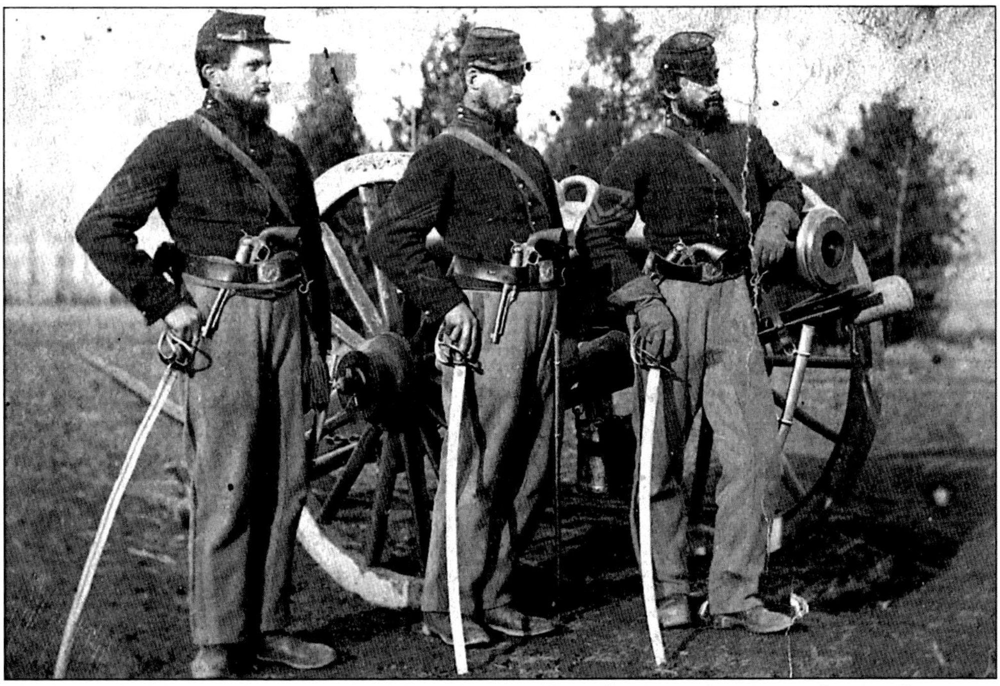

These three non-commissioned officers of Battery I/1st Illinois Volunteer Light Artillery were photographed at Springfield, Illinois, in 1862. They are Kankakee natives 1st Sgt. Jerome Slansom, Sgt. Harry Cox, and Q.M. Sgt. Albert Carlin. The field piece is an 1841 model, twelve-pound iron Howitzer, considered obsolete by the middle of the war. Battery I/1st Illinois was largely recruited in Kankakee. (Kankakee County Museum Photographic Collection, P2039.)

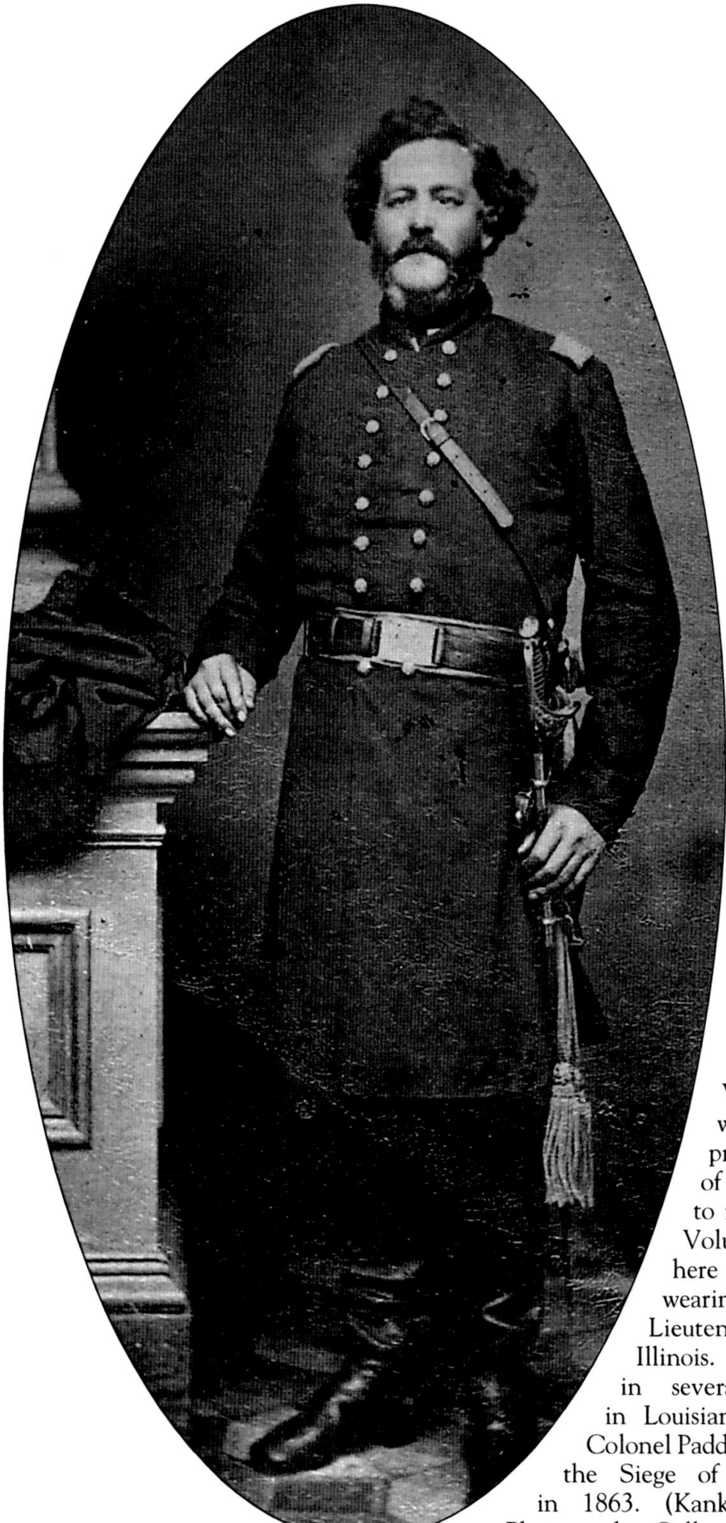

The Civil War was fought primarily with volunteers and prominent local leaders raised regiments. Their military abilities were not as important as their ability to encourage men to join the army. John Warren Paddock, who was a well-known attorney practicing law in the City of Kankakee, contributed to raising the 113th Illinois Volunteers. He is shown here in this 1862 photograph, wearing his uniform as Lieutenant Colonel/113th Illinois. His regiment served in several difficult campaigns in Louisiana and Mississippi, and Colonel Paddock would lead it through the Siege of Vicksburg, Mississippi, in 1863. (Kankakee County Museum Photographic Collection, P9565.116.)

An unidentified first sergeant in the Union cavalry displays his government-issue saber in this image, *c.* 1862. It is thought that he was from Kankakee. Photography was relatively new and early in their service soldiers rushed to have their image made for the folks at home, often posing with a variety of impressive weapons. Mounted volunteers from Kankakee served in the 4th, 5th, and 12th Illinois Volunteer Cavalry regiments. (Kankakee County Museum Photographic Collection, P1378.)

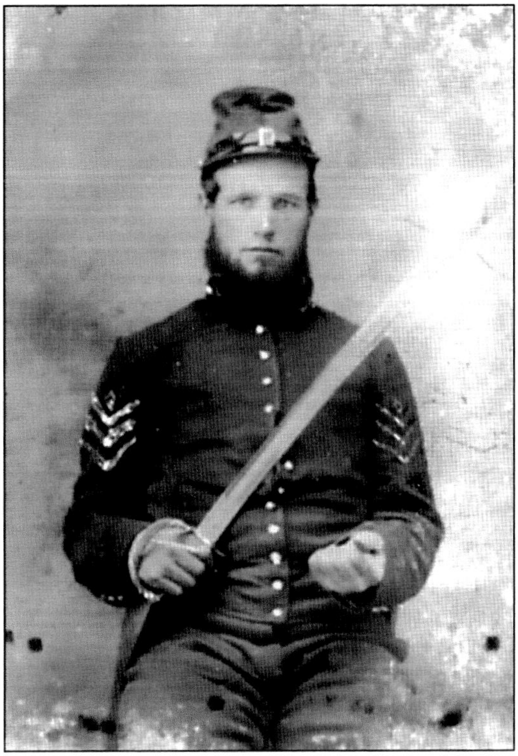

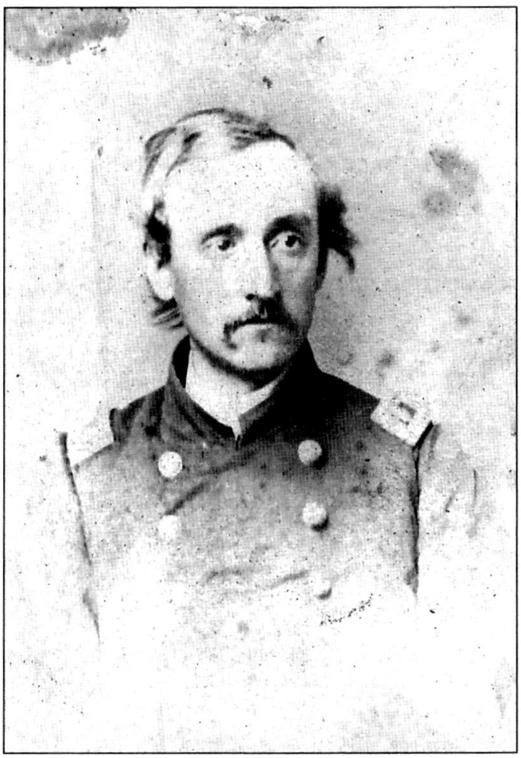

The 39th Illinois Volunteers, also known as the "Yates' Phalanx" for the state's governor, was one of the first three-year regiments raised in Illinois. At the start of the war, Charles Mather Clark was attending medical school in Chicago. His family lived in Kankakee. Clark joined the 39th Illinois as a medical officer and is shown here in this 1864 image as Major and Surgeon/ 39th Illinois. After the war, Dr. Clark would practice medicine in the City of Kankakee for over 40 years. (Kankakee County Museum Photographic Collection, P0332.)

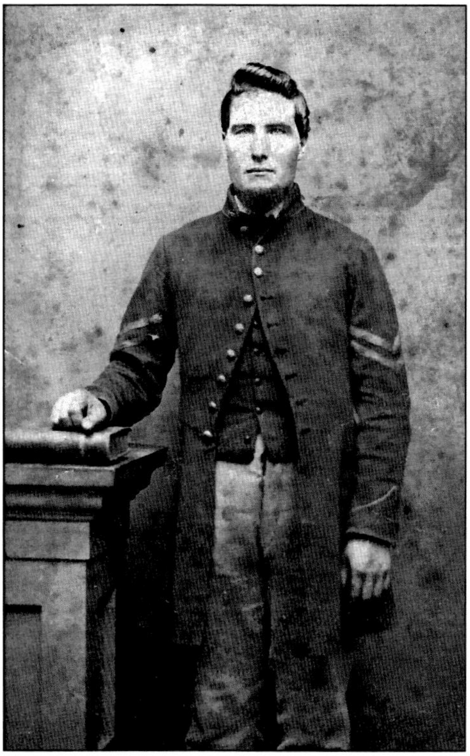

Kankakee farmer James Dennison had this image made at Springfield, Illinois, in 1862. He was serving as a corporal in Company K/113th Illinois Volunteers when he sent his picture, inscribed on the back "for Anne," to his wife Anne Harrison Dennison. Corporal Dennison was captured, with most of his regiment, at Brice's Crossroads, Mississippi, on June 10, 1864, and would spend the next three months at the Confederacy's Andersonville Prison, located in Georgia. (Kankakee County Museum Photographic Collection, P0110.)

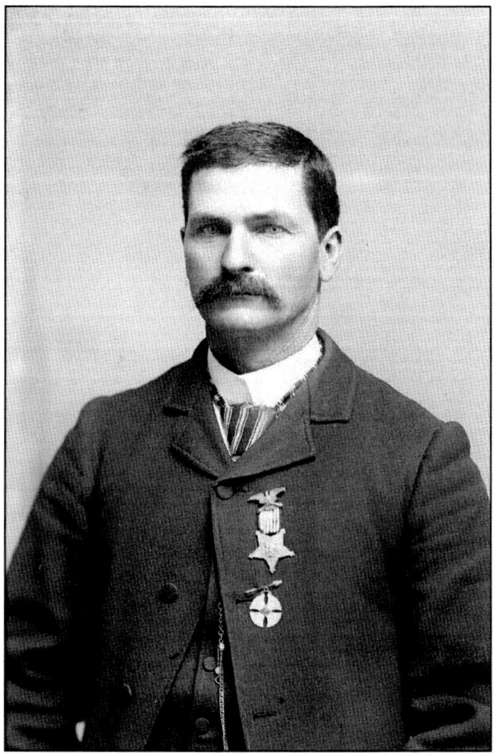

In this postbellum image, James Dennison proudly wears his Grand Army of the Republic veteran's badge. Below that, he wears the corps badges of the 16th Army Corps (the tilted Maltese Cross) and the 17th Army Corps (the arrow). Dennison served in both of these organizations with his regiment, the 113th Illinois Volunteers. He purchased 40 acres of unimproved land south of Kankakee and spent the remaining 43 years of his life farming, but he never forgot the three years he spent with "the boys in blue." (Kankakee County Museum Photographic Collection, P9565.115.)

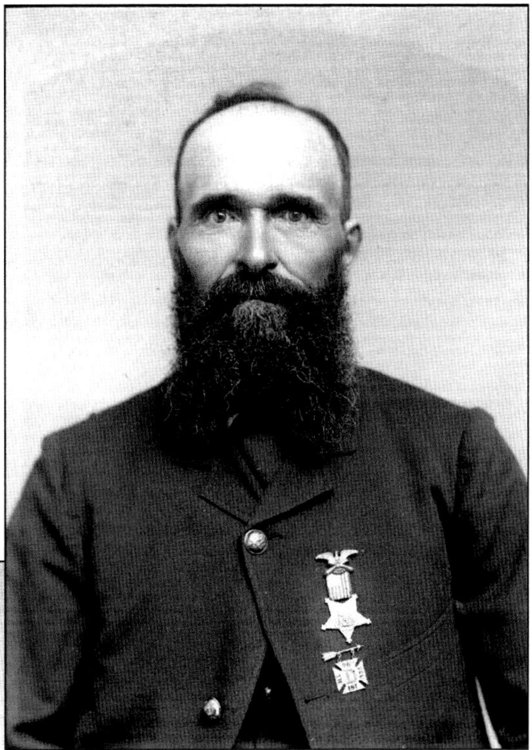

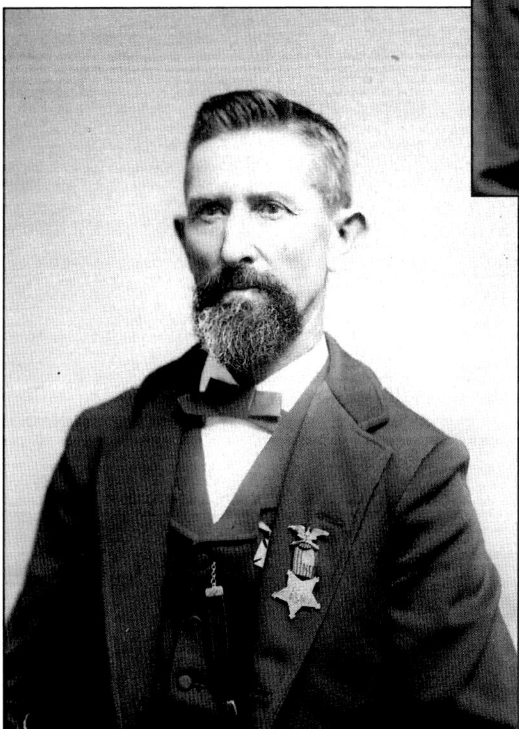

These Grand Army photographs of Kankakee Civil War veterans Stephen Cyrier (left) and Franklin Clark (right), both members of the 76th Illinois Volunteers, serve as reminders of the greatness latent in many men, which was made clear by their participation in the nation's great struggle. The 76th Illinois was heavily recruited in Kankakee County. The nation and Kankakee County would be led toward the 20th century by these men and their comrades. "In our youths," observed United States Supreme Court Justice Oliver Wendell Holmes, "our hearts were touched with fire." (Kankakee County Museum Photographic Collection, P9565.7 and P9565.4.)

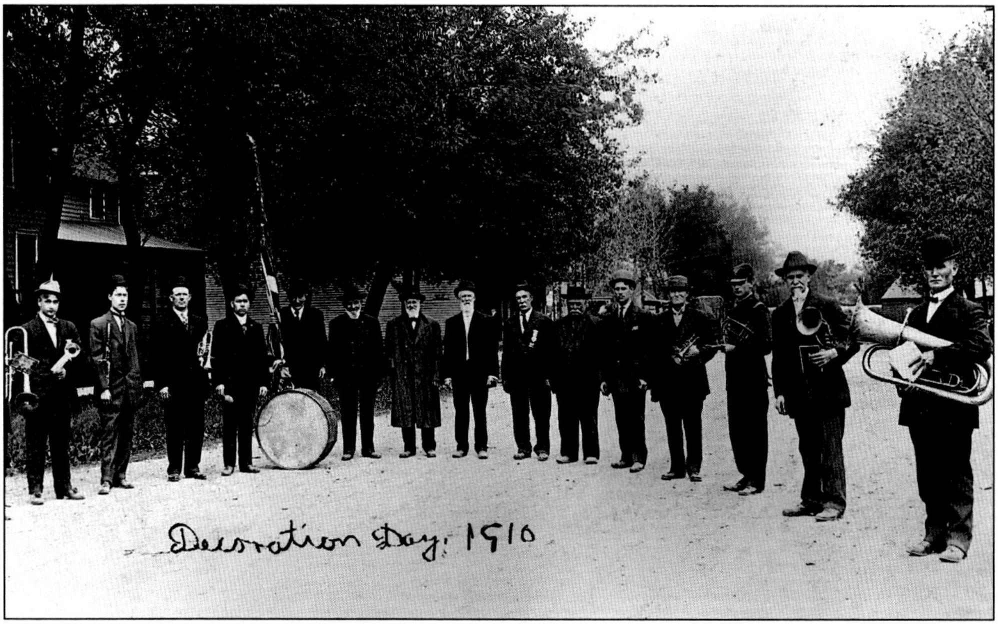

Only three years after the conclusion of the Civil War, Union Army veterans founded the Grand Army of the Republic (GAR) in Chicago in 1868. The first local GAR post in Kankakee County was organized on March 7, 1884, at the Kankakee County Court House with 38 members. The Whipple Post was named for Lewis Whipple, Captain of Company E/39th Illinois Volunteers. This photograph shows members of a brass band, some of them Kankakee Civil War veterans, at Decoration Day in 1910. (Kankakee County Museum Photographic Collection, P3496.)

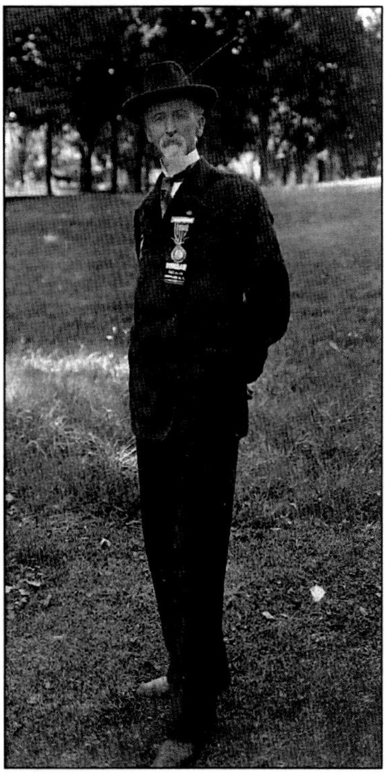

Kankakee's Whipple Post held their annual meetings generally in October, reaching their peak membership of 156 veterans in 1889. Kankakee's GAR Post passed out of existence in 1947 with the death of the area's last GAR veteran, William Perry Lockwood. Shown in this image is a member of the Whipple Post, identified only as Uncle Ed, with the photograph addressed to his niece Flora and inscribed, "Recalling the days of 1861 to 1865 and asking you not to forget the boys in blue." (Kankakee County Museum Photographic Collection, P2221.)

Two

Kankakee Businesses

"Making a go of it"

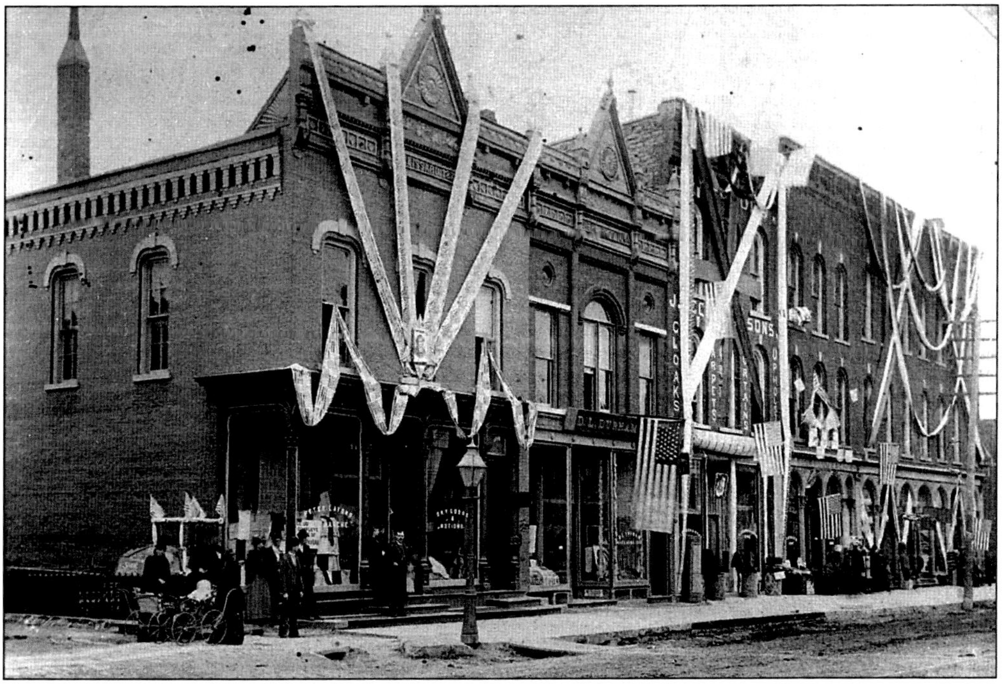

From the end of the Civil War through the early part of the 20th century, downtown merchants gave the City of Kankakee its character and, indeed, provided the city with its very reason for existence. Kankakee's merchants celebrated holidays and readily participated in the daily life of the town. This image shows the south side of Kankakee's Court Street, decorated in celebration of Columbus Day in October 1890. On the corner where the crowd is gathered is Peter LaFond's Dry Goods Store and next to it with the large American Flag is D.L. Durham's Book Store. The remainder of the block is occupied by Joseph Lecour's establishment, J. Lecour and Sons, which sold all types of clothing and was the single largest store in Kankakee. (Kankakee County Museum Photographic Collection, P1322.)

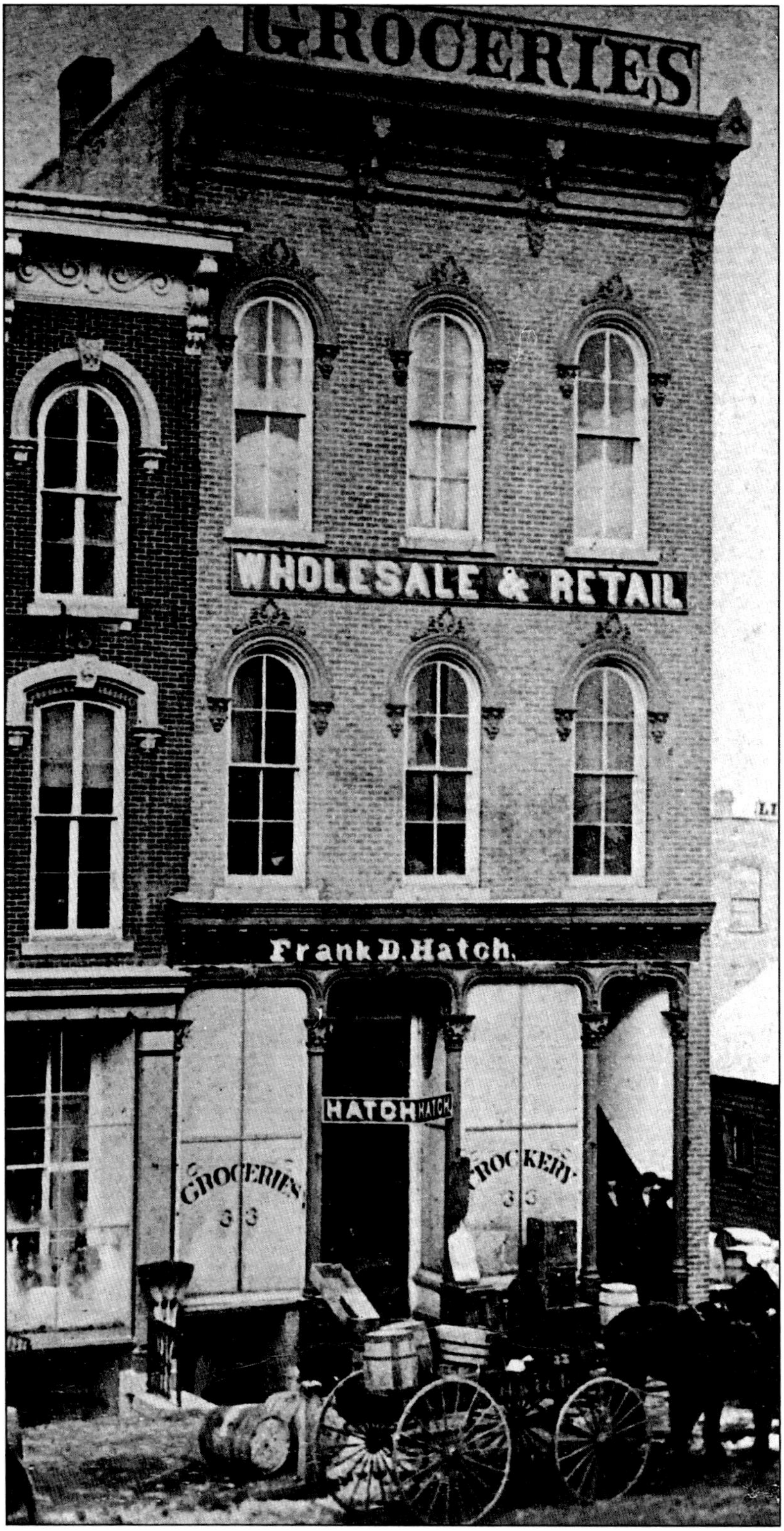

This is one of the oldest images of merchant activity on the streets of the City of Kankakee, taken in 1875. It shows the wholesale and retail grocery store of Frank Hatch, selling groceries and crockery, located on the north side of East Court Street. Frank Hatch occupied the building in 1869 and operated his business there until he was forced to declare bankruptcy in 1897. A variety of drug stores used the building at the left of the photograph, known as the "Hobby Building," until it burned in 1922. (Kankakee County Museum Photographic Collection, P1170.)

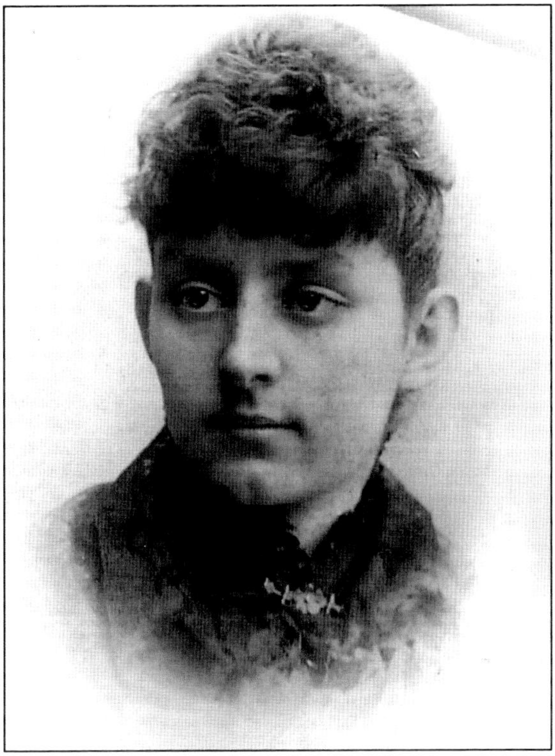

Perhaps the most prominent merchant in the City of Kankakee was Joseph Lecour, who, after working as a merchant in Canada, came to the Kankakee area in 1856 and established his Kankakee clothing store in 1859. His sons Edward and Louis Lecour joined the family business, J. Lecour and Sons. Louis Lecour married Miss Emma Caron Bachant in 1888, she is pictured in this image taken at the time of her marriage. (Kankakee County Museum Photographic Collection, P8696.)

The west side of Schuyler Avenue is seen in this photograph taken on November 25, 1899. The office of the *Kankakee Daily News*, at the left of the photograph, is advertising the advent of Festival Days. Just beyond the private residence with front stairs leading to the sidewalk is Labertram's Hardware Store, advertising paint. (Kankakee County Museum Photographic Collection, P1383.)

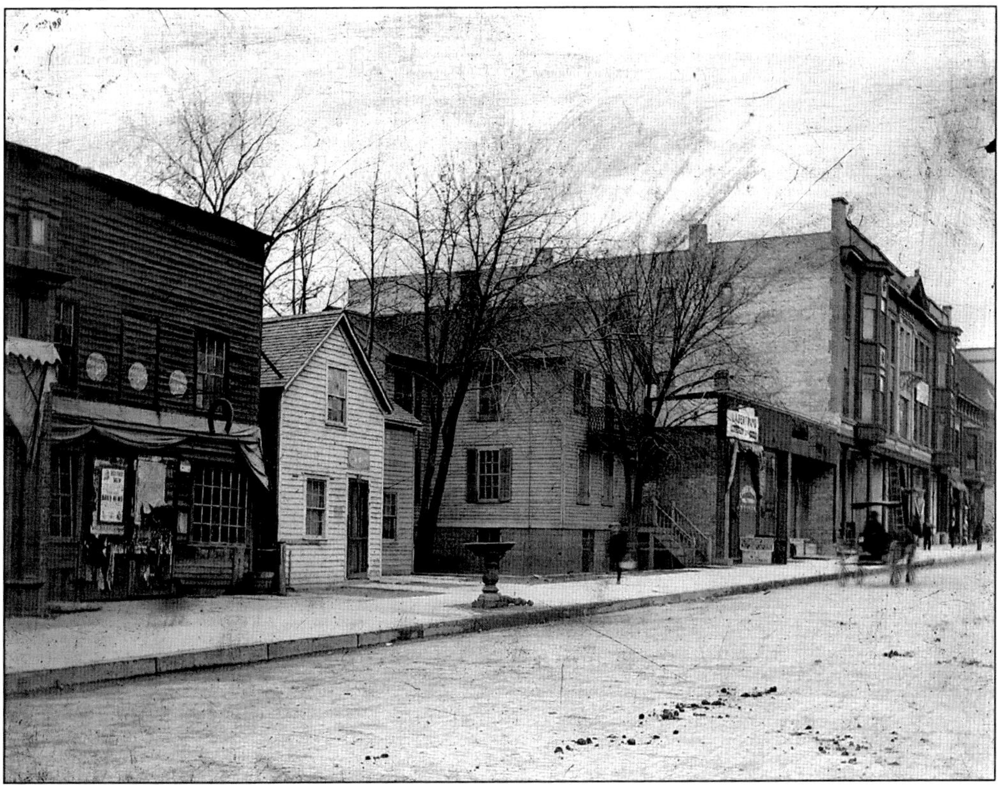

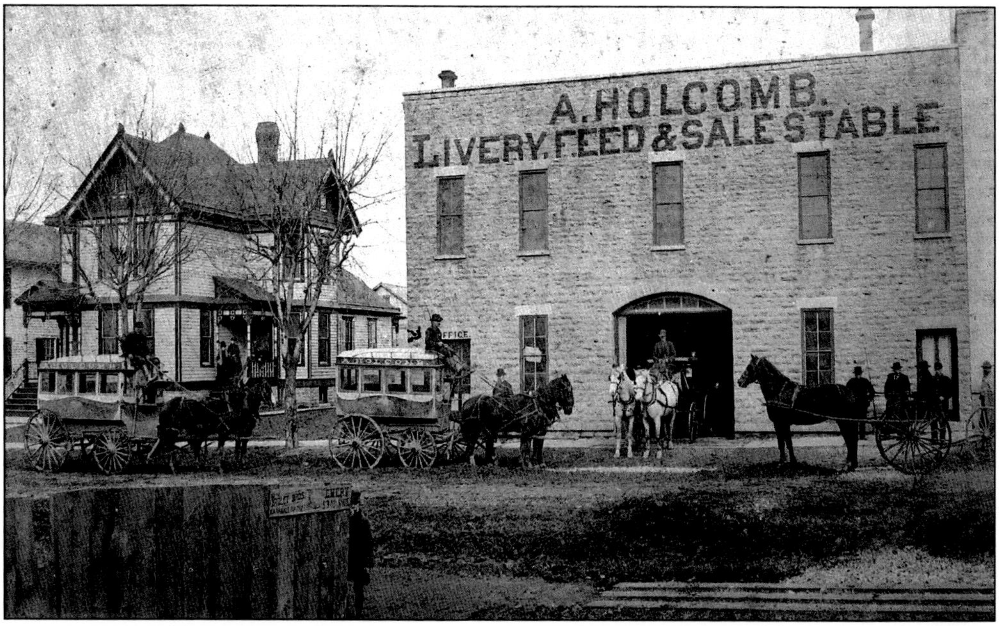

Amasa Holcomb's Livery Stable, located on Kankakee's North Schuyler Avenue, is shown here, *c.* 1880. Arriving from Connecticut in 1855, Holcomb started farming and then finally established Kankakee's largest livery stable in 1869. He operated it until 1888, when he devoted his energies to selling and judging horses. The horse-drawn buses, appearing in the center and left of the photograph, were used to transport people from the railroad depot to the Hotel Riverview and similar establishments. A sign on the fence to the left announces horse shoeing for $3. (Kankakee County Museum Photographic Collection, P3084.)

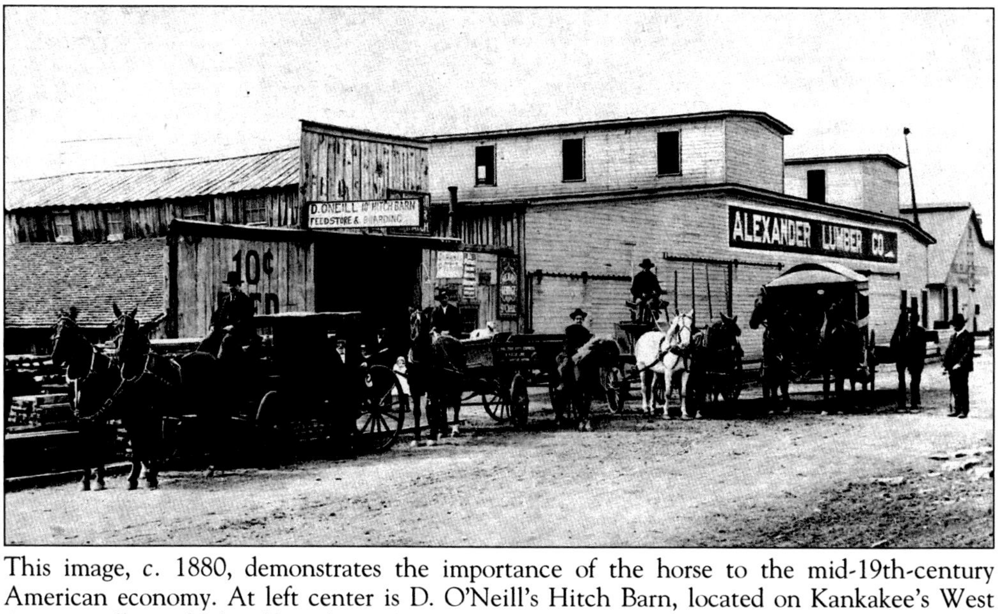

This image, *c.* 1880, demonstrates the importance of the horse to the mid-19th-century American economy. At left center is D. O'Neill's Hitch Barn, located on Kankakee's West Avenue, offering feed and boarding. The wagons, from the J. Palter Express and Hack Company, are engaged in moving people and freight about Kankakee. Note the large white dog on the open wagon. (Kankakee County Museum Photographic Collection, P0575.)

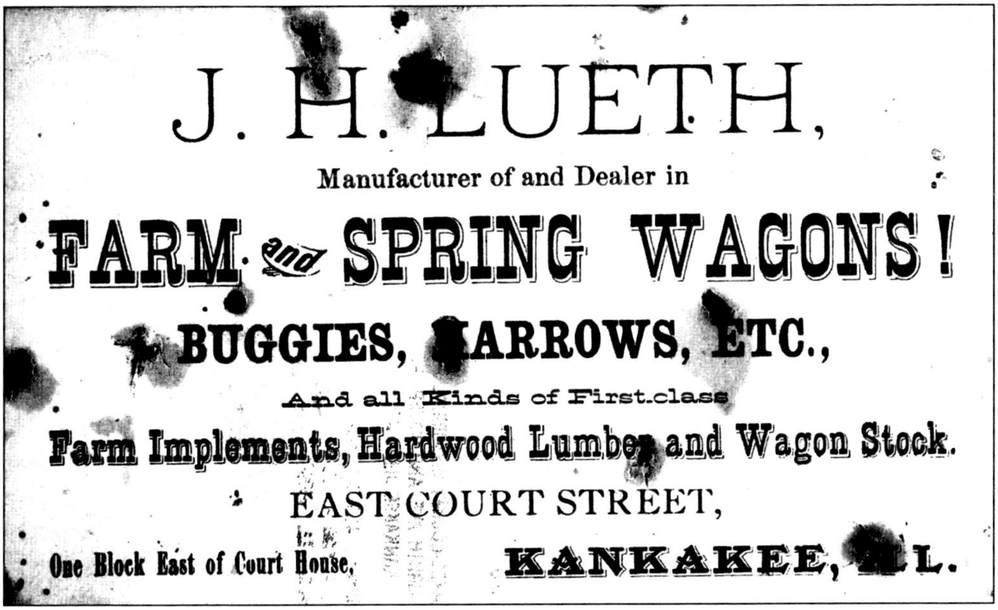

This advertisement for J.H. Lueth's wagon manufacturing company appeared in Kankakee papers, c. 1880. John Harold Lueth came to Kankakee in 1857 from Mecklenburg, Germany, where he learned the carriage trade. In 1867, he created the firm advertised here, that would build wagons, carriages, buggies, and assorted farm equipment in Kankakee for the next 50 years. From 1899, his company, now a Kankakee institution, would be operated by his sons George Carl and John Frederich Leuth. (Kankakee County Museum Photographic Collection, P5955.)

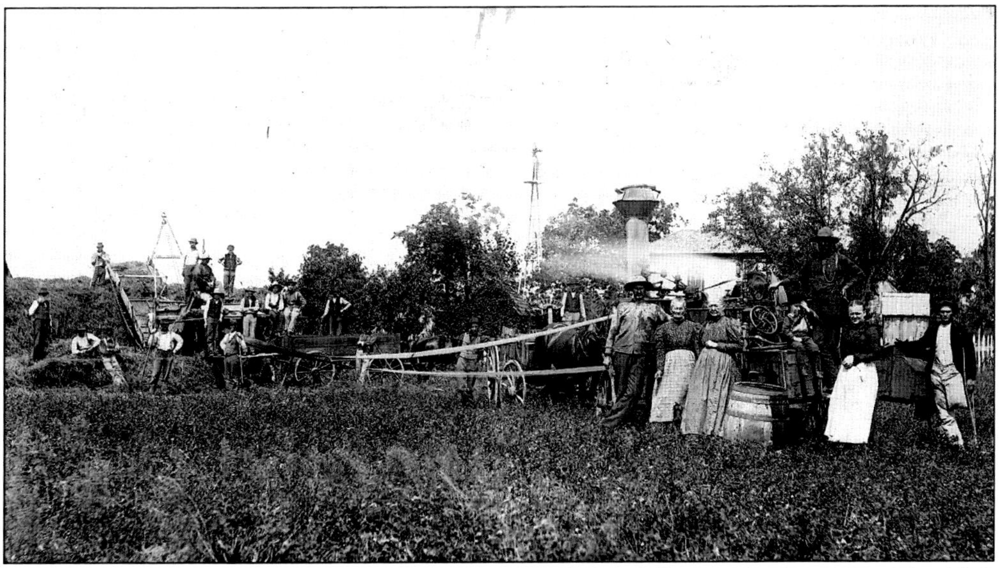

Commercial agriculture became more common in Kankakee following the Civil War. This 1872 photograph shows a threshing party using, for the period, innovative equipment. The work is being done on one of the many area fields owned by agrarian businessman Stephen Fitch Hanford, who built Kankakee's second and largest grain elevator in 1870. Hanford operated a large grain business through the rest of the century. (Kankakee County Museum Photographic Collection, P1340.)

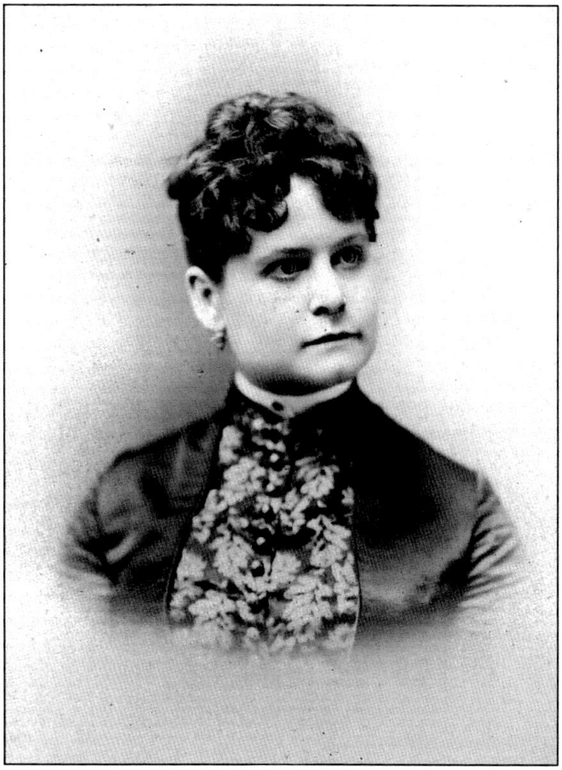

The Perry family was one of the most important farming families in the Kankakee area. Their "home place" was located in what was then known informally as North Kankakee, but would eventually be renamed Bradley in 1895. Miss Emma Perry had this wonderful portrait done during her visit to San Francisco in 1882. (Kankakee County Museum Photographic Collection, P0259.)

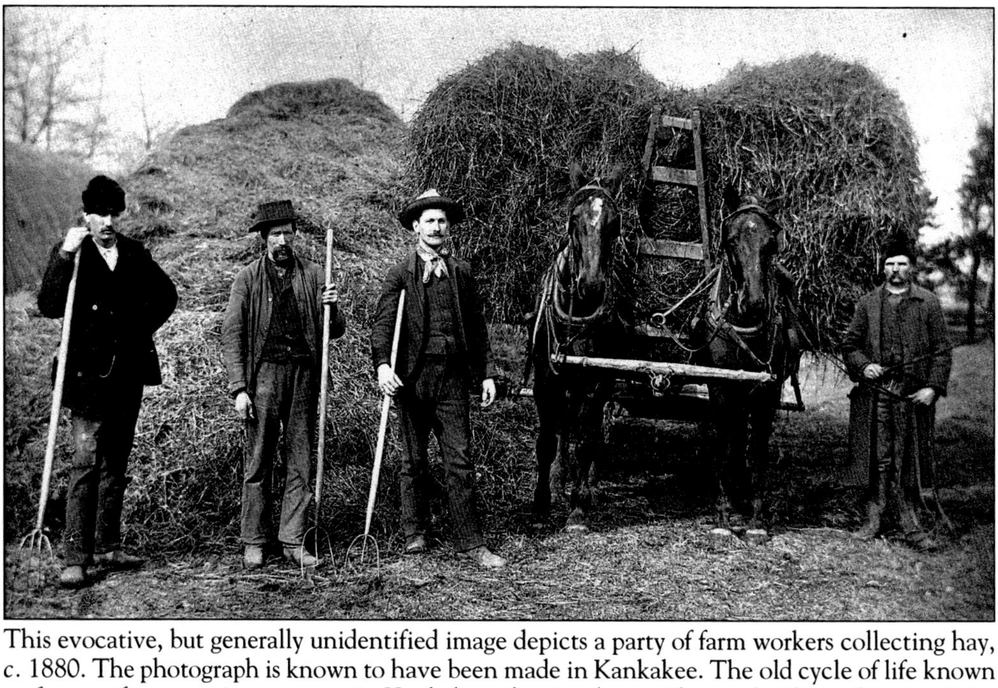

This evocative, but generally unidentified image depicts a party of farm workers collecting hay, c. 1880. The photograph is known to have been made in Kankakee. The old cycle of life known to farmers for centuries went on in Kankakee, despite the rapid growth of merchant activity and the eventual advent of the modern world. (Kankakee County Museum Photographic Collection, P5468.)

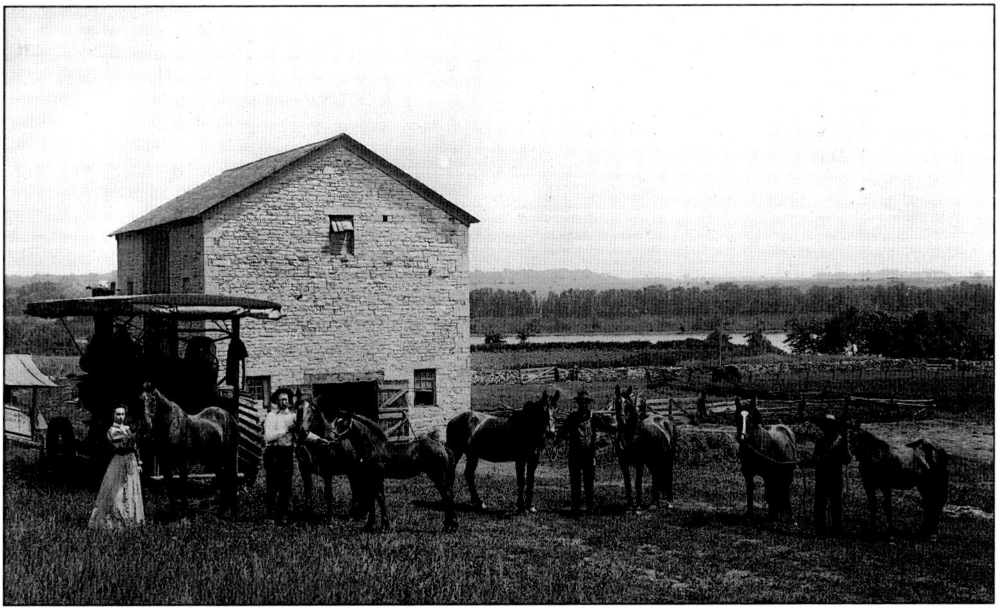

Sarah and Andrew Wiley are seen here (to the left) with their stone barn in 1910. The steam tractor was owned by their son, Merritt Wiley, who lived nearby and was a locally recognized, expert horse breeder. Sarah and Andrew's place, known as "Wiley Creek Farm," was located on the southern bank of the Kankakee River. (Kankakee County Museum Photographic Collection, P3031.)

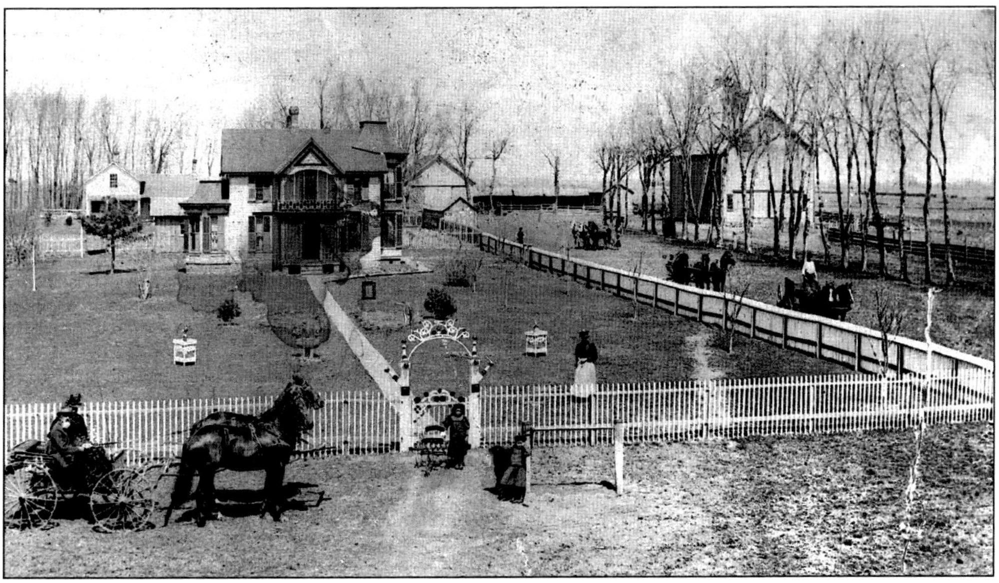

Just beyond the commercial center of the City of Kankakee, many neighborhoods still had a somewhat rural character. In this 1895 image, Mr. and Mrs. Semer Colman are seen arriving home in their carriage. The Colemans were one of the first families to settle the Norton Township section of Kankakee. (Kankakee County Museum Photographic Collection, P3133.)

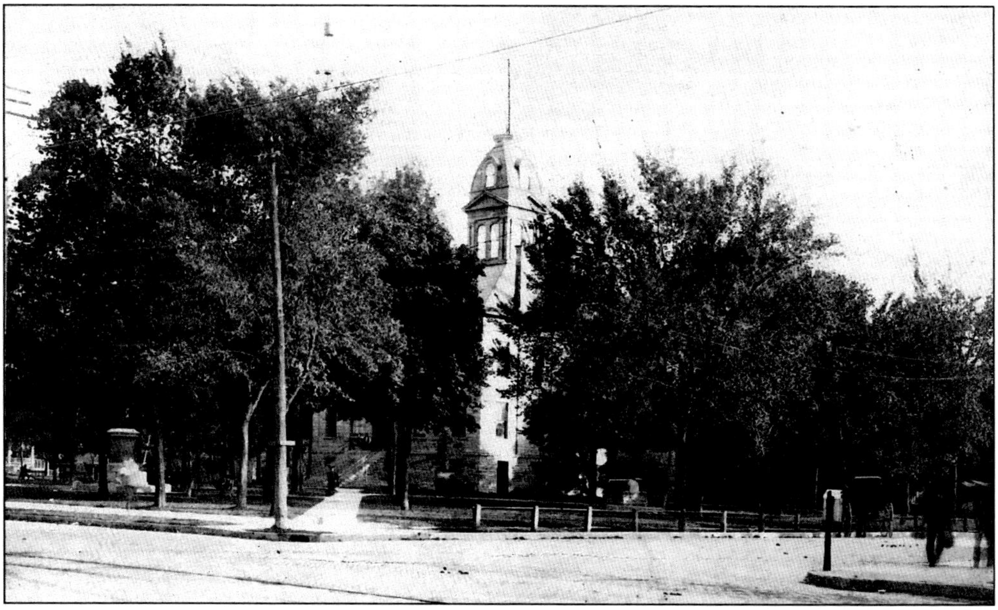

The center of the City of Kankakee was the Kankakee County Court House. This photograph shows the second court house, completed in 1873, in a view from the corner of Court Street and Indiana Avenue looking southeast. The Civil War Soldier's Monument can be seen at lower left. The second court house was razed in 1908, with construction completed on the third and present structure in 1912. (Kankakee County Museum Photographic Collection, P0836.)

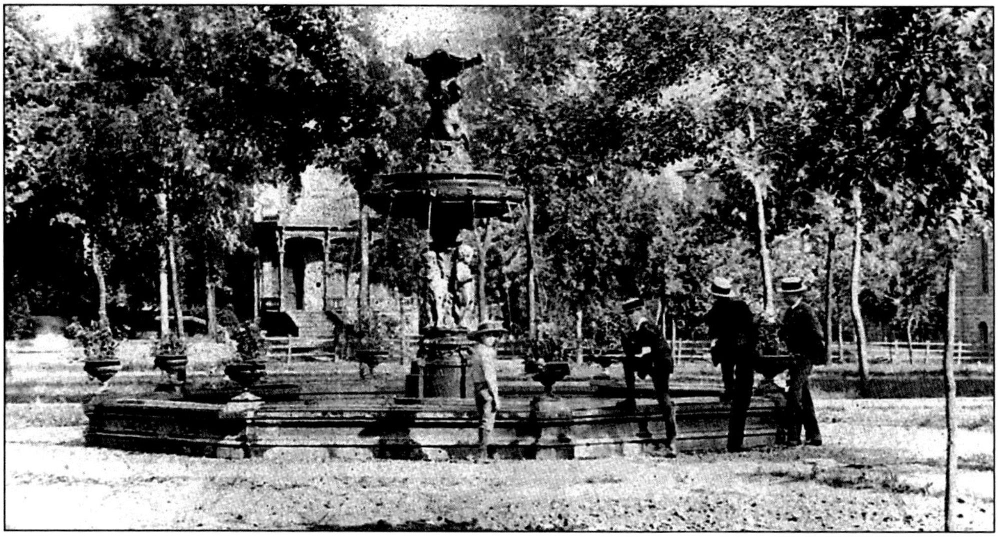

In late 1886, the county appropriated $500 for a fountain to beautify the courthouse square. Many thought it an unnecessary waste of money, but the *Kankakee Gazette* noted, "The plain truth of the matter is, the County ought to make a nice park out of the courthouse square. What cheek to fight against the expenditure of $500 for a public fountain!" It wasn't until 1890 that the 12-foot high fountain, with a jet of water a further 12-feet from the fountain's top, was completed. This image shows some young gentlemen at the fountain, c. 1900. During construction of the third court house in 1909, the fountain was removed to the grounds of Notre Dame Convent in Bourbonnais. (Kankakee County Museum Photographic Collection, P0835.)

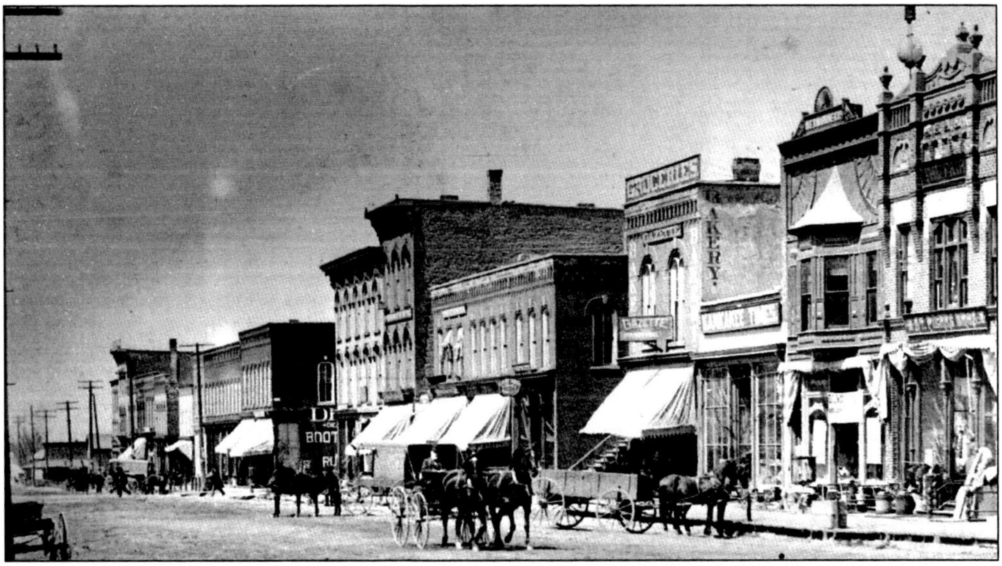

Lemuel Milk, an ice merchant and owner of the Waldron Ice House, can be seen in this image, driving his matched team of Morgan horses along Kankakee's Court Street in 1888. This photograph clearly shows the main commercial area of the City of Kankakee, *c.* 1880. To Mr. Milk's right is the *Kankakee Gazette*, located in the Hall Building, which was built in 1854 as the first brick structure in Kankakee. The *Gazette* was first published in 1853, with Augustin Chester setting up his press and printing his paper outside at the northeastern corner of Court Street and Schuyler Avenue under an oak tree. Editor Chester thought that a free press could not wait until the Hall Building was completed. (Kankakee County Museum Photographic Collection, P3132.)

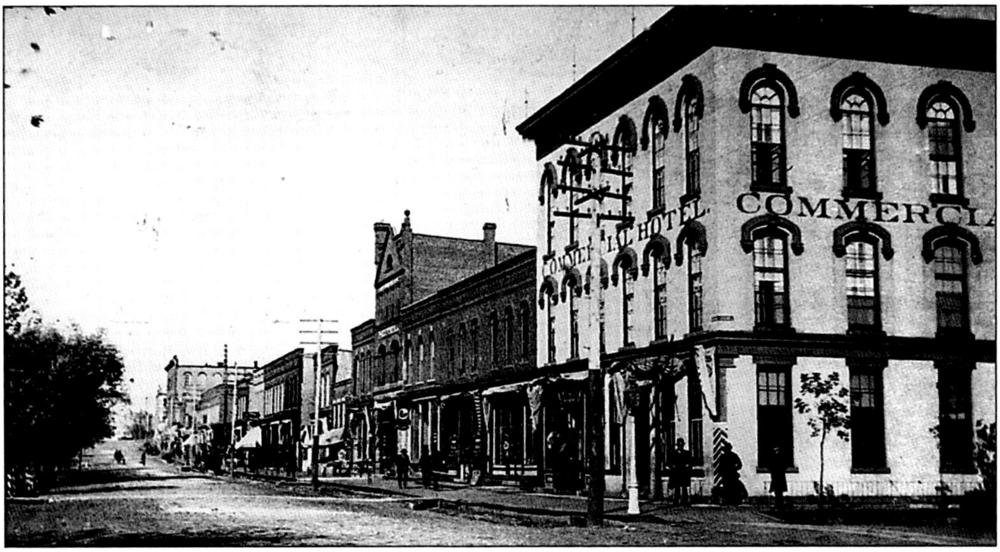

In another view of the main commercial area of the City of Kankakee, *c.* 1880, can be seen the Commercial Hotel, located at the corner of East Avenue and Station Street. In the second half of the 19th century, the Commercial Hotel, which was constructed in 1858, remained the most commonly used location in Kankakee for public and private meetings. It was originally intended to house the Kankakee County Bank. (Kankakee County Museum Photographic Collection, P0074.)

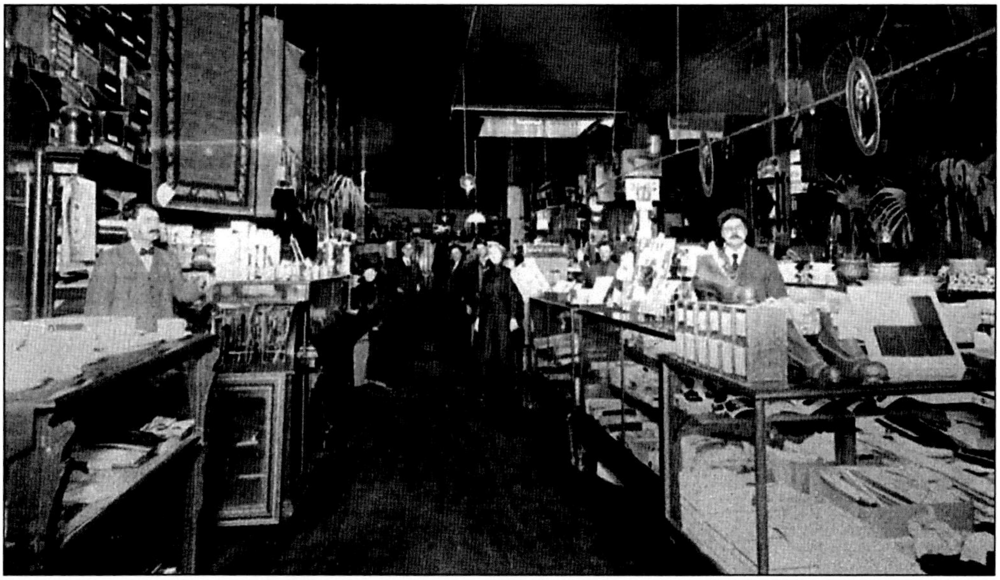

The interior of an unidentified Kankakee area merchant's store, which sold clothing and dry goods, was photographed in 1890. Ready-made clothing, shoe sizes, and even right and left shoes had only been developed as late as the Civil War. Note the wood floors and wood display cases. Store clerks stand ready to assist their customers with a shopping experience very different from that known only a generation before. (Kankakee County Museum Photographic Collection, P3207.)

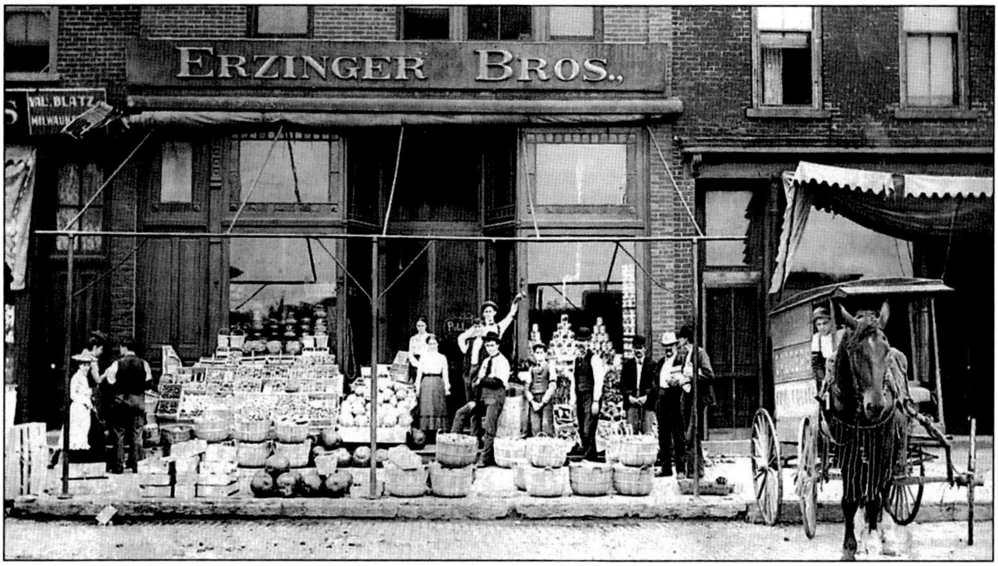

The employees of Erzinger Brothers, located on East Avenue and the largest grocery store in the City of Kankakee, were photographed displaying their wares on September 18, 1900. Their delivery wagon, advertising "Grocers, Fine Fruits," stands ready to send out orders, such as the watermelons on the sidewalk. Customers can be seen to the left of the photograph making their purchases. George Erzinger opened his grocery business in 1891. His father, Ulrich Erzinger, came from Germany in 1864 to work on the railroad. (Kankakee County Museum Photographic Collection, P0440.)

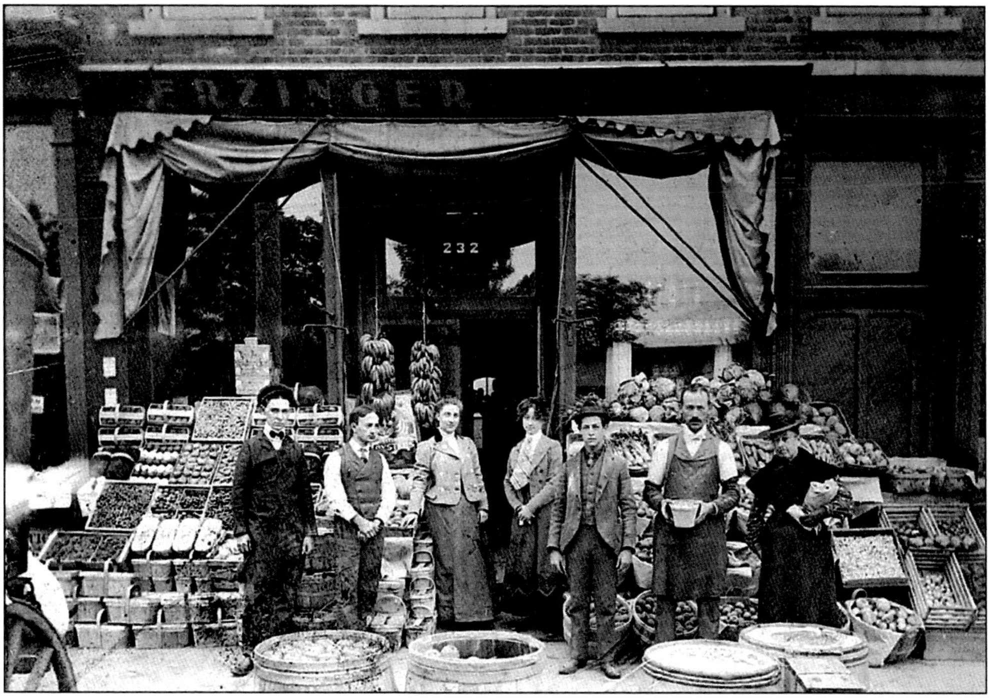

Erzinger Brothers employed 22 clerks, making it one of the largest employers in Kankakee. This photograph was taken in October 1905. The gentleman wearing an apron and holding a basket (second from the right) is William Erzinger, one of the owners. His wife, Laura Erzinger, is the woman standing in the doorway (fourth from the right). Bananas can be seen hanging in the doorway. (Kankakee County Museum Photographic Collection, P0487.)

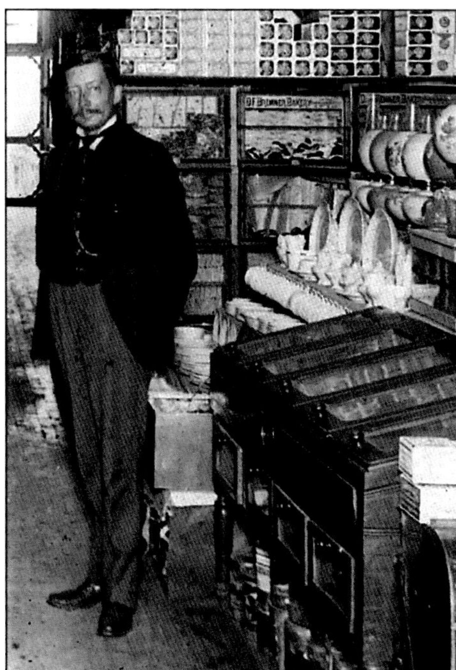

Another prominent Kankakee area grocer, August Ehrich, stands in the aisle of his Court Street store in this image made in 1901. Behind him is a display table of dishware and kerosene lamps. August Ehrich took an interest in the modernization of Kankakee's commercial district. He served as the treasurer of the North Kankakee Railroad Company, organized in June 1892, to operate electric street cars in the City of Kankakee. (Kankakee County Museum Photographic Collection, P3049.)

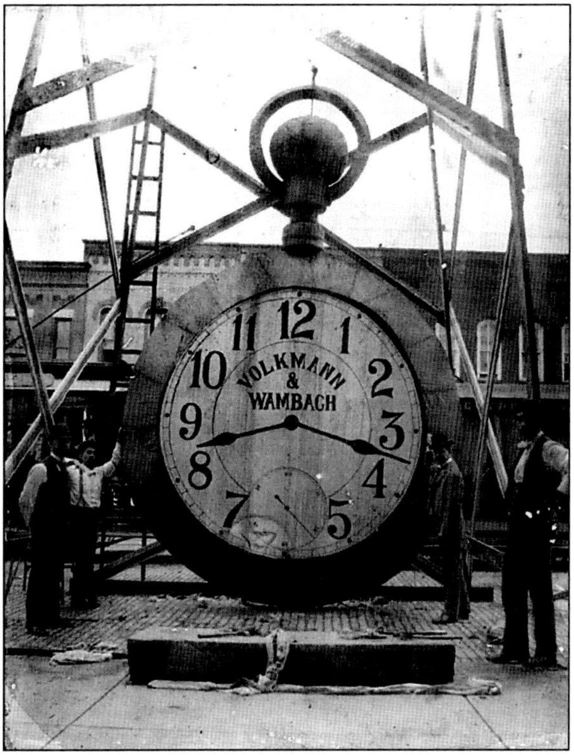

Kankakee area merchants organized street fairs to generate business, but also to maintain the interest of Kankakee residents in their thriving commercial district. In this photograph, workmen are preparing to hoist a large watch advertising Volkmann and Wambach, well-known Kankakee watchmakers and jewelers, at the 1899 Kankakee Street Fair. (Kankakee County Museum Photographic Collection, P3552.)

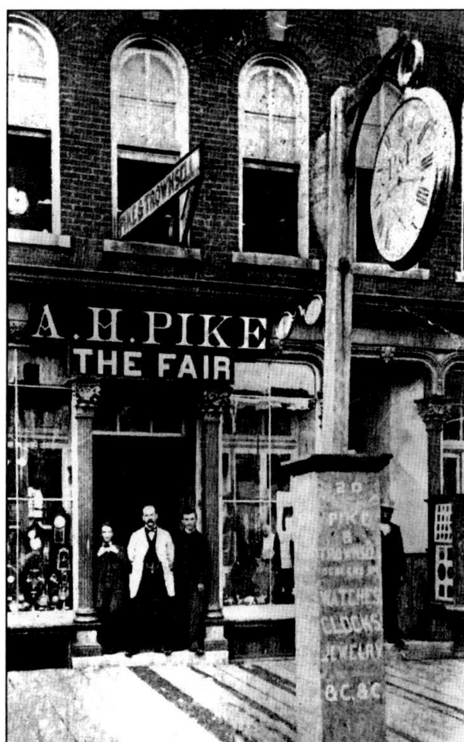

The Fair Building was located on the City of Kankakee's East Court Street. This photograph was taken in 1877. The main attraction at the Fair was the Pike and Trownsell Jewelry Store. Jeweler A.H. Pike, standing in the center of the doorway, also owned the Fair Building eventually purchased by his competitor Volkmann. Note the large clock advertisement, used to attract customers of limited literacy. (Kankakee County Museum Photographic Collection, P0552.)

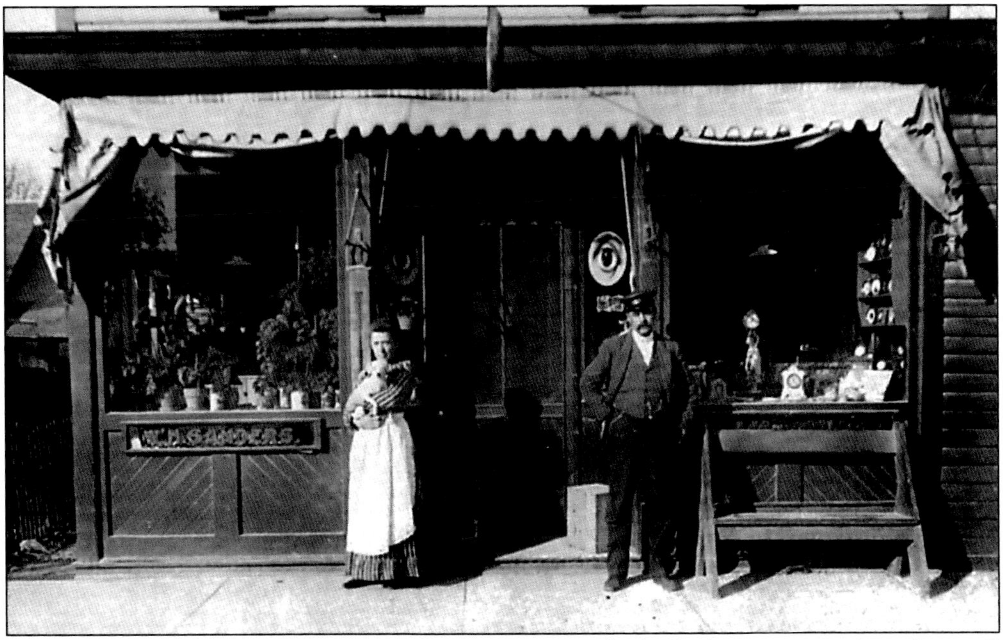

Kankakee's large jewelers, Volkmann, Pike, and Trownsell, also had competition from the small "mom and pop" jewelry store operated by William Sanders on Kankakee's Main Street. This photograph of him, his wife, and their dog was taken in 1897. Note their advertisement sign shaped like a watch appearing over their doorway. (Kankakee County Museum Photographic Collection, P5698.)

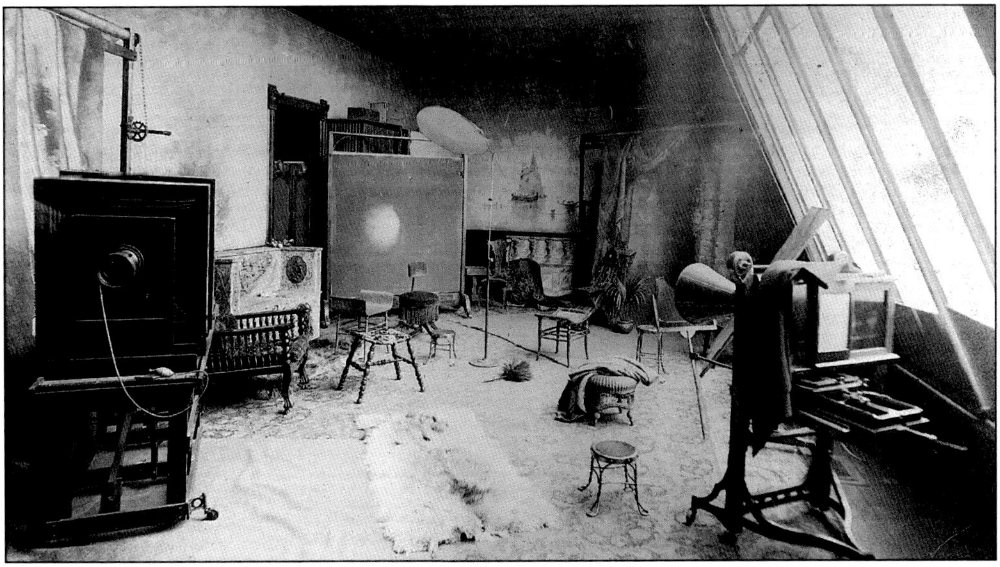

Photography arrived in America in 1839. In the antebellum era, daguerreotype shops and photographic artists, could be found in virtually any community. Studio photography became increasingly popular following the Civil War. The interior of Powell Studio, the most important photographer in the City of Kankakee, appears in this 1892 image. Note the painted backdrop and studio props littered about the room. (Kankakee County Museum Photographic Collection, P0790.)

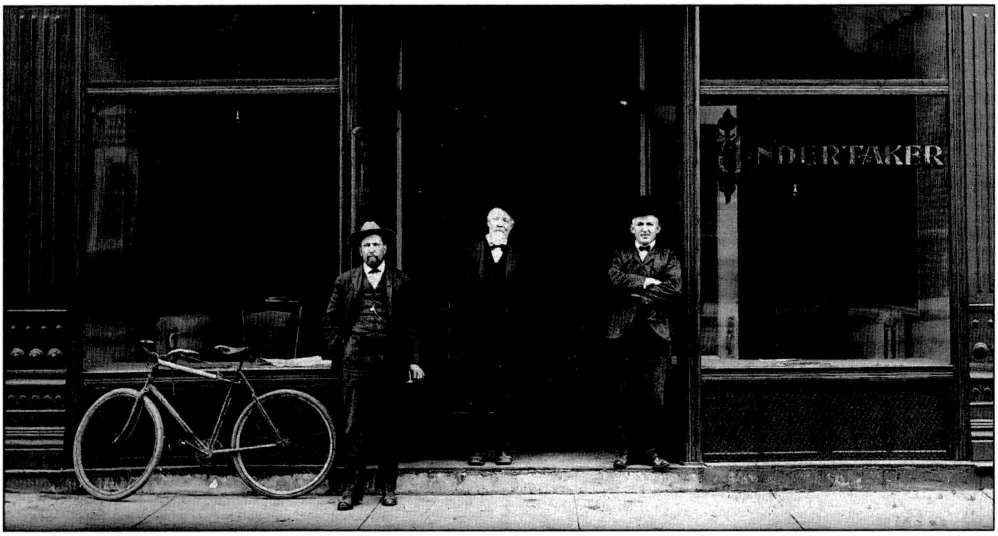

Flanked by his two assistant mortuary surgeons, David Lavery stands in the doorway of his undertaking establishment, located on Kankakee's East Merchant Street. The photograph was made, *c.* 1890, when Mr. Lavery or his employees would have gone to the home of the deceased. Toward the later part of the 19th century, professional morticians began to move the act of dressing the dead from the private home to the funeral parlor. Bereaved families came to expect morticians to deliver an antiseptically clean corpse, carefully presented with corpse cosmetics, to their cemetery of choice. (Kankakee County Museum Photographic Collection, P0794.)

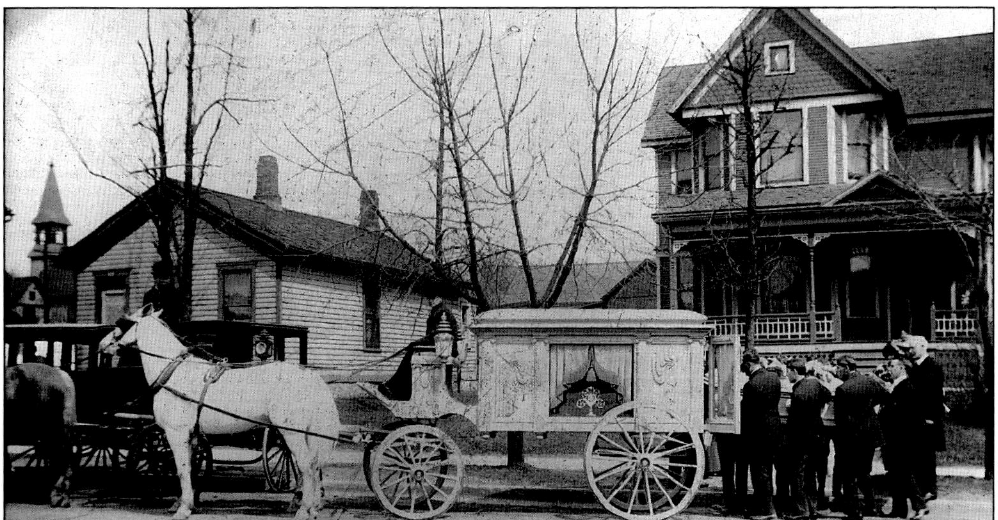

Kankakee area undertaker Harry Rehr organized this funeral, starting from a private home located at Kankakee's East Avenue and River Street. Traditional mourning colors were scarlet and white, rather than the more modern black, as is clearly evidenced in this 1900 photograph with pallbearers lifting a white casket into a white hearse drawn by a white horse to take the deceased to an area cemetery. Carefully manicured cemeteries were in fashion, where families could visit their dead. Such visitations were considered family outings and it was not uncommon to take Sunday dinner as a discreet picnic wherein all the family, both the living and the dead, could participate. (Kankakee County Museum Photographic Collection, P3088.)

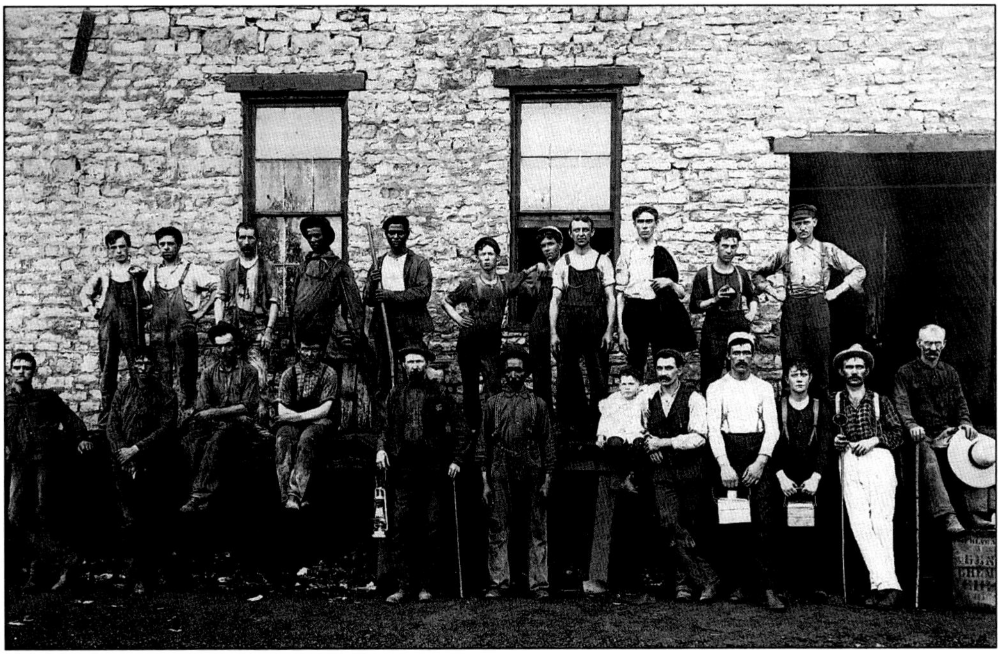

The employees of a Kankakee area paper mill gathered for this group photograph in 1910. Two workers at lower right are carrying their dinner pails. Interestingly for the period, it is a racially mixed work force with three African-American men appearing in the group. The gentleman holding the lantern is apparently the foreman. (Kankakee County Museum Photographic Collection, P2463.)

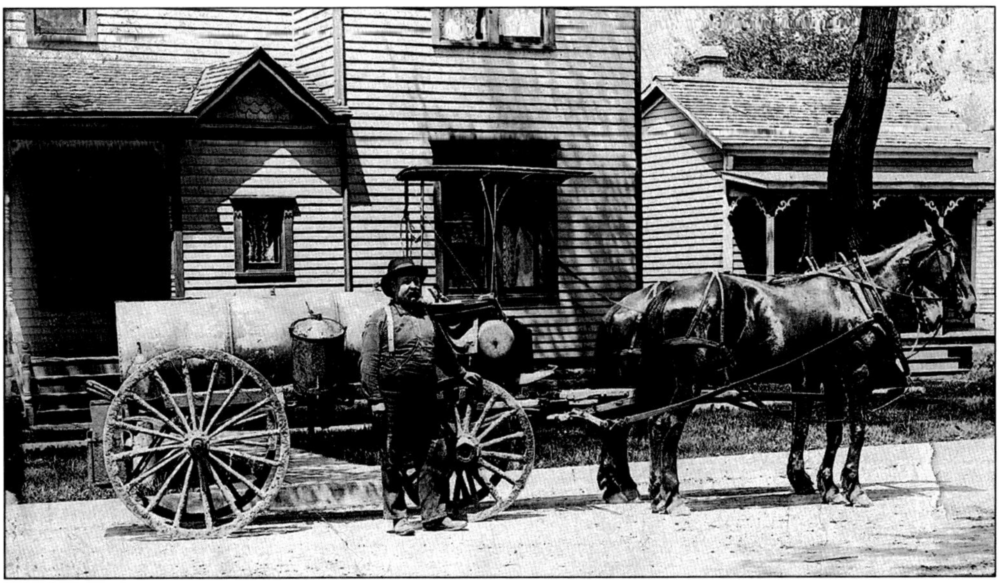

Stores and manufacturing firms came to dominate Kankakee's commercial areas, yet there still remained individual entrepreneurs. Samuel Newcomb, for example, continued to deliver individual shipments of kerosene and gasoline to his customers with a simple horse-drawn wagon at the turn of the 20th century. He is shown here in 1902. (Kankakee County Museum Photographic Collection, P8319.)

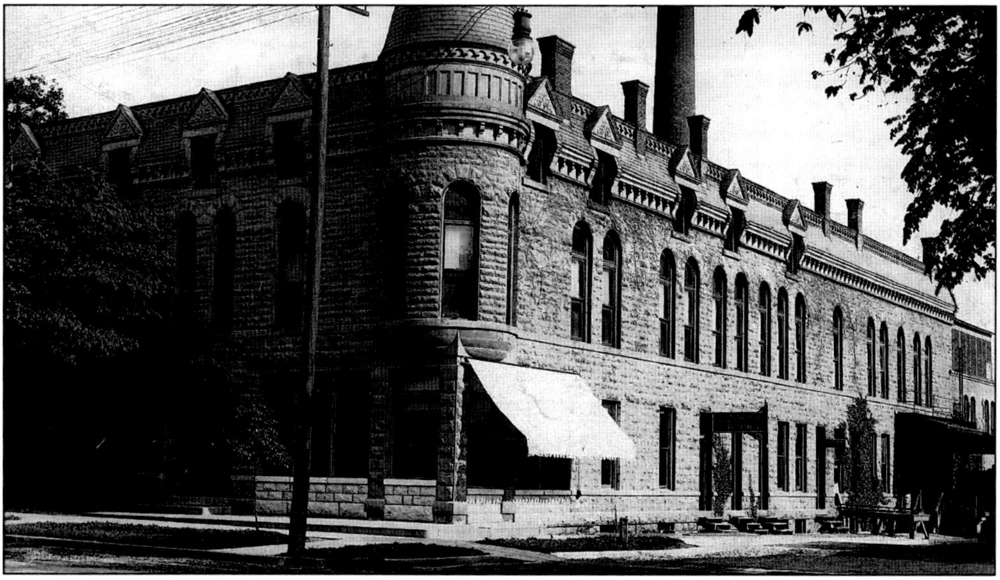

In 1875, Kankakee grocer Frederick Radeke created the F.D. Radeke Brewing Company. This photograph shows the Radeke office building, *c.* 1900. The entire Radeke complex was located on the southeast corner of River Street and Dearborn Avenue, right on the bank of the Kankakee River. At the beginning of the 20th century, Radeke employed 85 workers, annually producing 45,000 gallons of beer. (Kankakee County Museum Photographic Collection, P0302.)

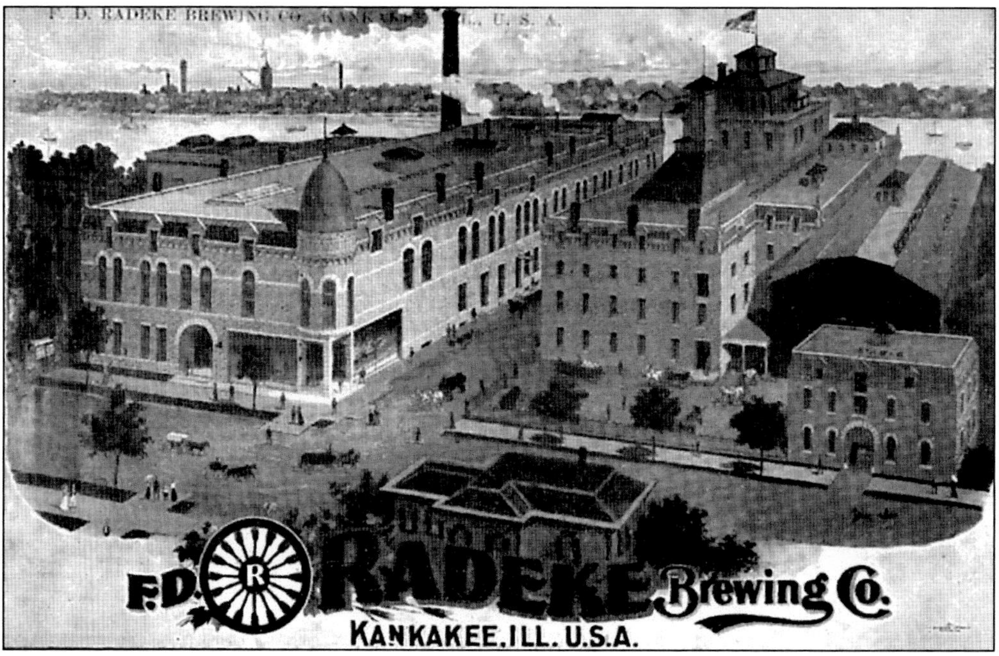

This view of the entire F.D. Radeke Brewing Company complex is taken from a late 19th-century postcard sold by Radeke as a piece of promotional literature. Contemporary Radeke publicity enthused that their brewery operation was, "one of the largest in this part of the state and occupies a high place in the consideration of the public, both for purity of product, honesty of purpose and for its large output." (Kankakee County Museum Photographic Collection, P8243.)

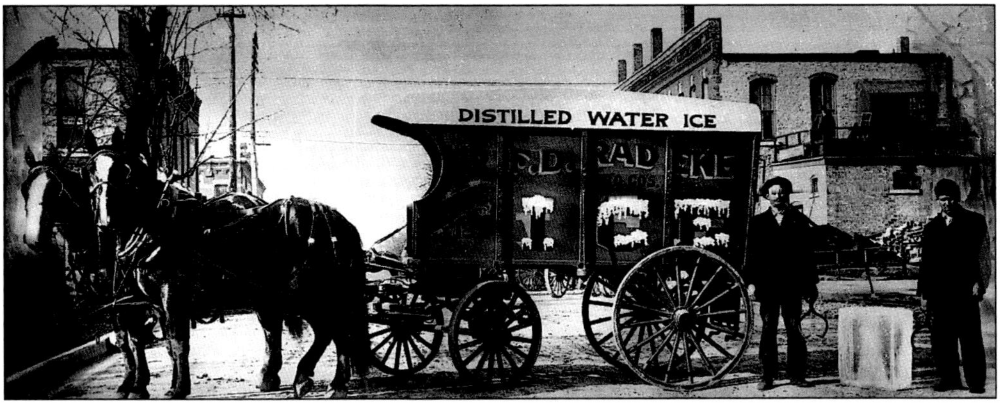

The F.D. Radeke Brewing Company, in conjunction with its brewing operations, maintained an ice plant capable of producing a daily capacity of 15 tons. By 1870, there was a large and lucrative natural ice business being conducted along the Kankakee River. Radeke employee Frederick Jennings (second from right) is shown here in this 1910 image in the process of loading Radeke Ice for local delivery. (Kankakee County Museum Photographic Collection, P3307.)

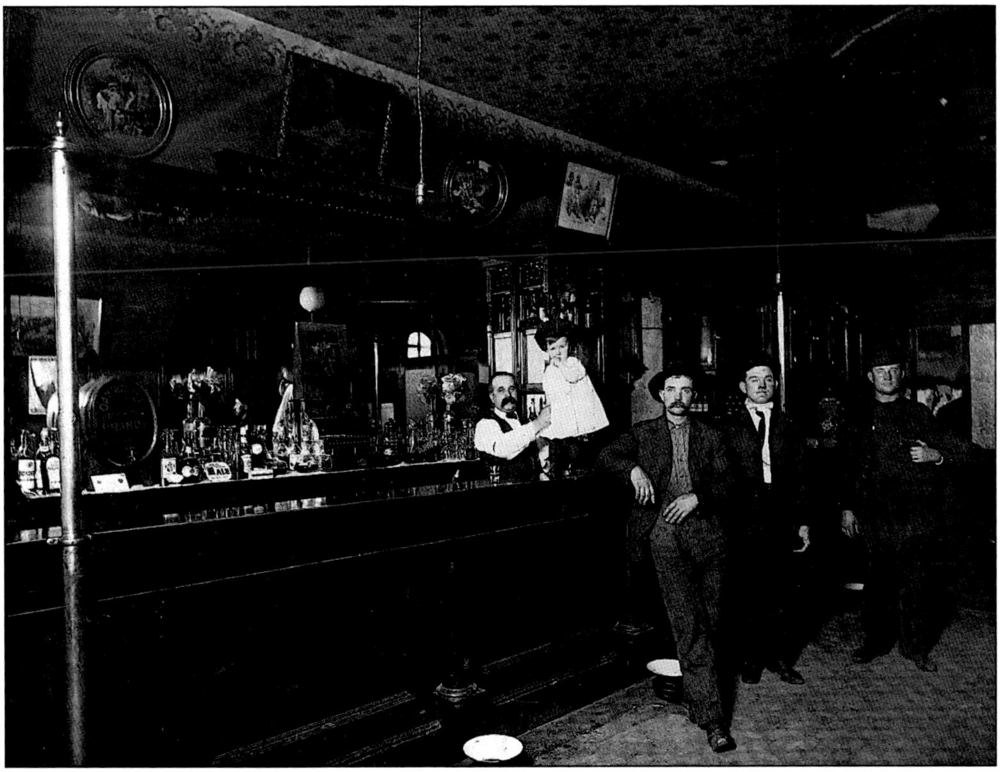

Radeke Beer was sold at local Kankakee bars and was doubtlessly available in this Court Street saloon, shown in this image, *c.* 1900. Bartender Neil Langlois holds his son Leo, while his working-class customers look squarely into the camera. The reclining female nude painting and the etching of bare knuckle prize fighters near the ceiling, as well as the metal spittoons on the floor, testify to the unique "manly" atmosphere of the saloon. (Kankakee County Museum Photographic Collection, P5682.)

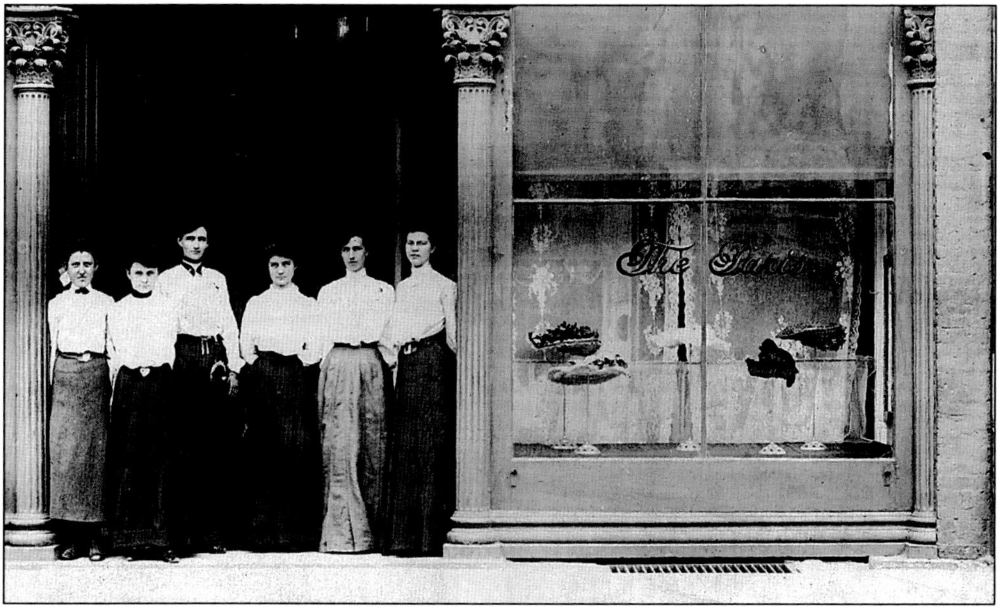

The main entrance of The Paris, Kankakee's exclusive millinery shop located on the south side of Court Street between Dearborn and Schuyler Avenues, is seen in this photograph taken in 1902. Mrs. Viola Henry, who owned and operated The Paris, stands at the left of the photograph next to five of her employees. (Kankakee County Museum Photographic Collection, P0550.)

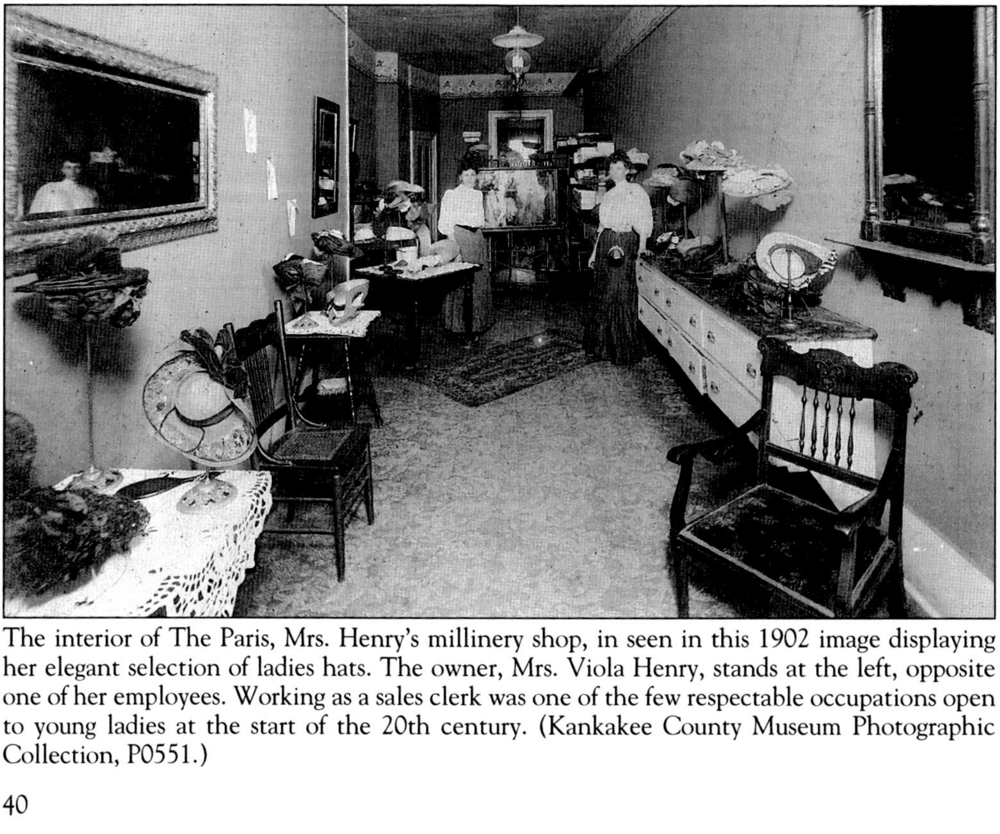

The interior of The Paris, Mrs. Henry's millinery shop, in seen in this 1902 image displaying her elegant selection of ladies hats. The owner, Mrs. Viola Henry, stands at the left, opposite one of her employees. Working as a sales clerk was one of the few respectable occupations open to young ladies at the start of the 20th century. (Kankakee County Museum Photographic Collection, P0551.)

The formally attired Mr. Jesse Thomas Murray appeared in this artful advertisement for H.A. Magruder, Clothier, c. 1890. The diversified Mr. Magruder was also employed as vice president of the Kankakee County Savings Bank. (Kankakee County Museum Photographic Collection, P6040.)

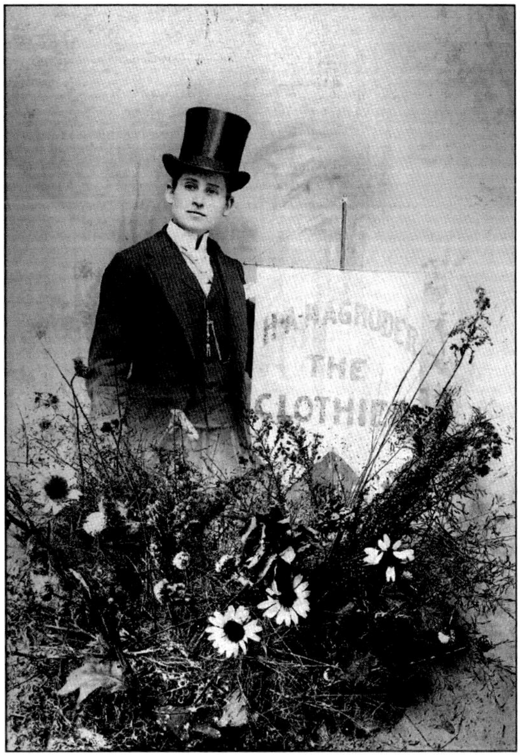

The Knecht Building, built in 1869 and located at the corner of Kankakee's Court Street and East Avenue, is seen in this photograph taken in May 1900. The Knecht Building was owned by John George Knecht, who operated a clothing store in two-thirds of the structure. To the left in the image, behind the two ladies, is F.E. Bellamy's art supply shop. On the second floor are insurance and real estate offices, and appearing at right in the photograph, toward the rear of the building, is an ice cream parlor. (Kankakee County Museum Photographic Collection, P0205.)

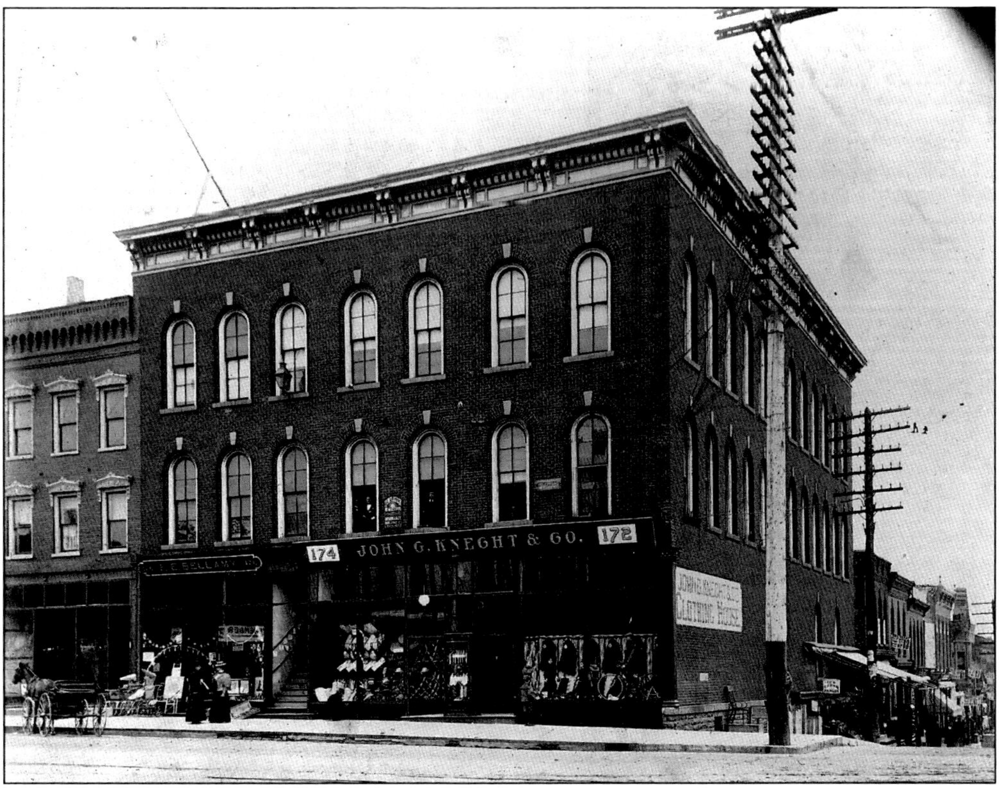

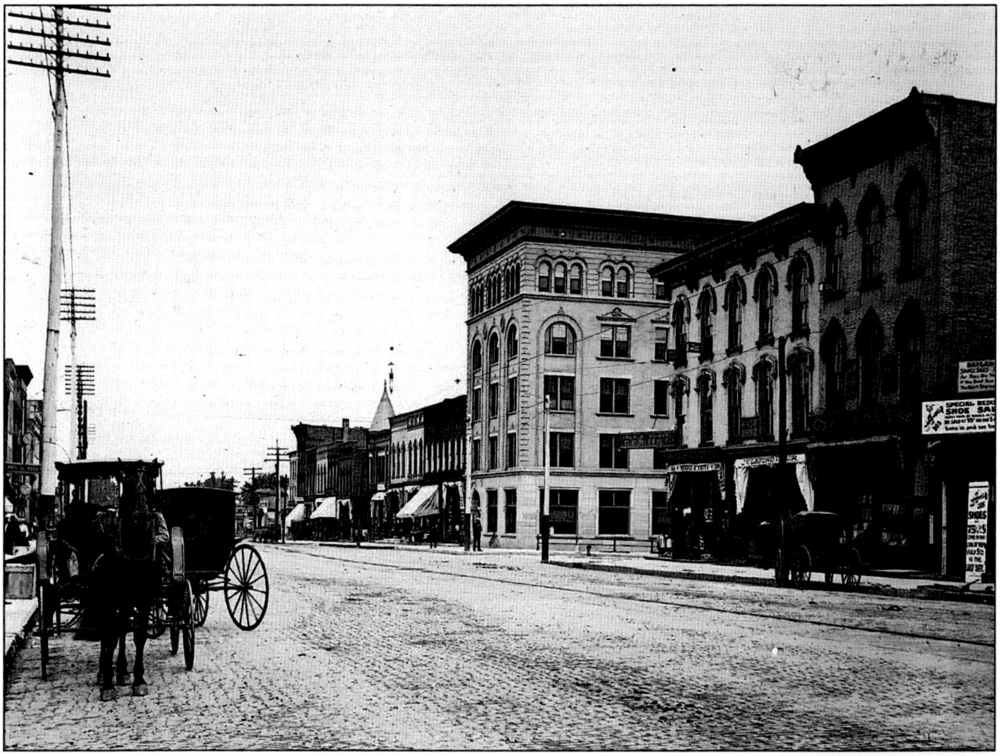

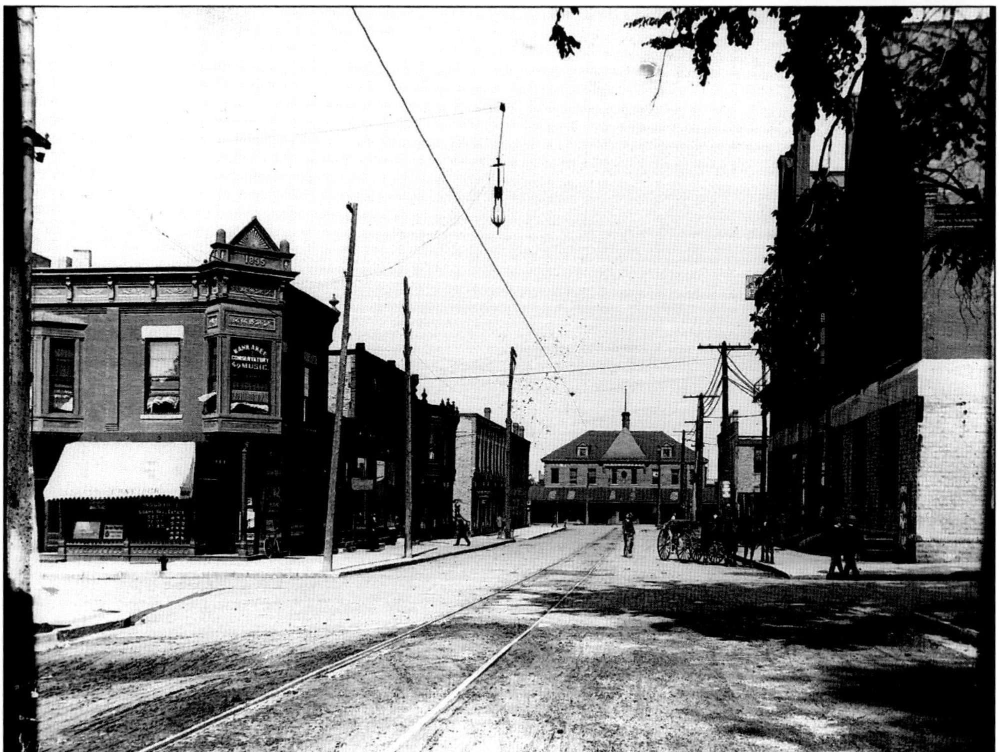
1895
KANKAKEE
CONSERVATORY
OF MUSIC

Opposite, top: By the turn of the 20th century, Kankakee had developed an impressive business district. This photograph shows the north side of Kankakee's Court Street, newly paved with cobblestones, looking west along Kankakee's main commercial district, *c*. 1900. The large edifice in the center of the photograph was owned by the City National Bank, which shared space with a sister financial institution, the Kankakee County Savings Bank. Various offices occupied upper floors, with the Kankakee Commercial Club, a social organization for Kankakee area businessmen, housed on the fifth floor. (Kankakee County Museum Photographic Collection, P1321.)

Opposite, bottom: It was the railroad that provided the initial impetus for the development of Kankakee Depot into the City of Kankakee, and at the turn of the 20th century the railroad was still important to the life of the city. This 1910 image shows the Illinois Central Depot Building, constructed in 1890, at the foot of Kankakee's Merchant Street. The Arcade Building appears to the right, and opposite on the southwest corner of Merchant Street and Schuyler Avenue is an 1895 building occupied by the Kankakee Conservatory of Music and the Kankakee Savings and Loan Association. (Kankakee County Museum Photographic Collection, P5939.)

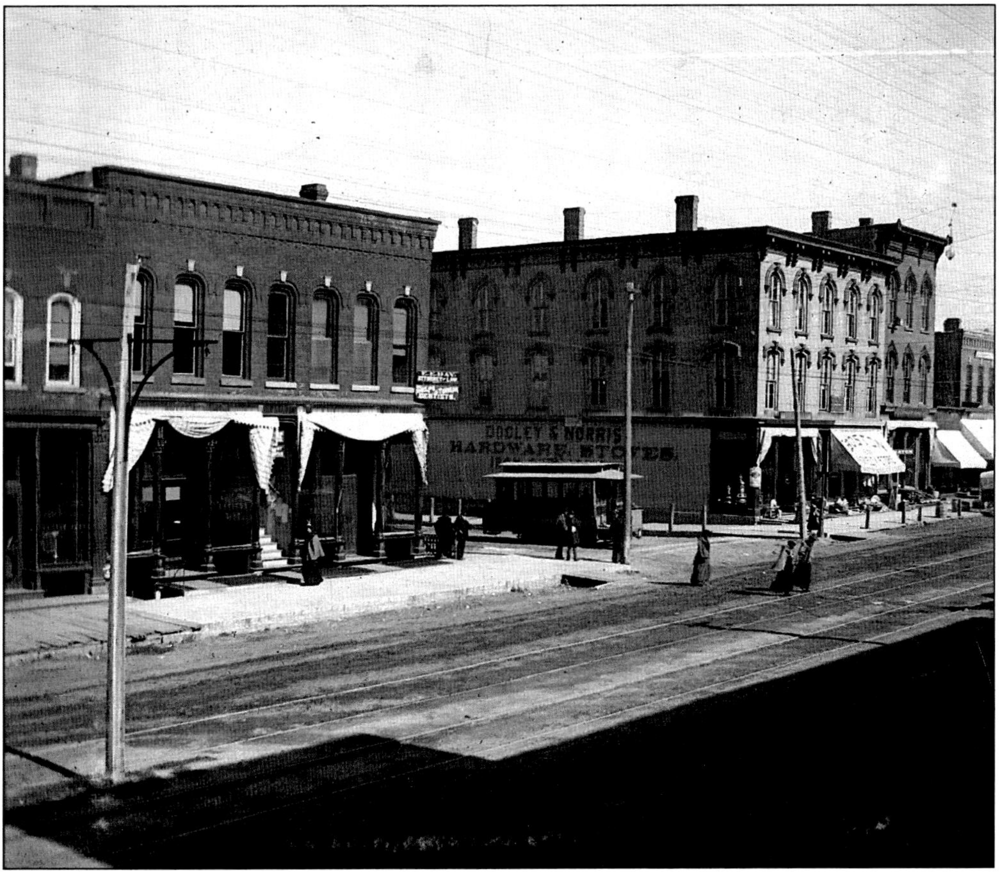

Daily life goes on in the City of Kankakee, illustrated in this photograph taken in 1891 of Court Street. The electric streetcar sits on Schuyler Avenue between the Dooley and Norris Store, selling hardware, and Dr. Phelps' dentist office. The lone woman crossing Court Street is Miss Minnie Albert, who worked at North Schuyler sewing for Mrs. Rinquette. (Kankakee County Museum Photographic Collection, P3554.)

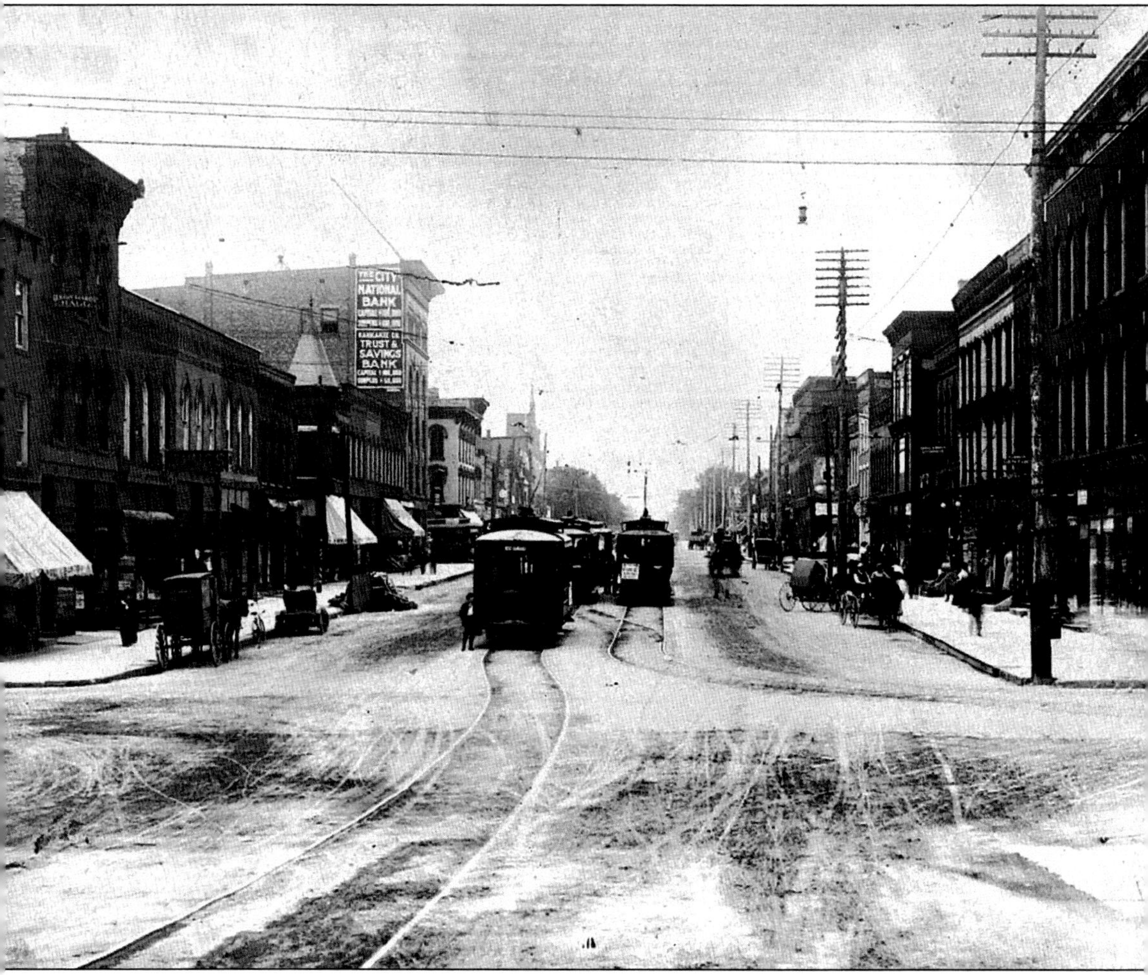

Looking east down Kankakee's Court Street, this 1910 image emphasizes the coming of modernity to the City of Kankakee's commercial district. The center of Court Street is occupied by electric street cars, their wires crossing overhead, and the street is bordered with telephone poles. Yet the continuity of the past is present too, represented by all the horse-drawn vehicles, the tracks made by their wheels clearly evident in the street. (Kankakee County Museum Photographic Collection, P3121.)

Opposite: The Kankakee River has always played an important part in the life of the Kankakee area. It has served both as a highway and as a vital component in the community's economic life. It has also been used by Kankakee's citizens as a site and vehicle for all types of recreational activity. These three gallants were photographed with their lady on the Kankakee in 1890, spending a lazy summer afternoon serenading her on the river. (Kankakee County Museum Photographic Collection, P3097.)

Three

THE KANKAKEE RIVER, STEAM BOATING, AND THE HOTEL RIVERVIEW

"The river is the essence of us"

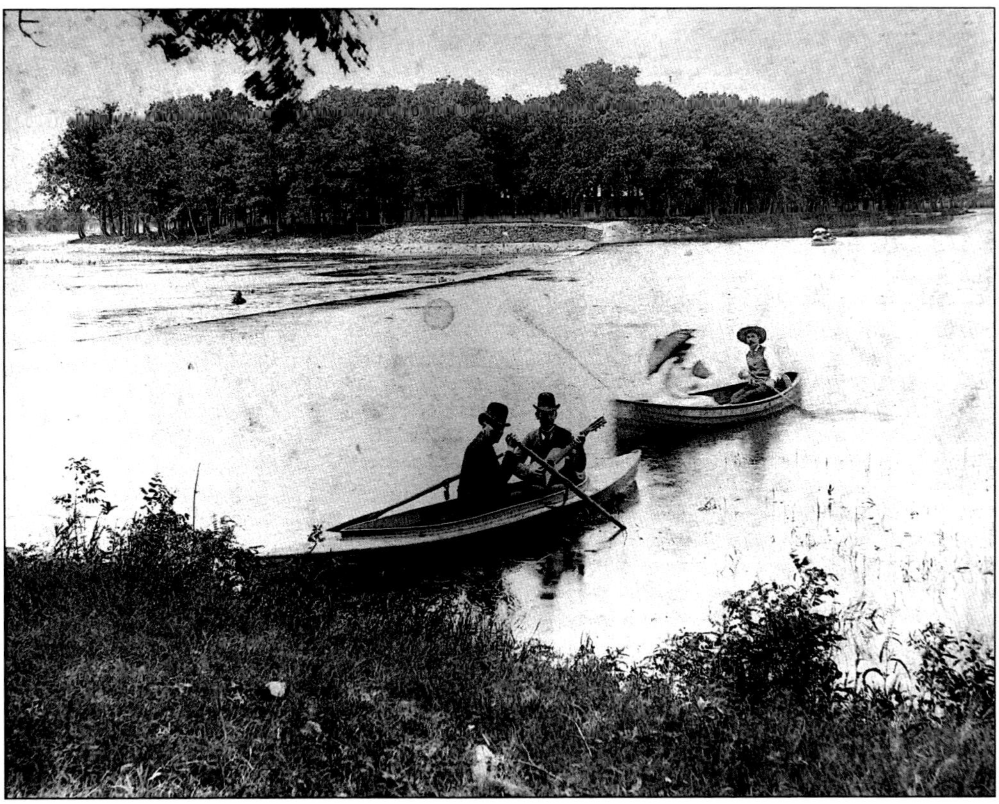

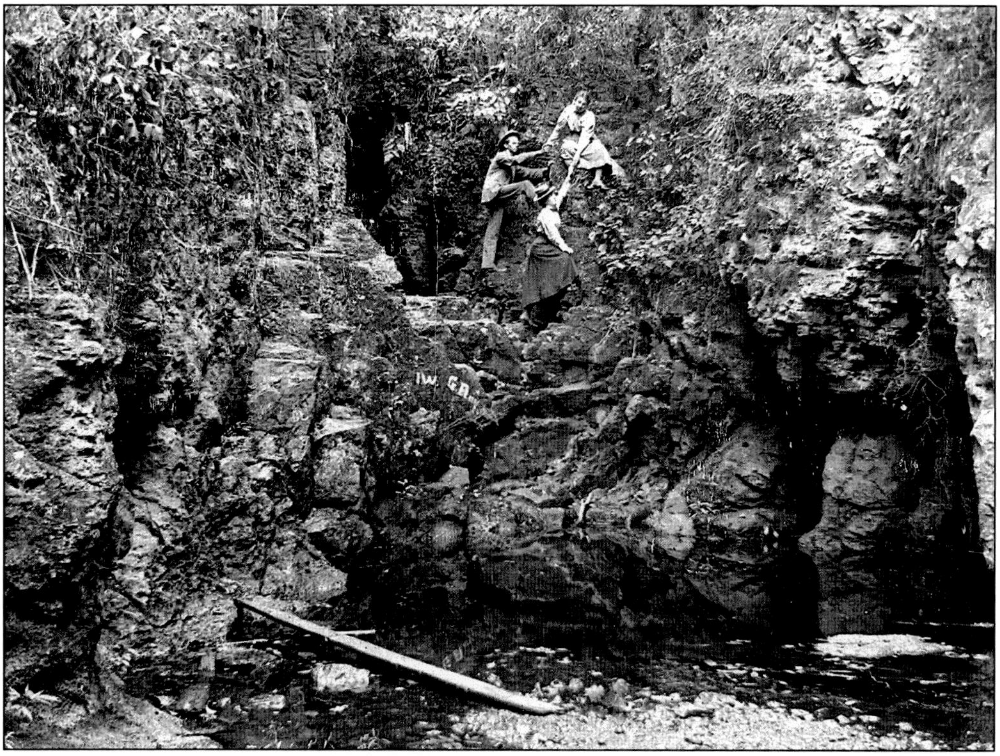

There is great natural beauty along the banks of the Kankakee River. It became very popular at the turn of the 20th century for Sunday excursionists to spend time exploring. The camera captured this trio in the summer of 1900 as they wandered along Rock Creek, which is located very near the eastern bank of the Kankakee. (Kankakee County Museum Photographic Collection, P8492.)

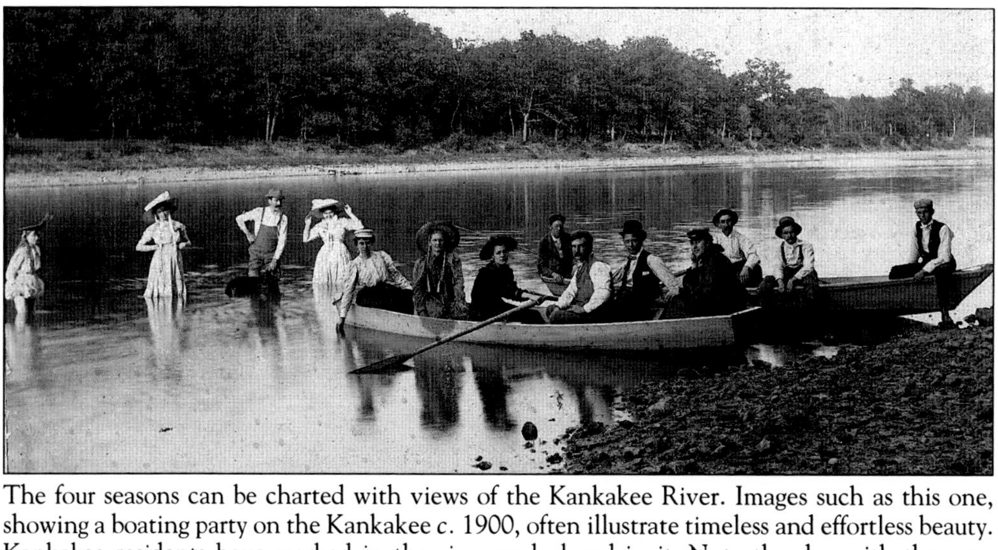

The four seasons can be charted with views of the Kankakee River. Images such as this one, showing a boating party on the Kankakee c. 1900, often illustrate timeless and effortless beauty. Kankakee residents have worked in the river and played in it. Note the dog with the man standing knee deep in the water, third from left in the photograph. (Kankakee County Museum Photographic Collection, P8527.)

Family entertainment was simple at the turn of the 20th century. Sitting before their family cottage on the bank of the Kankakee River, Nina Allison was photographed in the summer of 1892 reading to her sisters Mary and Caroline. Their father, an area attorney, represented Kankakee in the Illinois State House of Representatives. (Kankakee County Museum Photographic Collection, P0371.)

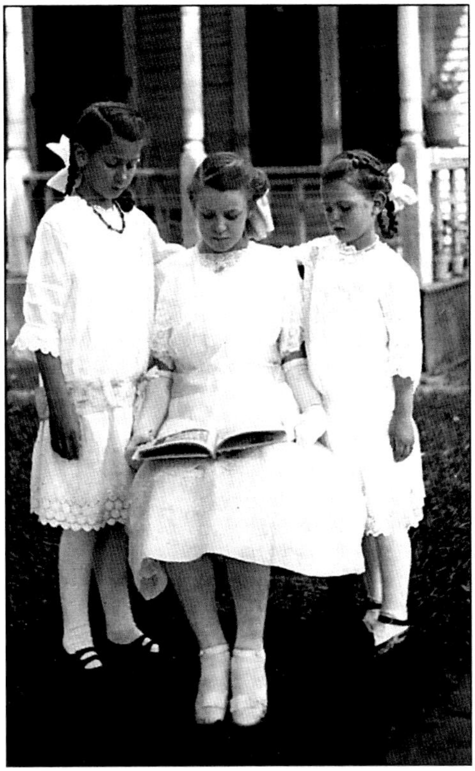

Seemingly less than enthusiastically, Oscar Kuntz poses with his family, consisting of his wife, four daughters, mother-in-law, the family dog, and, likely the real leader of the household, the family cat, in this image taken in 1896. They are on the porch steps of a rented cottage along the Kankakee River. Taking the family on summer vacation was a new concept. (Kankakee County Museum Photographic Collection, P3792.)

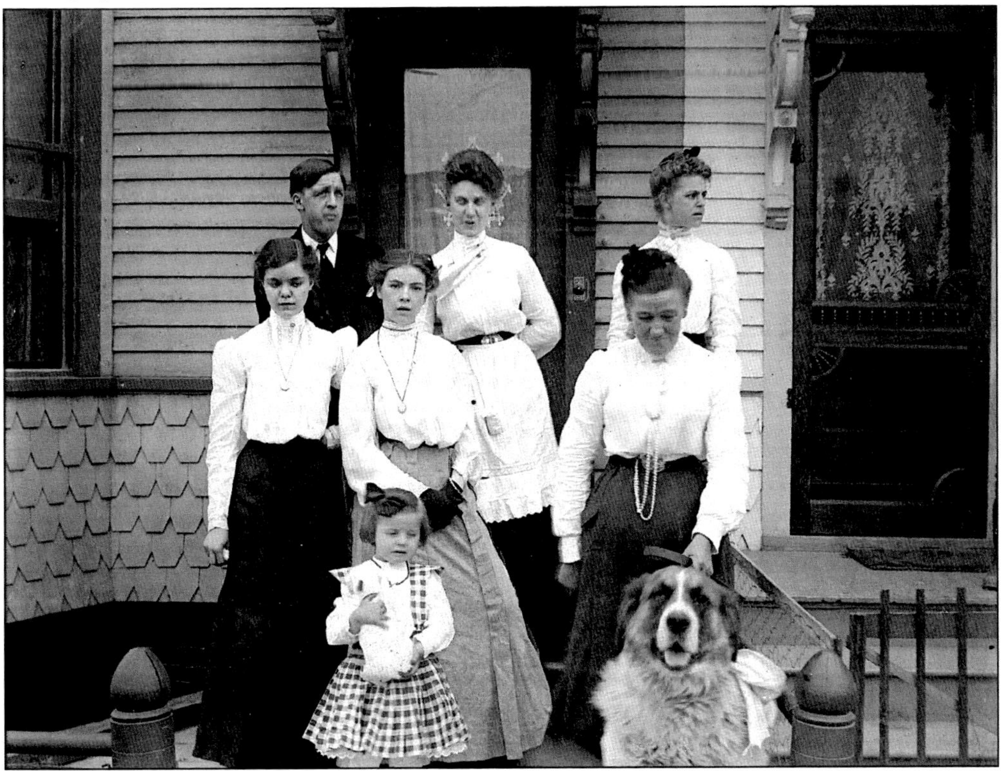

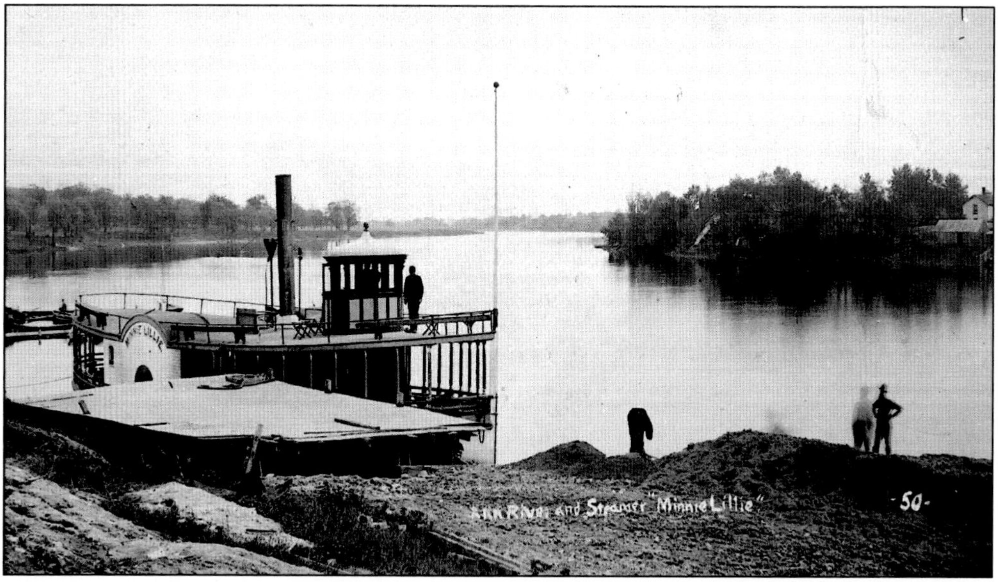

The steamer *Minnie Lillie* is shown here at her dock at the foot of Kankakee's Schuyler Avenue in 1885. William Gougar originally built her in 1883 to tow barges carrying his coal and sand for local architect James Lillie, busily overseeing the construction of the new state mental hospital. Gougar quickly found out how popular and lucrative she could be by taking area tourists on river excursions. The *Minnie Lillie* became a Kankakee fixture. She was hit by lightening and burned at her dock in 1896. (Kankakee County Museum Photographic Collection, P3443.)

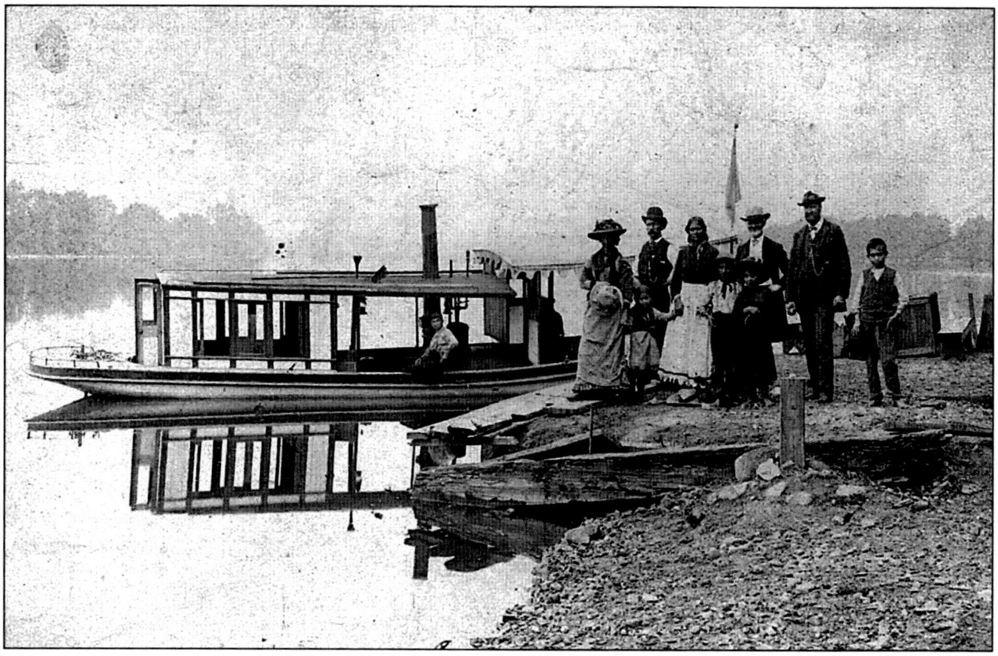

The success of the *Minnie Lillie* encouraged William Gougar in 1887 to purchase another pleasure boat, the steam launch *Shaubanee*. Capable of carrying 20 passengers, she operated on the Kankakee for the next 20 years. A group of excursionists are shown in this image prepared to board the *Shaubanee* in 1889. (Kankakee County Museum Photographic Collection, P3682.)

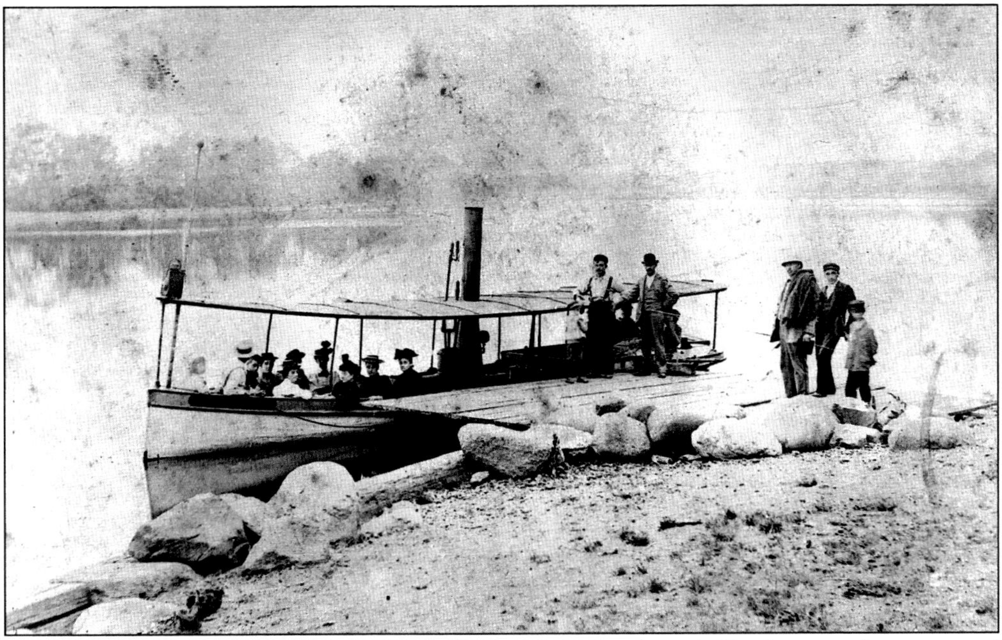

These passengers were photographed embarked on the steam launch *Shaubanee* in the summer of 1890. She made regular runs on the Kankakee River, carrying tourists to Gougar's Grove, where families could picnic and couples would spend romantic summer evenings dancing under the stars in an era before the advent of the automobile. (Kankakee County Museum Photographic Collection, P0764.)

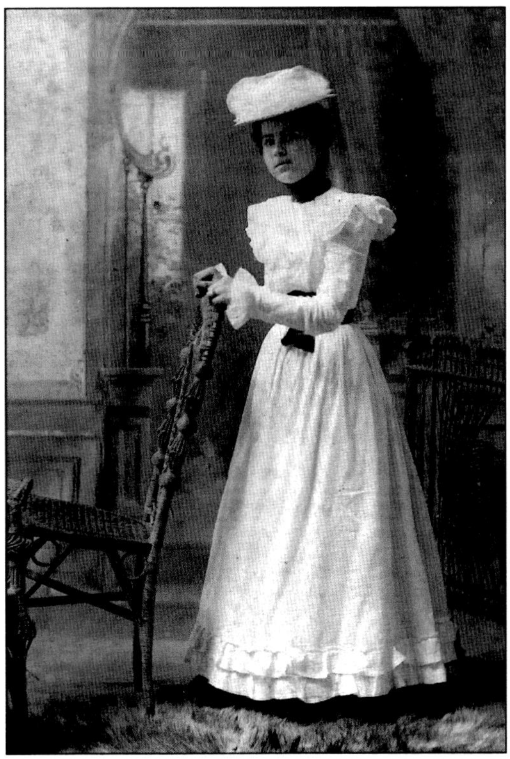

Perhaps one of the excursionists using Captain Gougar's steamboats was Miss Emma Kunde, shown wearing a new summer frock and posing for a formal portrait in 1895. (Kankakee County Museum Photographic Collection, P5593.)

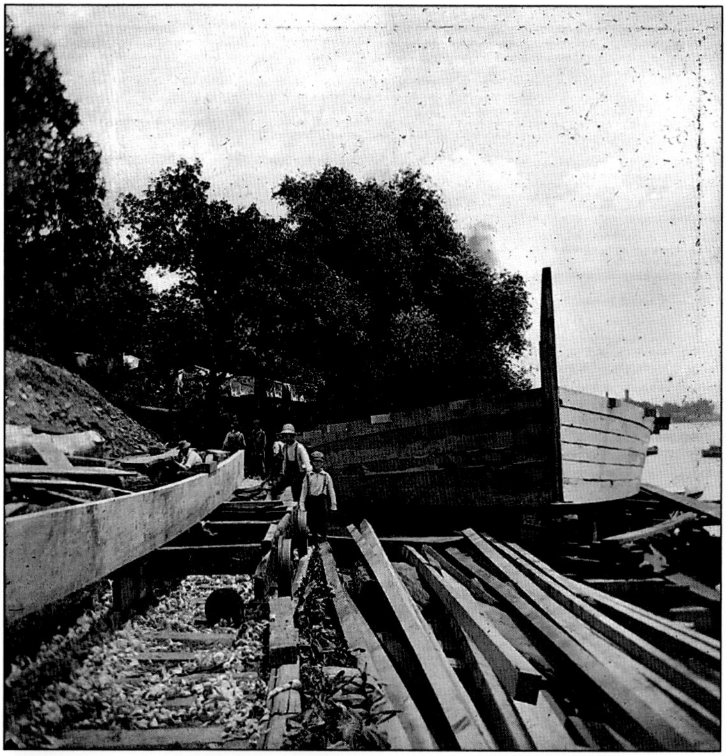

In the spring of 1898, Captain Gougar commenced construction of his largest and best excursionist steamer. Eventually christened the *Margaret*, she was laid down on the north bank of the Kankakee River, just west of Schuyler Avenue. In this photograph, her lower hull is completed and caulked. The primitive rail tracks appearing at left led to the nearby Wenzelman Saw Mill, which provided the *Margaret*'s timbers. (Kankakee County Museum Photographic Collection, P0808.)

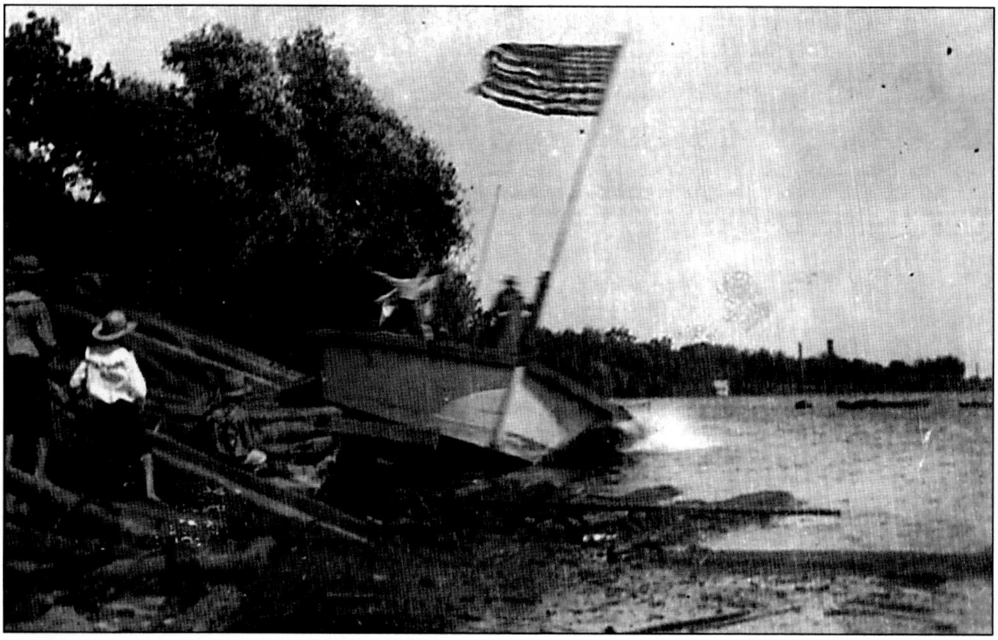

On June 9, 1898, *Margaret* was launched into the Kankakee River. With the ways lubricated with soft soap and tallow, she slid sideways into her natural element in the procedure usually employed in this era to launch small vessels into rivers. The American flag is seen proudly flying on her prow. The Spanish-American War was only a month old. (Kankakee County Museum Photographic Collection, P0810.)

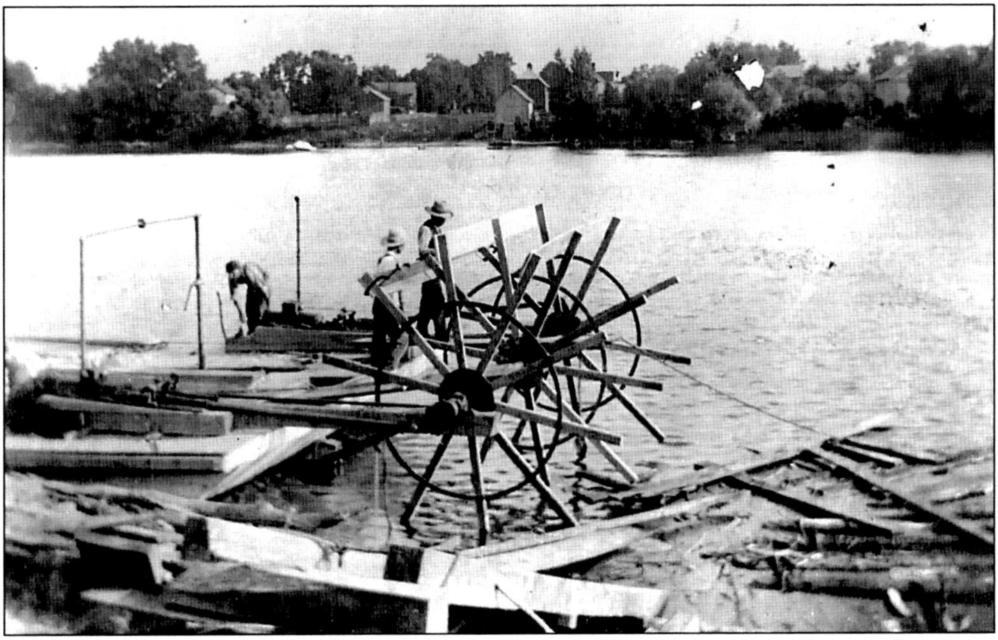

Once afloat, work commenced on *Margaret's* deck and planking, and on the installation of her power plant. In this image, workmen can be seen placing the paddles on her stern wheel, used to propel her up and down the Kankakee River for the next 17 years. (Kankakee County Museum Photographic Collection, P0812.)

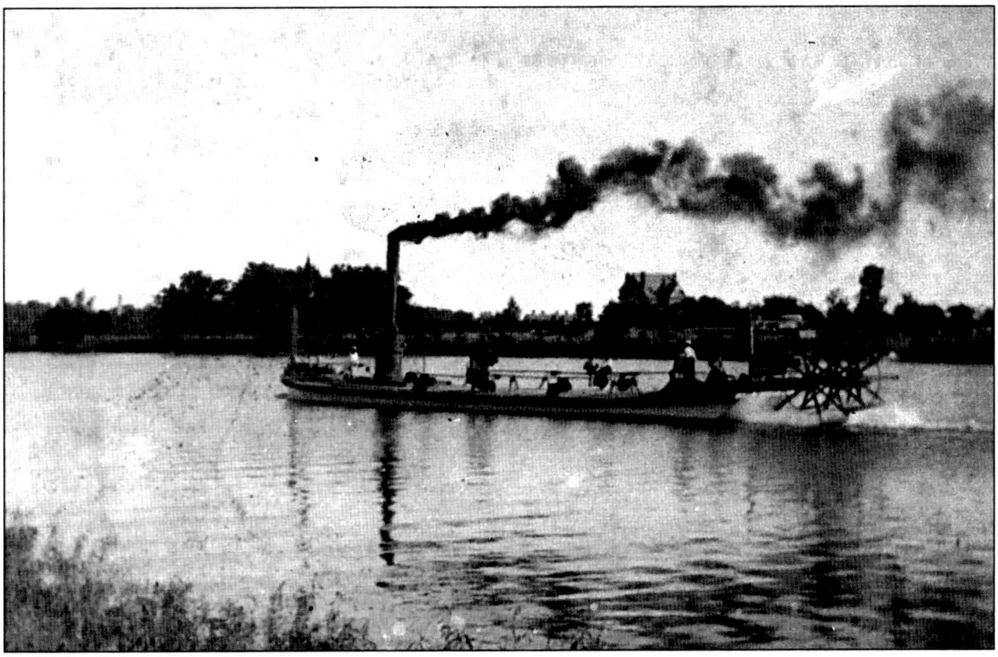

By the middle of July 1898, *Margaret's* propulsion system was completely installed. She is shown here making her shakedown cruise on the Kankakee River. She has not yet had her upperworks even started, which would have a carrying capacity of 300. (Kankakee County Museum Photographic Collection, P1332.)

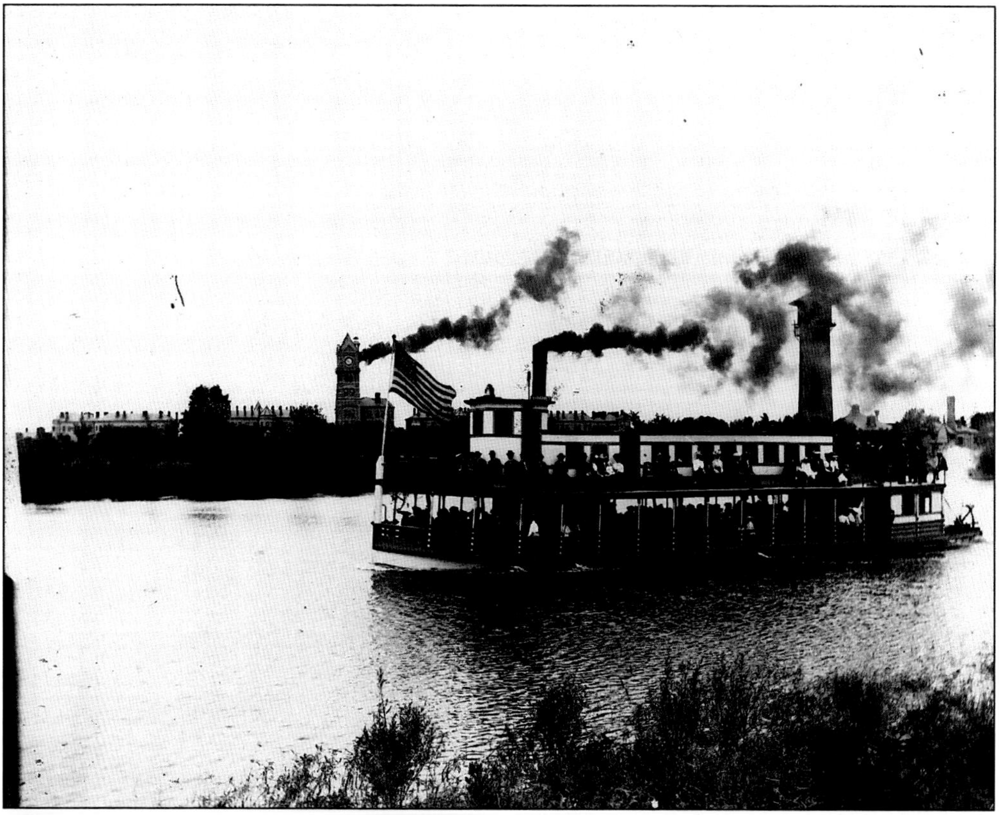

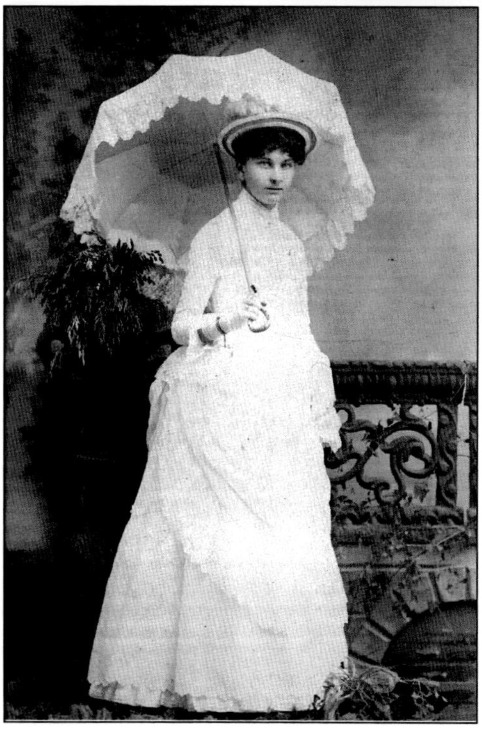

Margaret was captured in this photograph carrying a load of excursionists up the Kankakee River on July 4, 1901. She is passing the distinctive clock tower of the Illinois Eastern Hospital for the Insane, which can be seen along with the institution's other buildings. Captain Gougar named his new steamer for his wife, Margaret Gougar. (Kankakee County Museum Photographic Collection, P5949.)

Wearing a lovely summer dress and demurely carrying her parasol against the sun, Mrs. Julia Fink Lillie appears here in June 1887, in an image made by Charles Knowlton, a Kankakee photographer. Her husband was architect James Mateer Lillie, who had recently been awarded a contract from local entrepreneur Emory Cobb to build a large new elegant hotel. In May 1887, he started directing work at the site, located near the Kankakee River at Chicago and South Greenwood Avenues. (Kankakee County Museum Photographic Collection, P0266.)

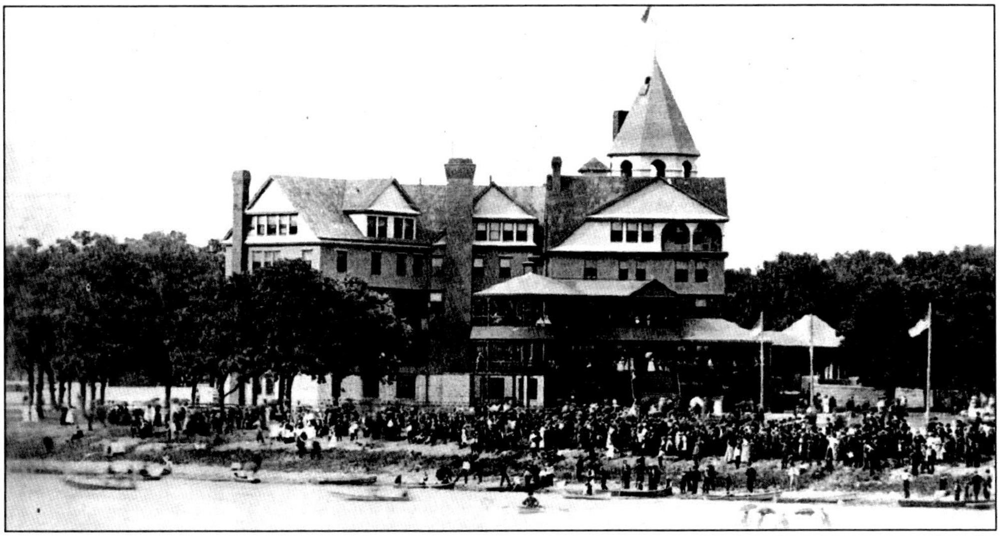

The majestic Hotel Riverview opened for business in July 1887 under the direction of well-known hotel manager Captain Jewett Wilcox. This photograph was taken during the Wholesale Grocers of Chicago Convention, held at the Riverview in the summer of 1887. Interestingly, the sale and consumption of alcoholic beverages (except wines served during dinner) were prohibited at the Hotel Riverview. Emory Cobb's new hostelry, nonetheless, housed over 1,500 guests by the end of its first season in September 1887. (Kankakee County Museum Photographic Collection, P4055.)

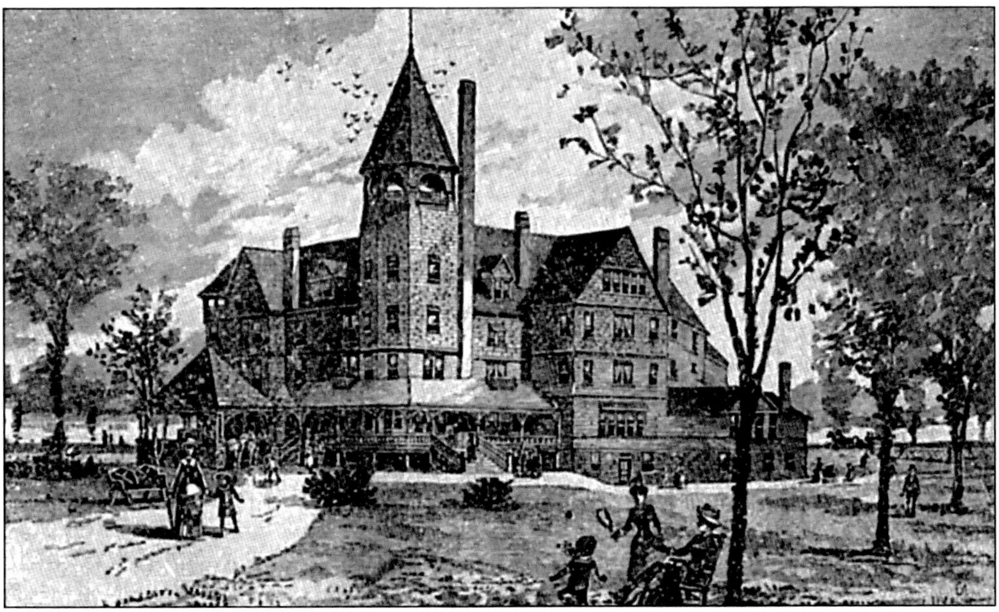

Within a decade, the Hotel Riverview became the most well-known building in the City of Kankakee. The Hotel Riverview's instant success is partly explained by the massive promotional campaign launched by Emory Cobb, the Illinois Central Railroad, and the Big Four Railroad, all of which had financial interests in the Hotel Riverview. This etching comes from such promotional literature, enthusing that the Hotel Riverview, "is as elegant as the most fastidious guest could ask for." (Kankakee County Museum Photographic Collection, P0406A.)

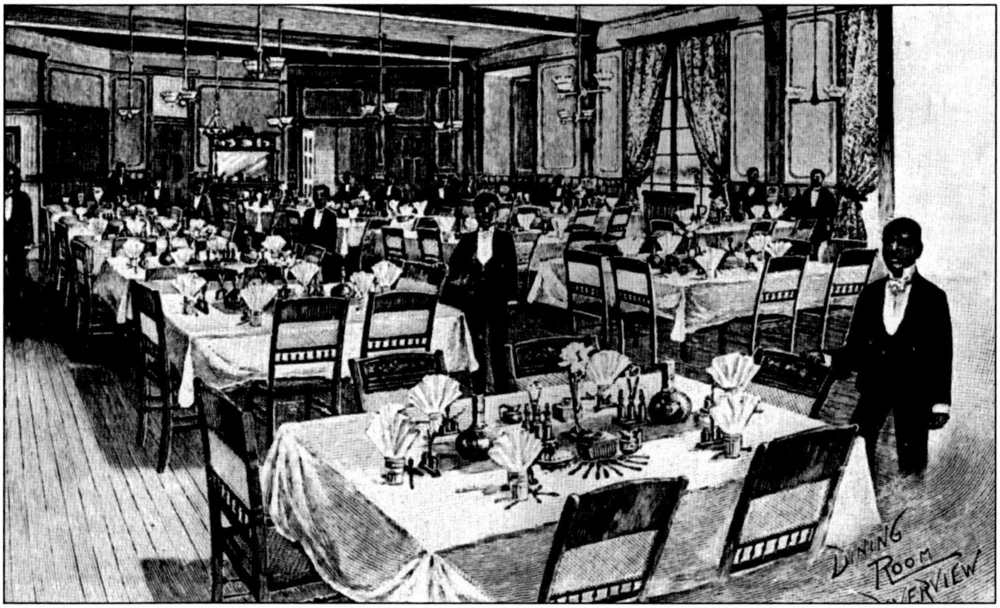

The Hotel Riverview operated on the "American Plan," with full-course meals available in the hotel dining room, pictured here in another piece of promotional literature prepared by Cobb and the railroad companies. These etchings date from 1895. (Kankakee County Museum Photographic Collection, P0406B.)

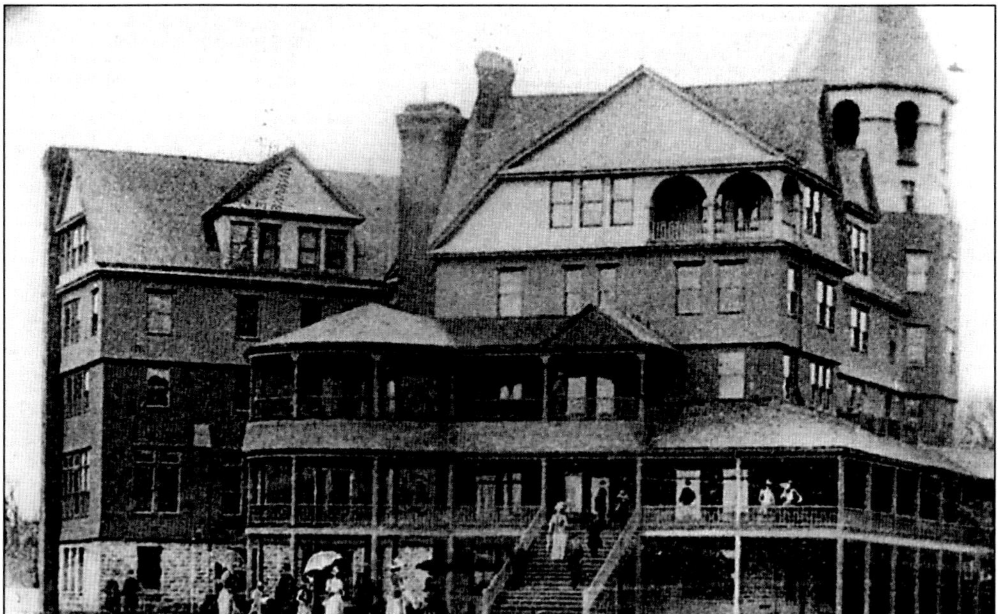

Guests are seen in this 1890 image enjoying the large double veranda around the Hotel Riverview. Built at a cost of $85,000, the Riverview brought thousands of summer vacationers to Kankakee. Patrons of the Hotel Riverview could enjoy several "parlors fitted with handsome red silk plush furniture" and spend their nights in hundreds of rooms, "handsomely carpeted and furnished with rich antique oak sets." (Kankakee County Museum Photographic Collection, P5941.)

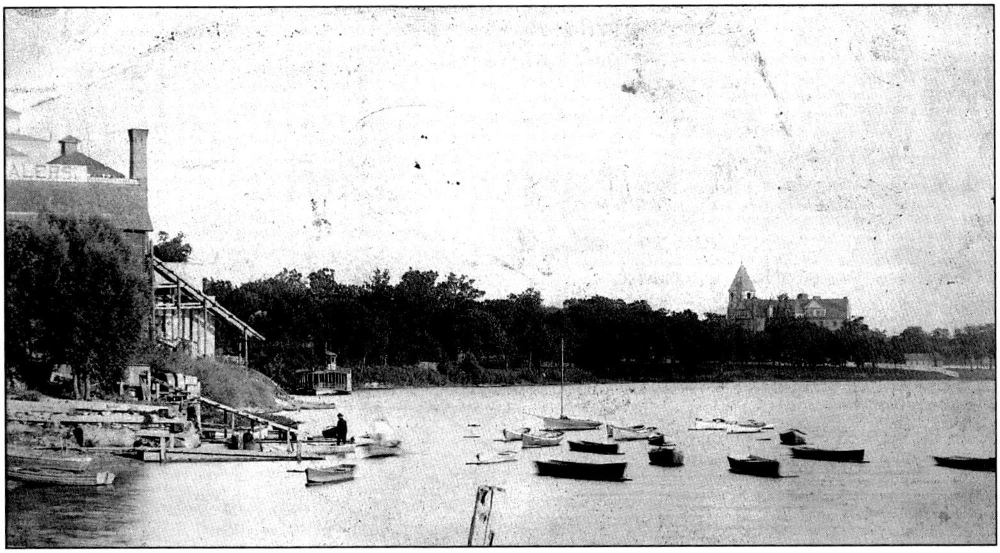

This image is a view of Shekey's Landing located at the foot of Schuyler Avenue, c. 1890. Several small pleasure boats can be seen in the center of the photograph and to the left center can be seen Captain Gougar's steamer *Minnie Lillie*. The imposing Hotel Riverview appears in the right center of the image. (Kankakee County Museum Photographic Collection, P0075.)

This image shows an opposite view, looking down the Kankakee River from the Hotel Riverview, c. 1890. The Illinois Central Railroad Bridge appears toward the center of the photograph and Captain Gougar's steamer *Minnie Lillie* can be seen docked at the left of the image, just below the Wenzelman Saw Mill. (Kankakee County Museum Photographic Collection, P0073.)

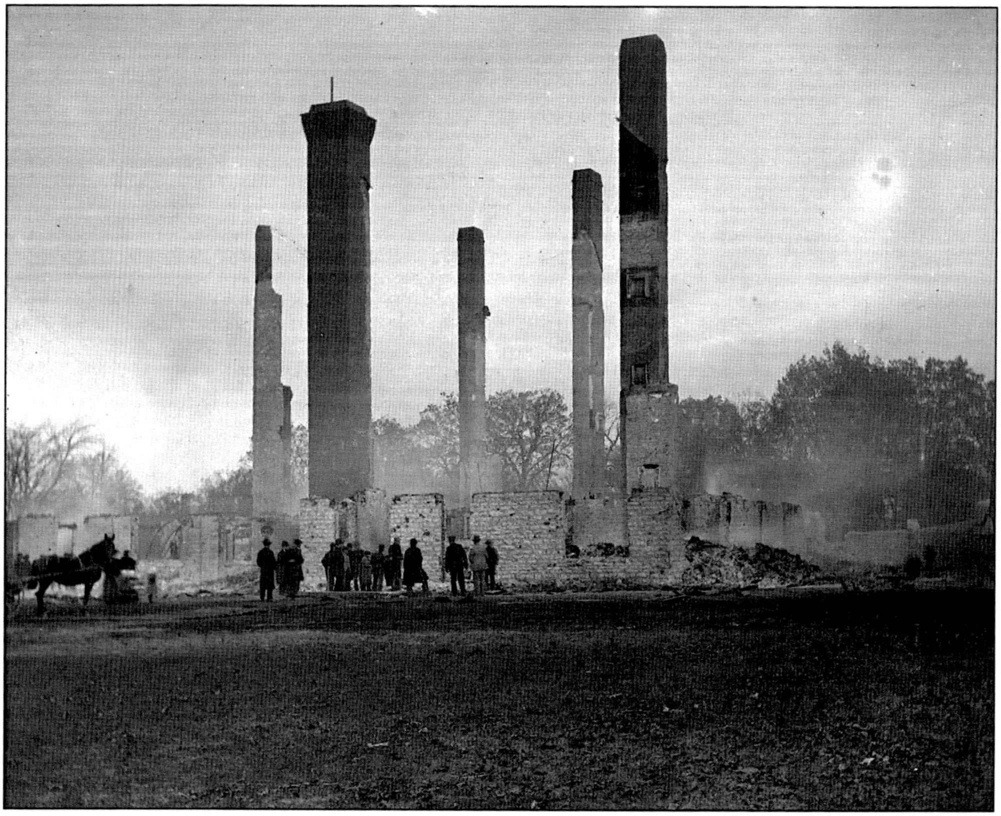

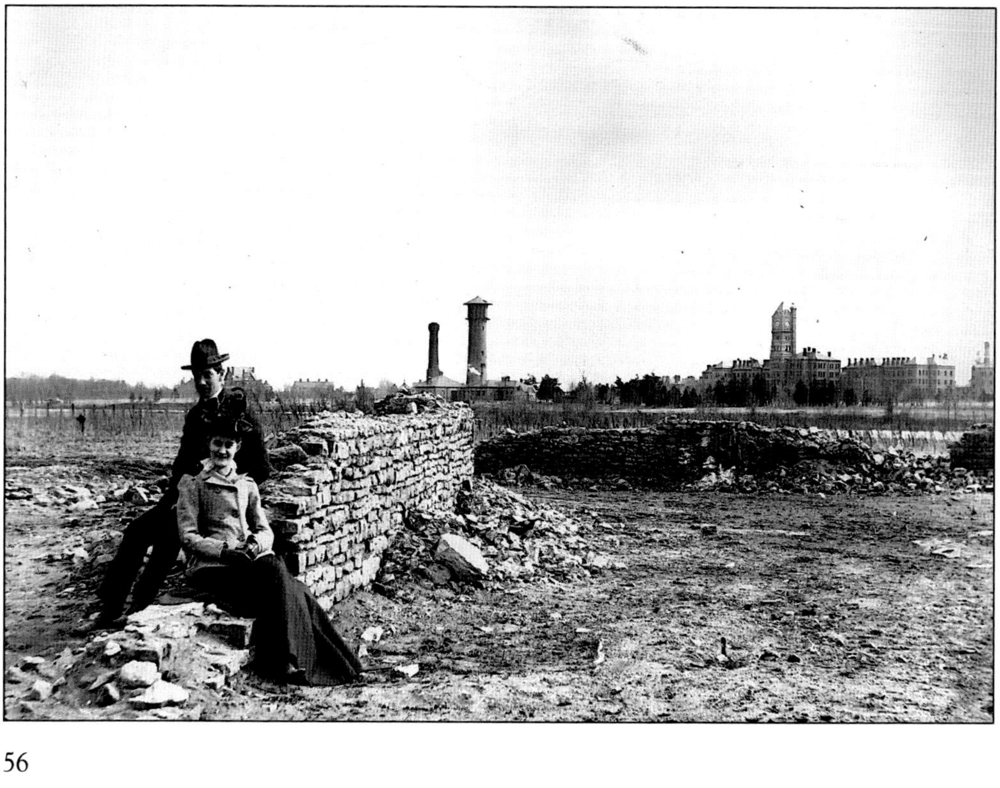

Opposite, top: The Hotel Riverview was destroyed by an early morning fire on November 12, 1897, that apparently started in a basement storeroom. The owner, Emory Cobb, was staying in the Riverview that night and narrowly escaped. By dawn, only the four large chimneys and the foundation walls remained of the once magnificent structure. This photograph of the still smoking hotel ruins was taken that morning. (Kankakee County Museum Photographic Collection, P1171.)

Opposite, bottom: The owners of the Hotel Riverview received only $20,000 of insurance money and they decided not to rebuild. Within a few years, the four large chimneys and the foundation walls that remained were taken down. In this image, an attractive Kankakee couple was photographed sitting amid the remnants of the Hotel Riverview's foundation wall, *c.* 1900. The Illinois Eastern Hospital for the Insane's distinctive clock tower and the other buildings of the hospital complex can be easily seen in the background. (Kankakee County Museum Photographic Collection, P1161.)

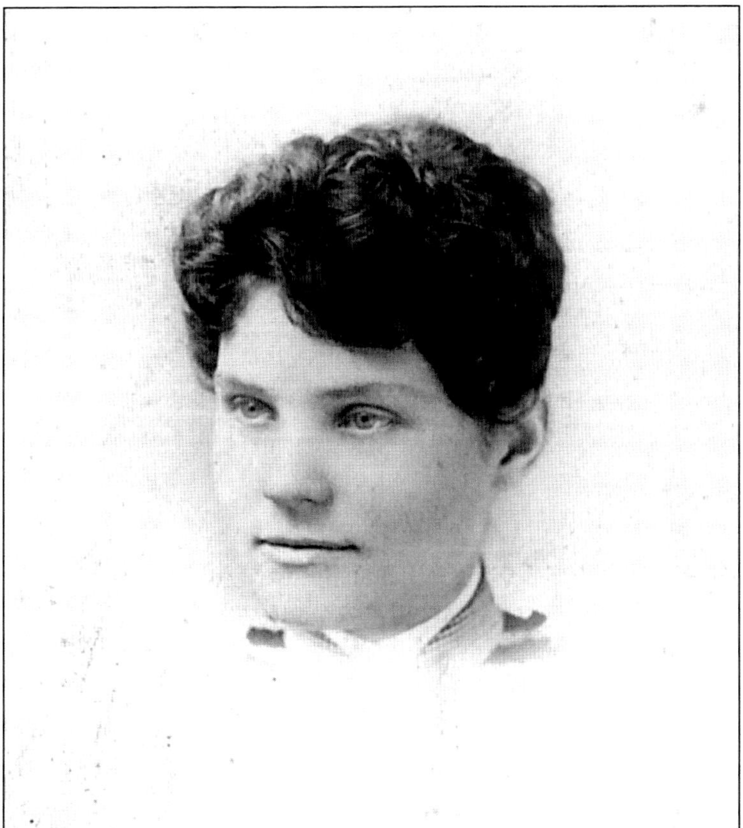

Kankakee residents would continue to enjoy the Kankakee River, despite the destruction of the Hotel Riverview, for many decades to come. People such as the lovely Miss Emma Colentha Little, appearing here in this 1899 image, would still recreate on and around the scenic Kankakee River. Miss Little's father, William Little, was a prosperous farmer. (Kankakee County Museum Photographic Collection, P0082.)

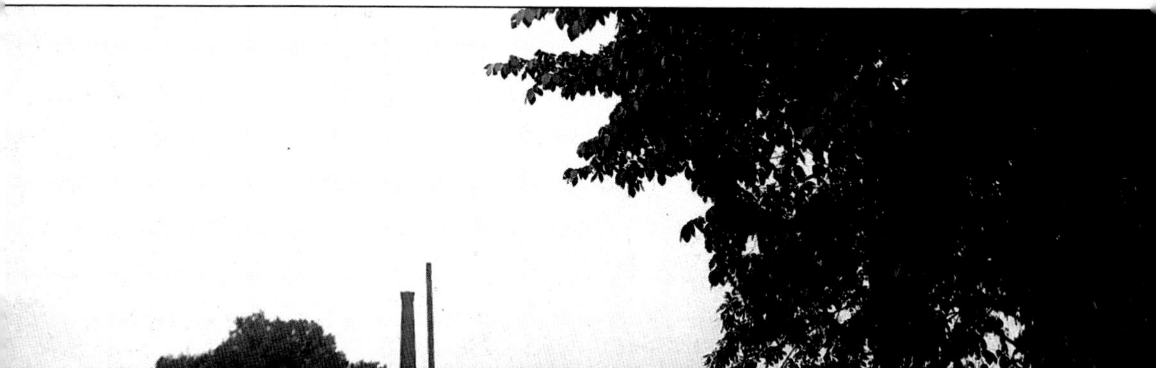

The essential beauty of the Kankakee River, coupled with the resonance of eternity it provided, truly helped to define the City of Kankakee's nature during the first 50 years of the community's existence. The Kankakee always remains for area residents to enjoy, just as these two young ladies seem to be doing in this photograph taken *c*. 1910. (Kankakee County Museum Photographic Collection, P0348.)

Opposite: On May 25, 1877, the Illinois State Legislature authorized a committee to find a location for a new large mental health facility. The City of Kankakee was selected. Well-known local architect and contractor James Lillie was awarded the contract to construct the hospital's buildings, the first of which he completed in 1879. Dr. Richard Dewey was chosen as the first superintendent of the newly created Illinois Eastern Hospital for the Insane in August and the institution's first patient was admitted in December 1879. At the beginning of January 1893, the facility housed 1,850 patients and by 1906 the Illinois Eastern Hospital for the Insane served the needs of 2,300 patents, making it the second largest mental health facility in the United States. The hospital complex, with its distinctive clock tower administration building shown here in 1893, fronted on the Kankakee River. The hospital grounds and buildings were, "considered among the handsomest of those of any public institution in the United States." (Kankakee County Museum Photographic Collection, P2975.)

Four

The Illinois Eastern Hospital for the Insane

"Great credit is due our committee of citizens in acquiring this project"

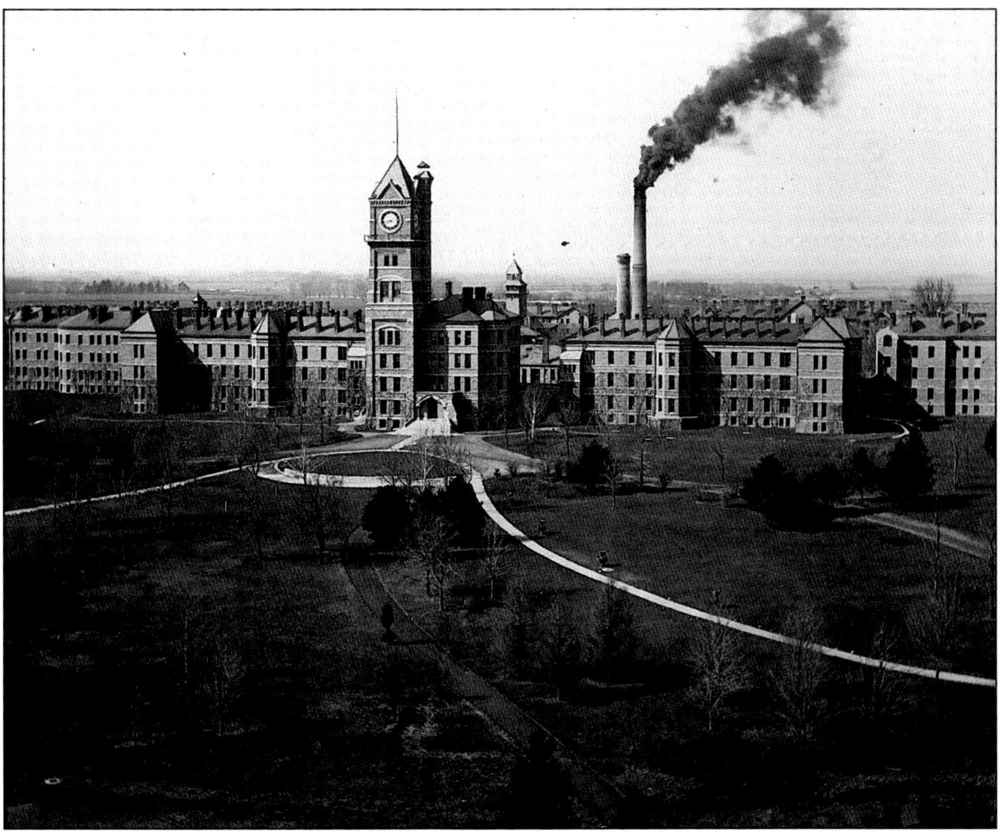

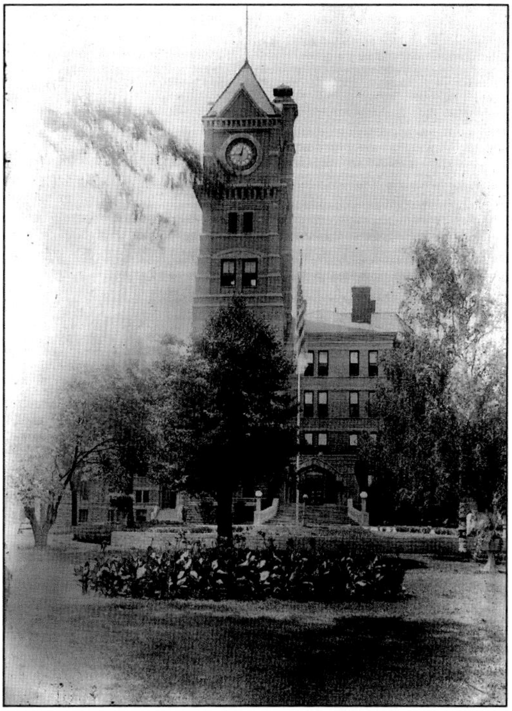

The distinctive clock tower, part of the Illinois Eastern Hospital for the Insane's main administration building, immediately became an area icon. Contemporary Kankakee residents thought it a great compliment that the Illinois State Legislature had placed the new facility in their city. On January 21, 1879, a public celebration was held at Kankakee's Presbyterian Church, announced as, "A Diagnosis of the First Serious Mental Disturbance, A Mild Kind of Celebration in Honor of the Near Completion of the Asylum." This photograph of the clock tower was taken in 1901. The two open windows appearing just above the tree standing next to the flag pole is where the hospital's operating room was located. With all four windows open there was excellent lighting. (Kankakee County Museum Photographic Collection, P8209.)

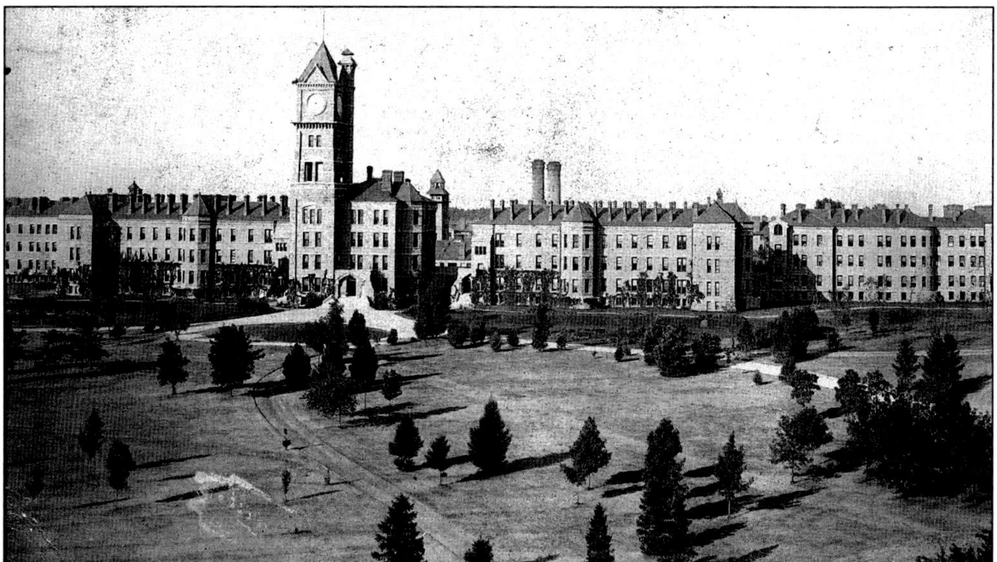

By 1890, the Illinois Eastern Hospital for the Insane maintained 18 wings, or main building wards, 20 cottage wards, and 52 buildings for various purposes. The 250 acres that comprised the hospital grounds were purchased for $14,000. The Illinois Eastern Hospital for the Insane was constructed with a combination of the older Kirkbride Plan where all wards were connected to the main building and the newer cottage system, where patients were housed in smaller detached buildings maintaining smaller wards. The latter system allowed patients with like disorders to be housed together. This photograph shows the hospital complex as it appeared in 1889. (Kankakee County Museum Photographic Collection, P0076.)

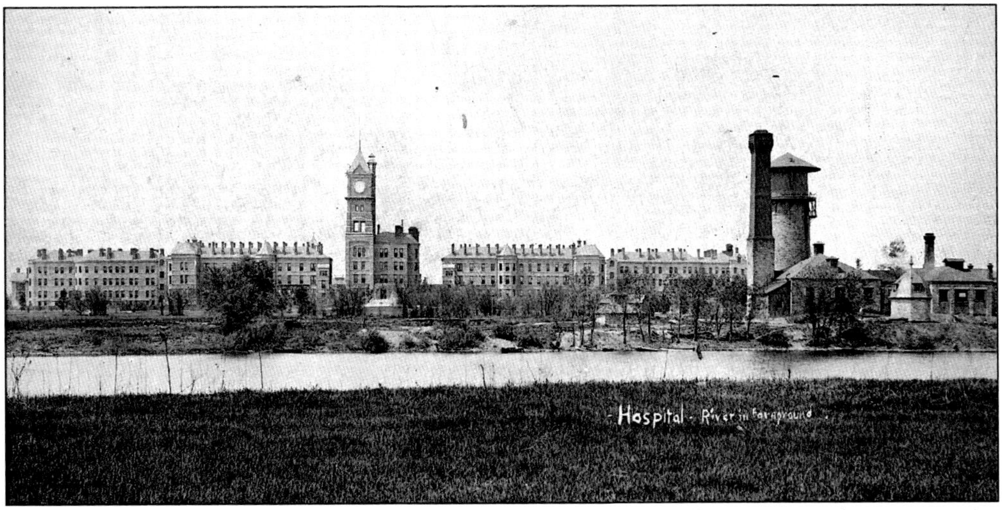

This view of the Illinois Eastern Hospital for the Insane was taken in 1888 from across the Kankakee River in Riverview Park. One piece of persistent local folklore is that Kankakee was offered a choice by the Illinois State Legislature of having either the new mental hospital or Illinois Industrial University (eventually the University of Illinois). Kankakee selected the hospital. There is, however, no truth to this story. (Kankakee County Museum Photographic Collection, P0369.)

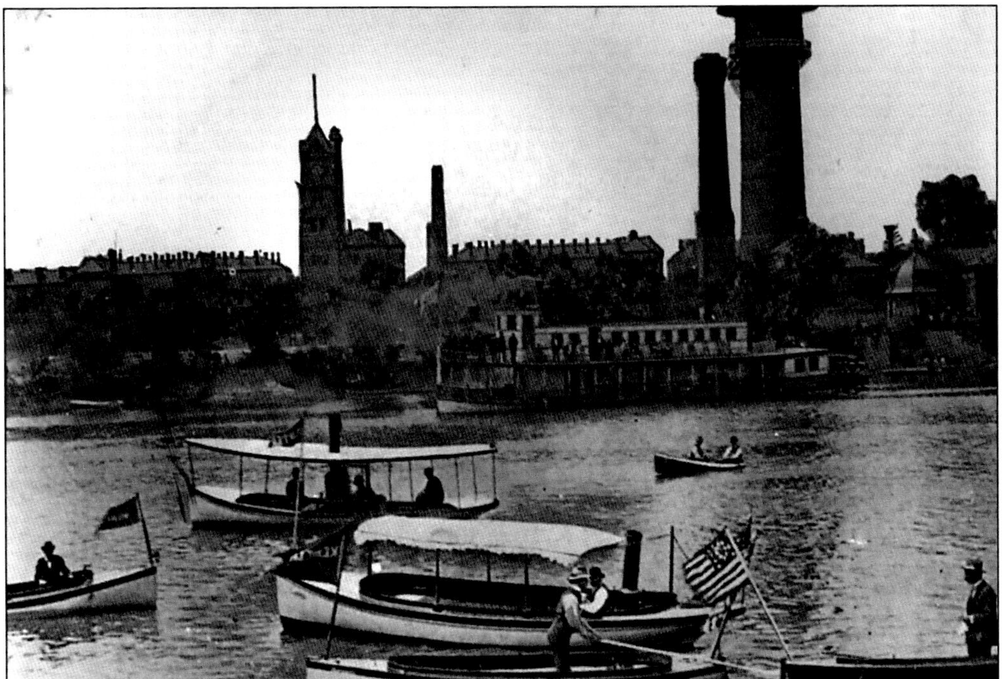

Captain Gougar's steamer *Margaret* and other smaller pleasure craft are seen in the Kankakee River in this 1893 image. The buildings of the Illinois Eastern Hospital for the Insane appear in the background. A serious disagreement between hospital officials and local citizens took place when Captain Gougar and others wanted to take tourists to the hospital's grounds to amuse themselves by staring at the patients. The practice was stopped. Hospital officials refused to allow their facility to be viewed as entertainment. (Kankakee County Museum Photographic Collection, P0839.)

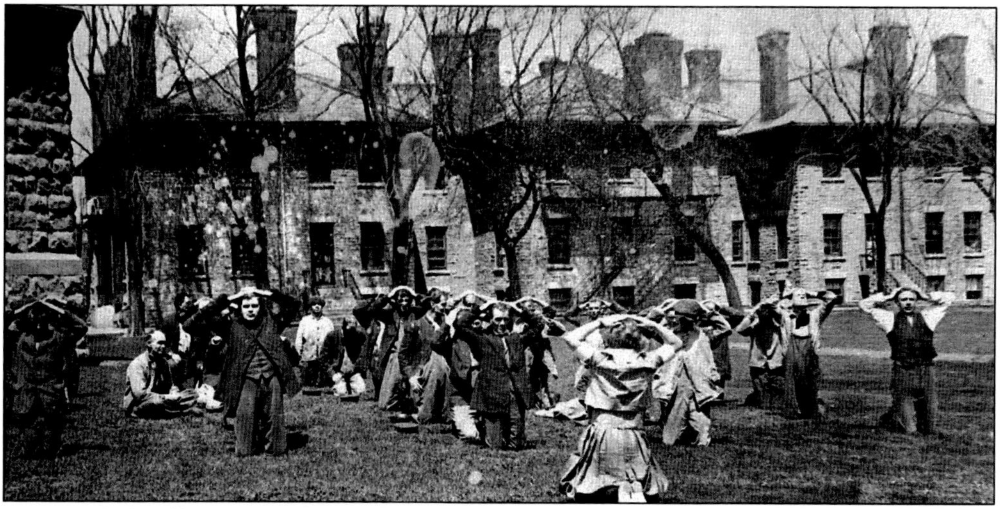

In general, the Illinois Eastern Hospital for the Insane's patients experienced little restraint. In conformity with prevailing 19th-century attitudes toward exercise and outdoor recreation the hospital's patients were exercised daily, as has been captured in this image made in 1900. The hospital buildings to the rear of the group closely resemble mid-19th-century military barracks, all built to a common pattern. (Kankakee County Museum Photographic Collection, P3175.)

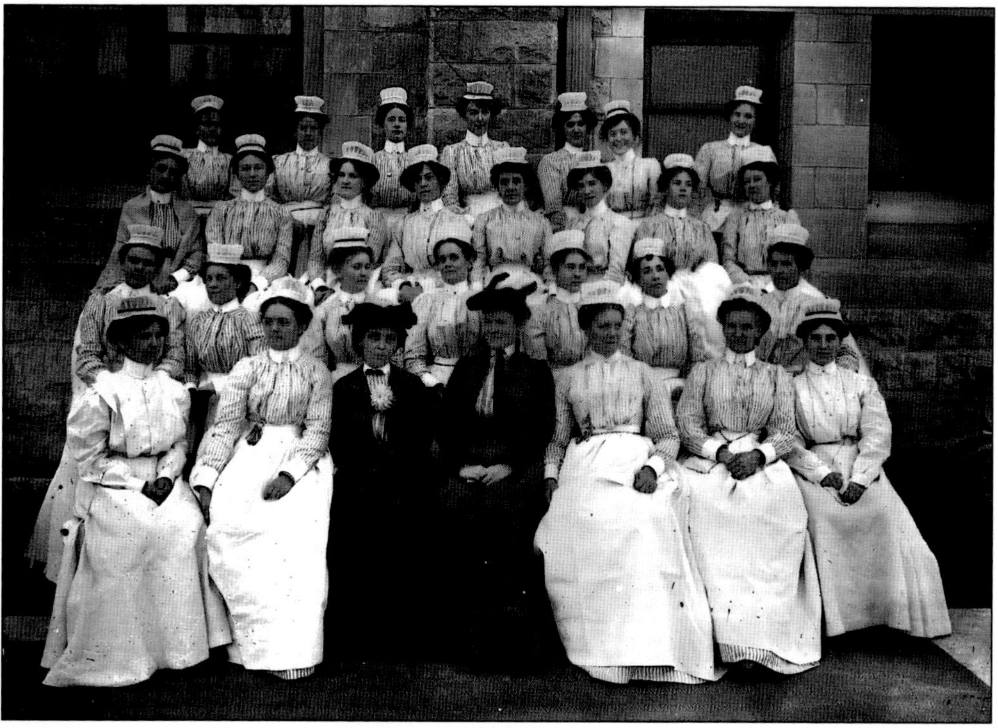

The Illinois Eastern Hospital for the Insane's medical staff was led by the senior resident physician, who also served as superintendent. His staff consisted of eight assistant physicians and the nursing contingent, who appear here in this group portrait made in 1900. The two ladies dressed in black are the hospital matrons, who directed the activities of the 27 uniformed nurses surrounding them in the photograph. (Kankakee County Museum Photographic Collection, P3173.)

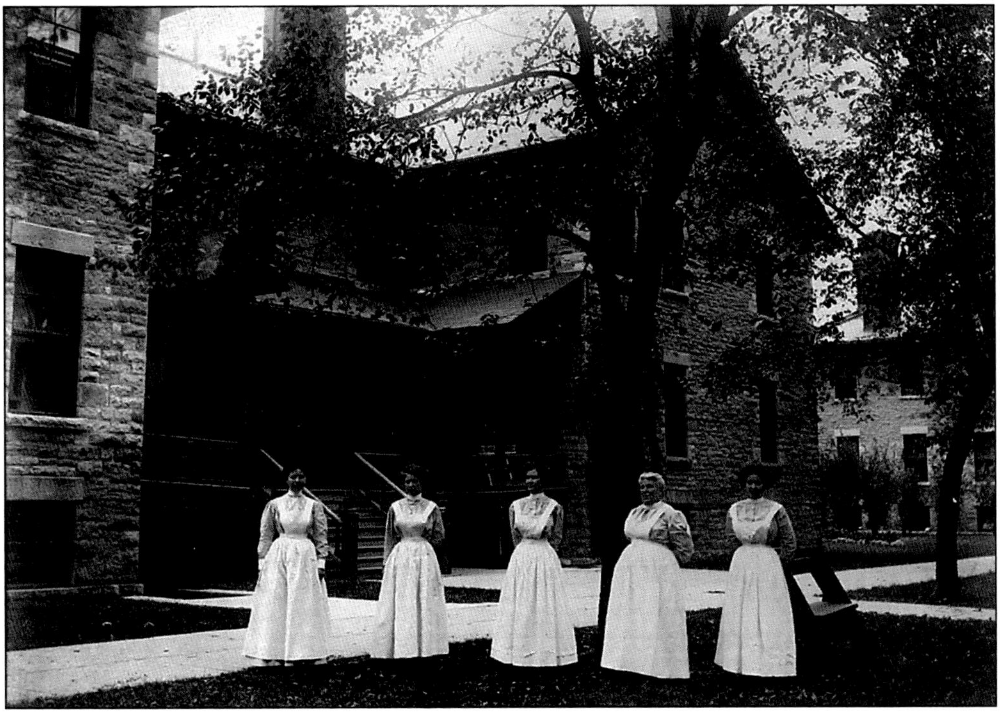

These members of the Illinois Eastern Hospital for the Insane's nursing contingent were photographed at the rear of one of the Institution's detached cottages in 1902. They are very likely the nurses assigned to this particular cottage. Patients were housed in cottages grouped by the nature of their mental ailments and by their ability to function. (Kankakee County Museum Photographic Collection, P4262.)

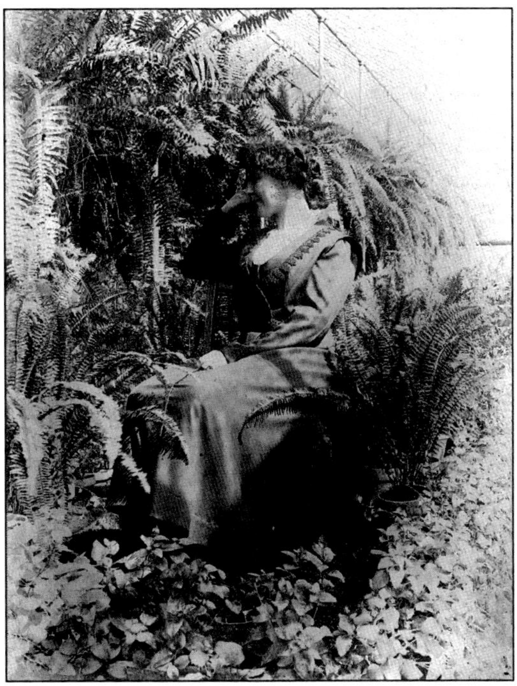

It was thought that flowers and other natural beauties had therapeutic value. The Illinois Eastern Hospital for the Insane maintained 50 acres as lawn for recreation, 50 more acres as gardens, and a large hot house to produce "calming" flowers and plants for the Hospital's wards. In 1910, Mrs. Ruth Goll, wife of one of the hospital's assistant physicians, was photographed relaxing in the hospital green house. (Kankakee County Museum Photographic Collection, P8190.)

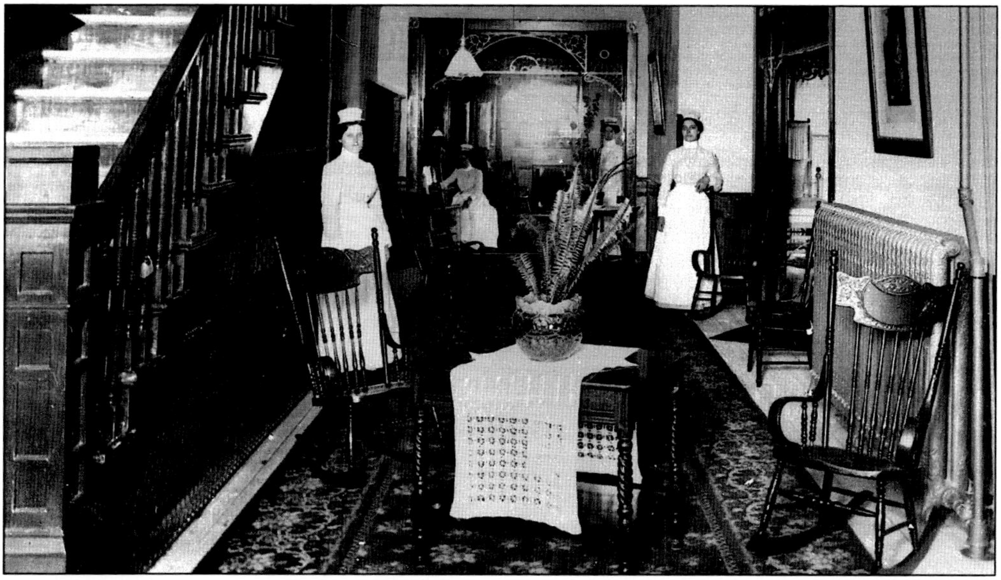

This 1900 image shows the interior hallway of a typical detached cottage at the Illinois Eastern Hospital for the Insane. Six nurses were assigned permanently to each cottage, operating three eight-hour shifts, each with two nurses. The cottages were steam heated and provided with gas lighting. Note the ceiling fixture in the center of the photograph. (Kankakee County Museum Photographic Collection, P3172.)

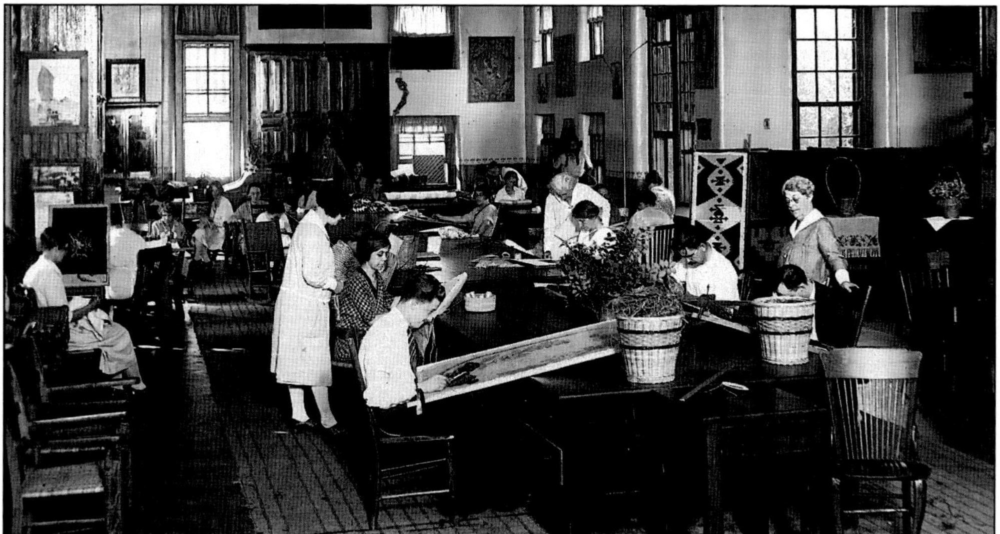

The Illinois Eastern Hospital for the Insane offered its patients a variety of activities intended to serve as occupational therapy. The hospital maintained gardens and a thousand-acre farm, where some patients worked producing fruits, vegetables, and meat for the hospital staff and their fellow patients. They could also be employed making chairs, brushes, brooms, repairing shoes, or more creatively making baskets, painting, or embroidering, as is depicted in this 1910 photograph. The woman to the right of the photograph is Mrs. Adele Keister, superintendent in charge of occupational therapy, and the woman to the left of the photograph is one of her instructors, Alice McIntosh. (Kankakee County Museum Photographic Collection, P4871.)

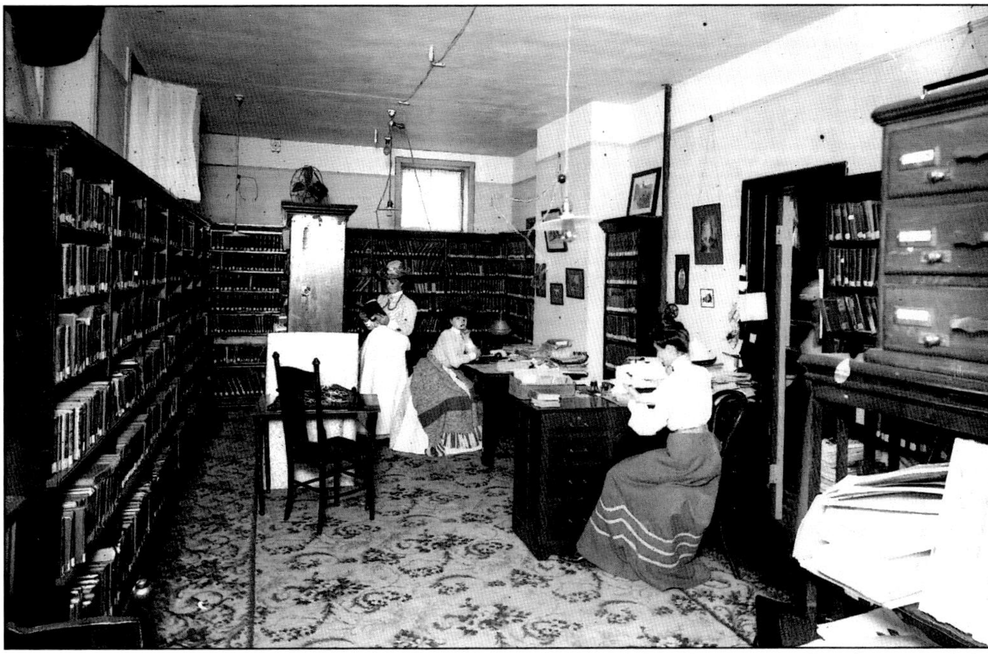

A library was maintained at the Illinois Eastern Hospital for the Insane for the use of the hospital staff and those patients able to make use of it. The library contained over three thousand volumes of general interest, the leading magazines and periodicals of the period, and a collection of over 1,300 medical texts. This 1900 image shows three members of the hospital's nursing contingent posed in the library for a piece of promotional literature. (Kankakee County Museum Photographic Collection, P3181.)

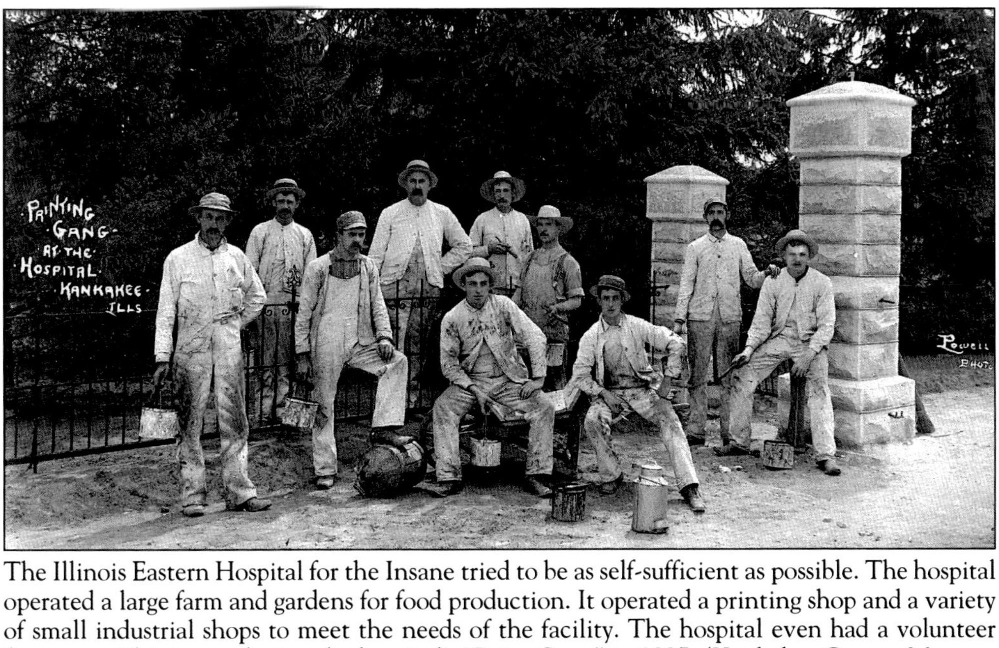

The Illinois Eastern Hospital for the Insane tried to be as self-sufficient as possible. The hospital operated a large farm and gardens for food production. It operated a printing shop and a variety of small industrial shops to meet the needs of the facility. The hospital even had a volunteer fire group. This image depicts the hospital's "Paint Gang" in 1897. (Kankakee County Museum Photographic Collection, P2934.)

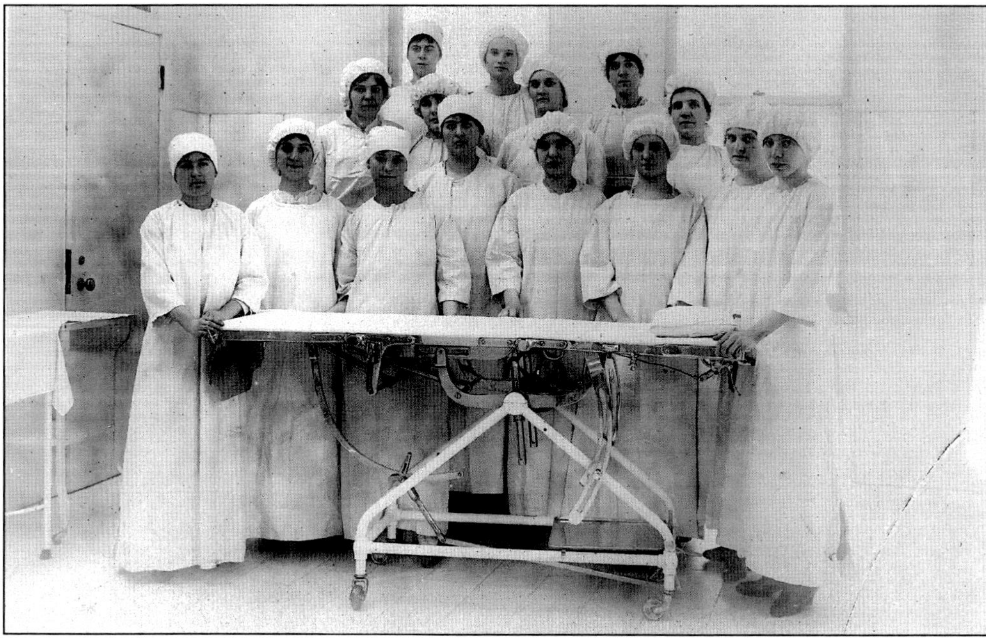

A large pathological laboratory was an important component of the Illinois Eastern Hospital for the Insane. The hospital superintendent and his assistant physicians were very much interested in research to discover the causes of various types of mental illness. A large portion of the hospital patients were indigent and it became standard procedure to perform autopsies in an effort to assemble scientific data. This group of gowned hospital nurses was photographed in one of the hospital's operating theaters in 1900. (Kankakee County Museum Photographic Collection, P6138.)

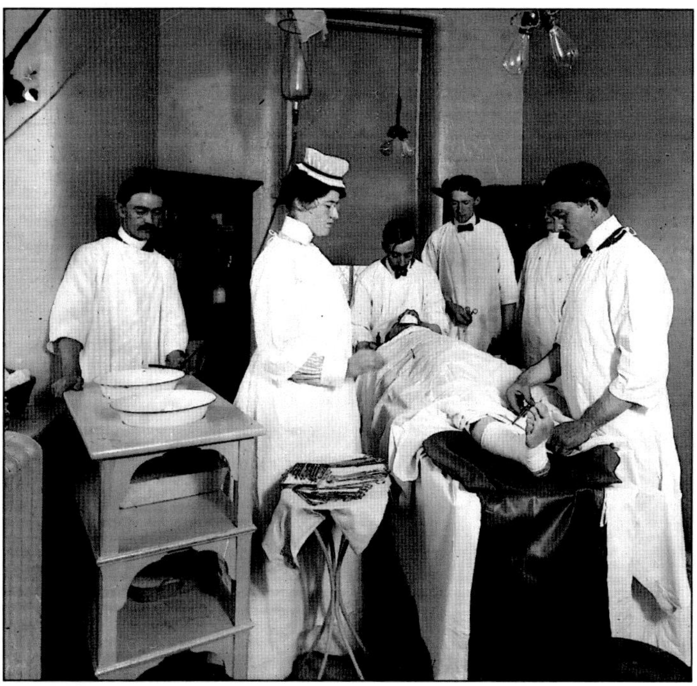

The Illinois Eastern Hospital for the Insane was fully equipped with modern surgical facilities, which included an elaborate x-ray machine—at the time considered quite an innovation. Minor surgeries were performed on a routine basis, such as removing a cast from a set fractured limb shown in this 1900 image. Note that the patient has been anesthetized, necessary for even minor procedures for the mentally ill. (Kankakee County Museum Photographic Collection, P3174.)

Five

SUPPORTING THE COMMUNITY

THE POLICE, FIRE FIGHTERS, CHURCHES, AND SCHOOLS

"The needs of our community are easily answered"

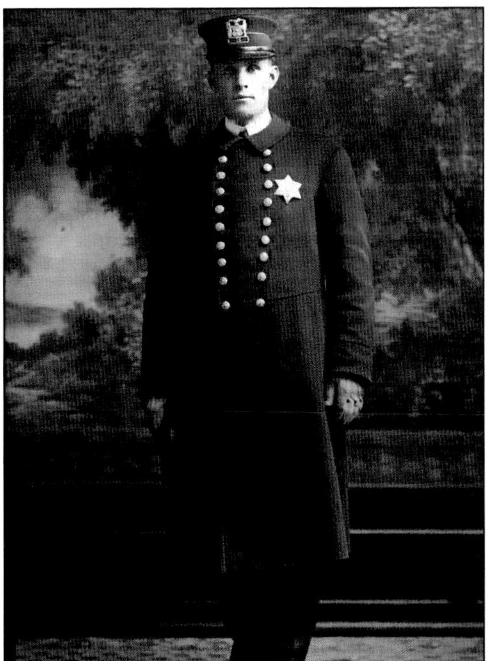

In this posed studio photograph, Joseph Kohl, patrolman no. 3 of the City of Kankakee Police Department, stares squarely at the camera. Walking city streets on a regular basis, he is a symbol of authority. Grasping his billy club in his right hand, Patrolman Kohl represented law and order in the City of Kankakee, *c*. 1900. (Kankakee County Museum Photographic Collection, P9710.)

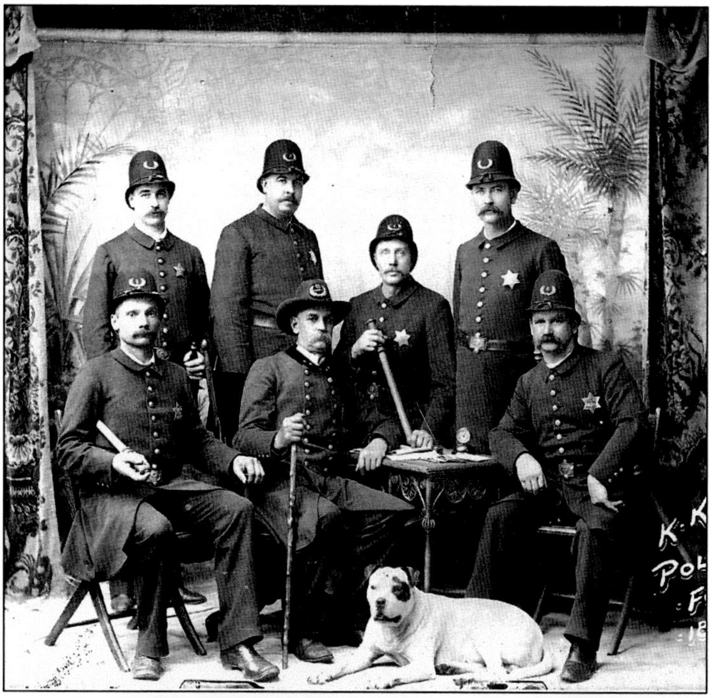

The seven-member police force of the City of Kankakee and their mascot "Pug" (for Pug-ugly) appear in this group photograph taken in 1892. The man seated in center is the chief of police. The man to his right, patrolman no. 1, is Weston Boule, who will become chief of police in 1902. The patrolmen's belt buckles are inscribed "C.P.," for city police and they are all carrying their billy clubs as a symbol of their office. (Kankakee County Museum Photographic Collection, P2812.)

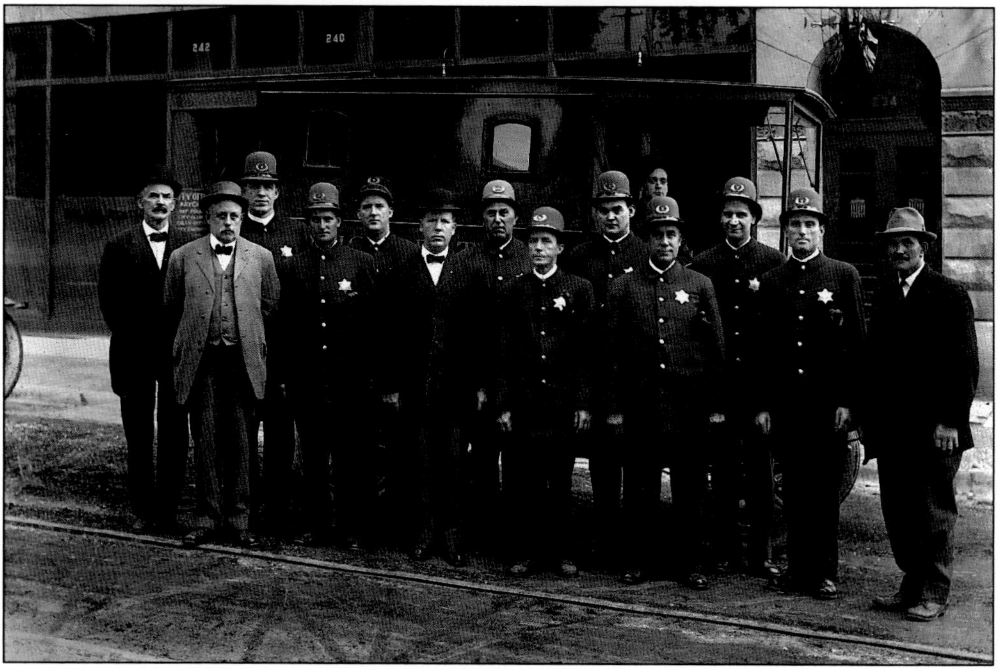

In 1910, the police force of the City of Kankakee is shown here proudly exhibiting their brand new motorized "Paddy Wagon," which is parked in front of the City of Kankakee Police Department's office. The gentlemen wearing suits, to the right and left of the uniformed group, are J.H. Bell, Frank Walkley, and Edwin Brazill. They also represent something new in Kankakee in 1910—"Plain Dicks,"or plain clothes detectives. (Kankakee County Museum Photographic Collection, P0108.)

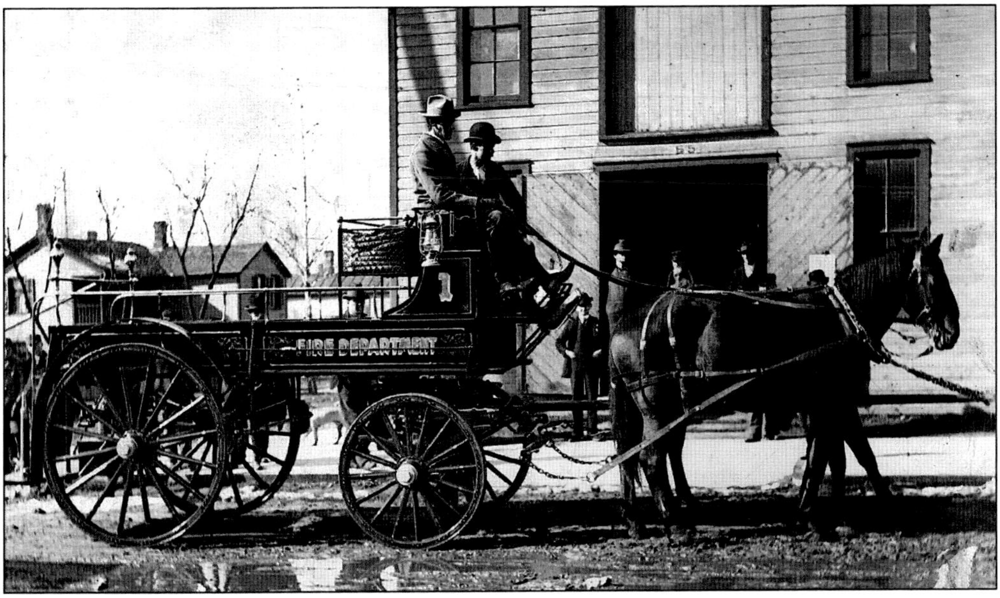

Louis Schneider, a blacksmith by trade, was manufacturing wagons in Kankakee from 1861. In October 1892, he created Schneider and Son Wagon and Carriage Shop. The Schneiders are shown here in this 1898 image in front of their factory establishment, trying out the brand new fire wagon, engine no. 1, that they have built for the City of Kankakee Fire Department. The horse came as an extra. (Kankakee County Museum Photographic Collection, P3083.)

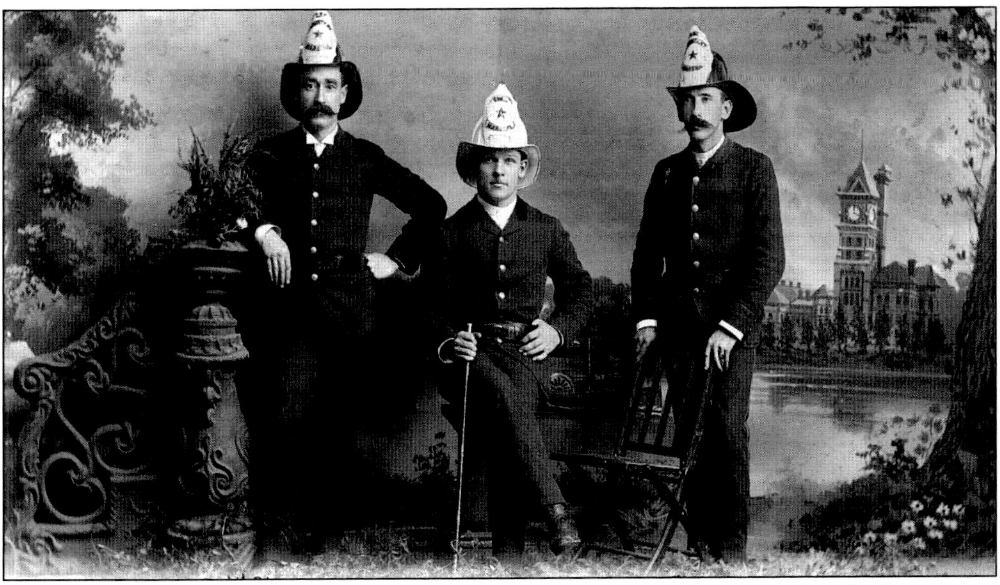

Chief Fire Marshall Dr. L.H. Prince, flanked by his two assistant fire marshals, J.H. Shields and C.W. Eastman, shown here *c.* 1890, are the officers of the volunteer fire company formed from the employees of the Illinois Eastern Hospital for the Insane. They were photographed in front of a painted backdrop depicting the hospital's distinctive clock tower, appearing behind the Kankakee River. Their leather belts display the letters I.E.H.I., for Illinois Eastern Hospital for the Insane. One of the hospital's attending physicians, Dr. Prince, led the hospital's volunteer fire company as a "gentleman's club." (Kankakee County Museum Photographic Collection, P1286.)

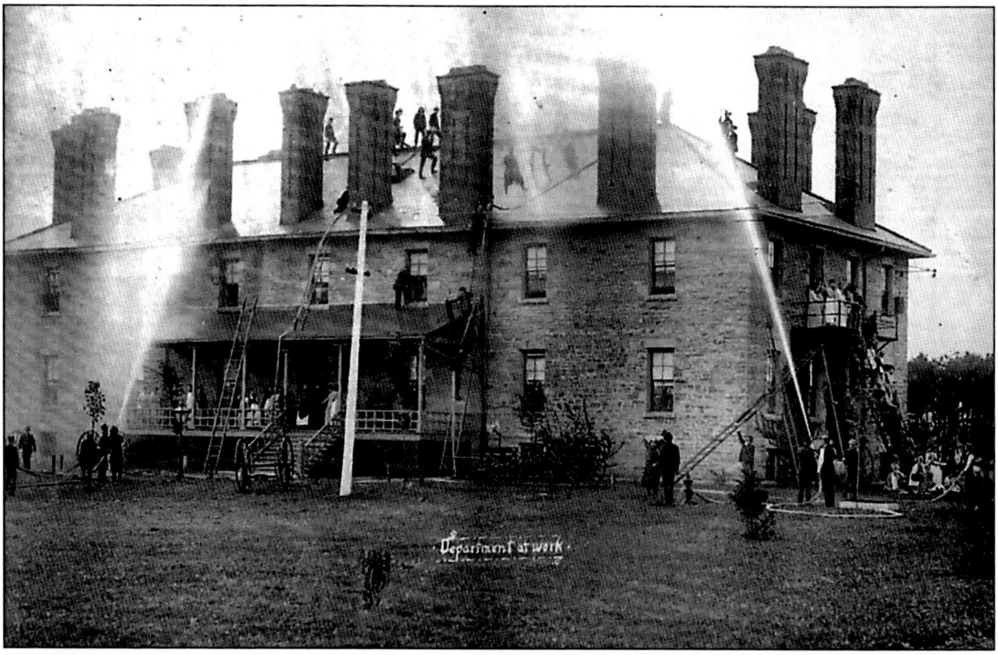

The Illinois Eastern Hospital for the Insane's Volunteer Fire Company hold a seemingly realistic fire drill, complete with ladders, hoses, and real water, at one of the hospital's administrative buildings in 1900. Displaced from their normal activities, hospital nurses and office workers stand on the porch and side stairs, observing the proceedings. (Kankakee County Museum Photographic Collection, P6148.)

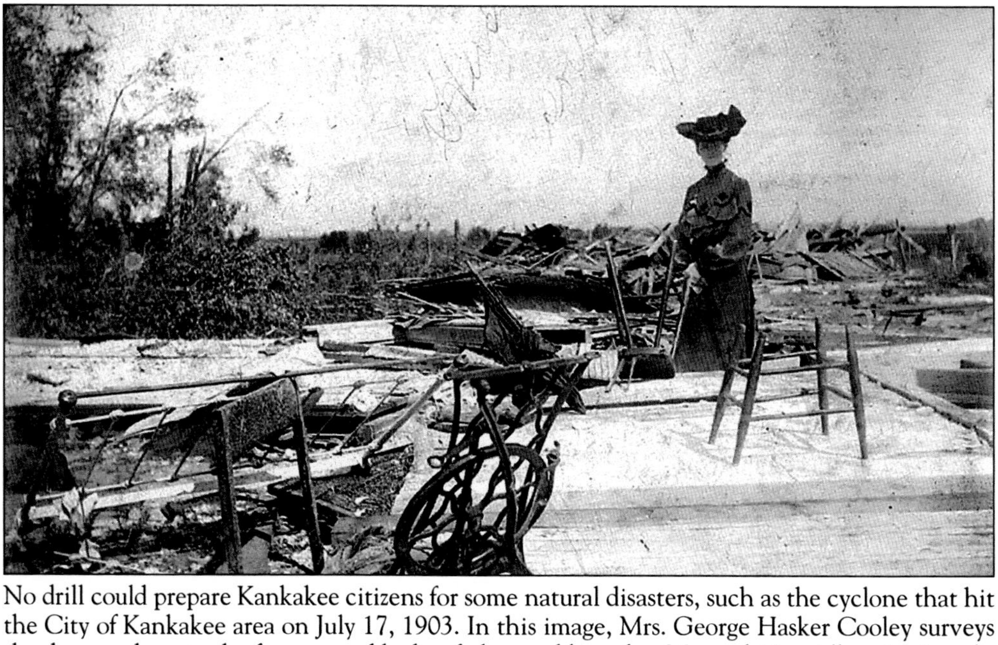

No drill could prepare Kankakee citizens for some natural disasters, such as the cyclone that hit the City of Kankakee area on July 17, 1903. In this image, Mrs. George Hasker Cooley surveys the damage done to the farm owned by her father and leased to Mr. and Mrs. Albert McIntosh, who died during the storm with their eight-year-old son Lester. (Kankakee County Museum Photographic Collection, P4875.)

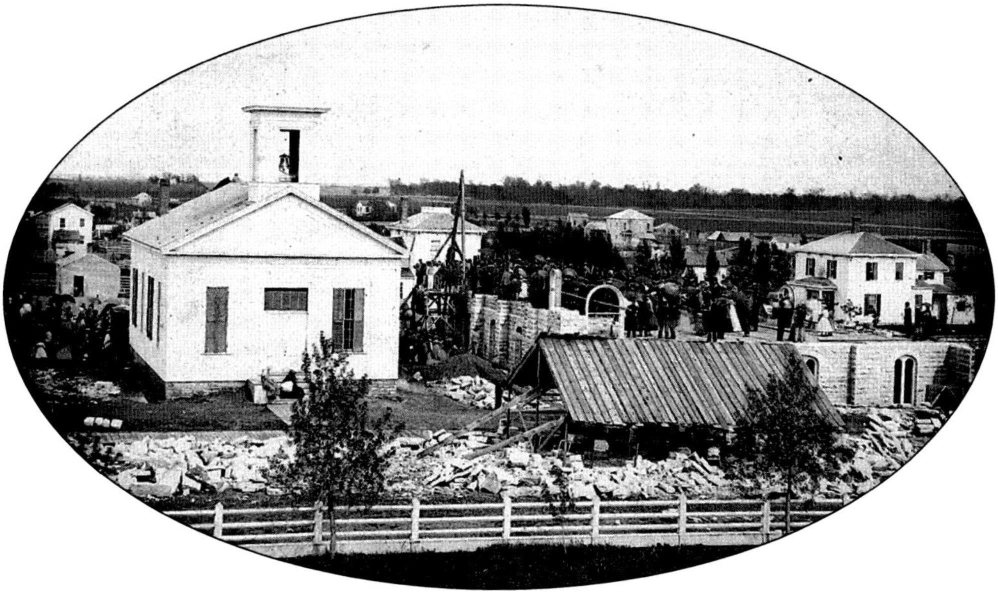

Captured in this mid-19th-century image is the crowd attending the ceremonies at the laying of the corner stone of the First Methodist Church of Kankakee on the afternoon of Thursday, May 28, 1867. The view was taken from a second-story window on the east side of the court house. The small white church building appearing to the left in the photograph, the First Congregational Church of Kankakee, is no longer in existence. (Kankakee County Museum Photographic Collection, P0072.)

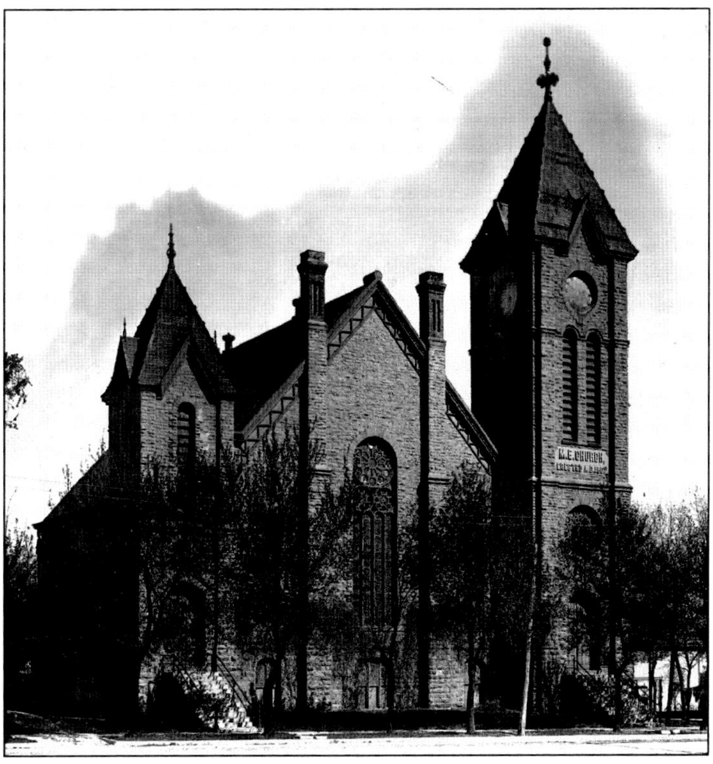

The completed First Methodist Church of Kankakee is shown in this photograph taken in 1890. Stone for the construction of the church was donated in 1867 by David Woodard's Kankakee Stone Quarry. Services were first held in the completed basement, even before the structure was finished. In 1890, the Methodist Church property, still located at the northeastern corner of Harrison Avenue and Merchant Street, was valued at $52,000. (Kankakee County Museum Photographic Collection, P0209.)

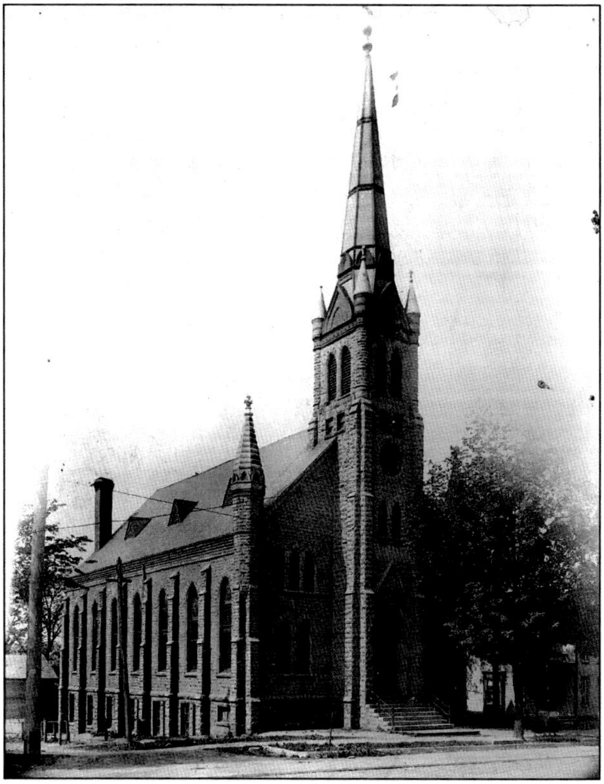

The recently built Saint Paul's Lutheran Church shows its stately appearance in this photograph taken in the summer of 1900. Erected in 1888 east of the southeast corner of East Merchant Street and South Dearborn Avenue, the "new" Saint Paul's was the third German Lutheran Church in the City of Kankakee. On Sunday, the large congregation often included as many as 650, making it one of the largest in the City of Kankakee. Saint Paul's operated a parochial school with five teachers and a hundred students in the church basement. In 1890, the church's property was assessed at $34,000. (Kankakee County Museum Photographic Collection, P0313.)

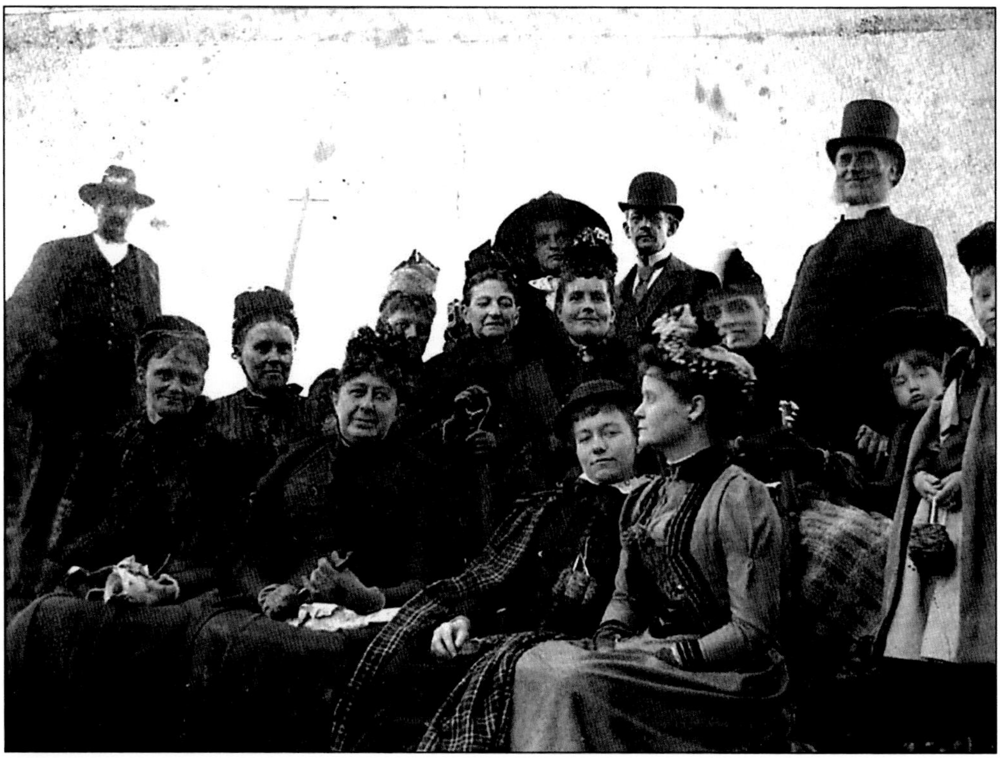

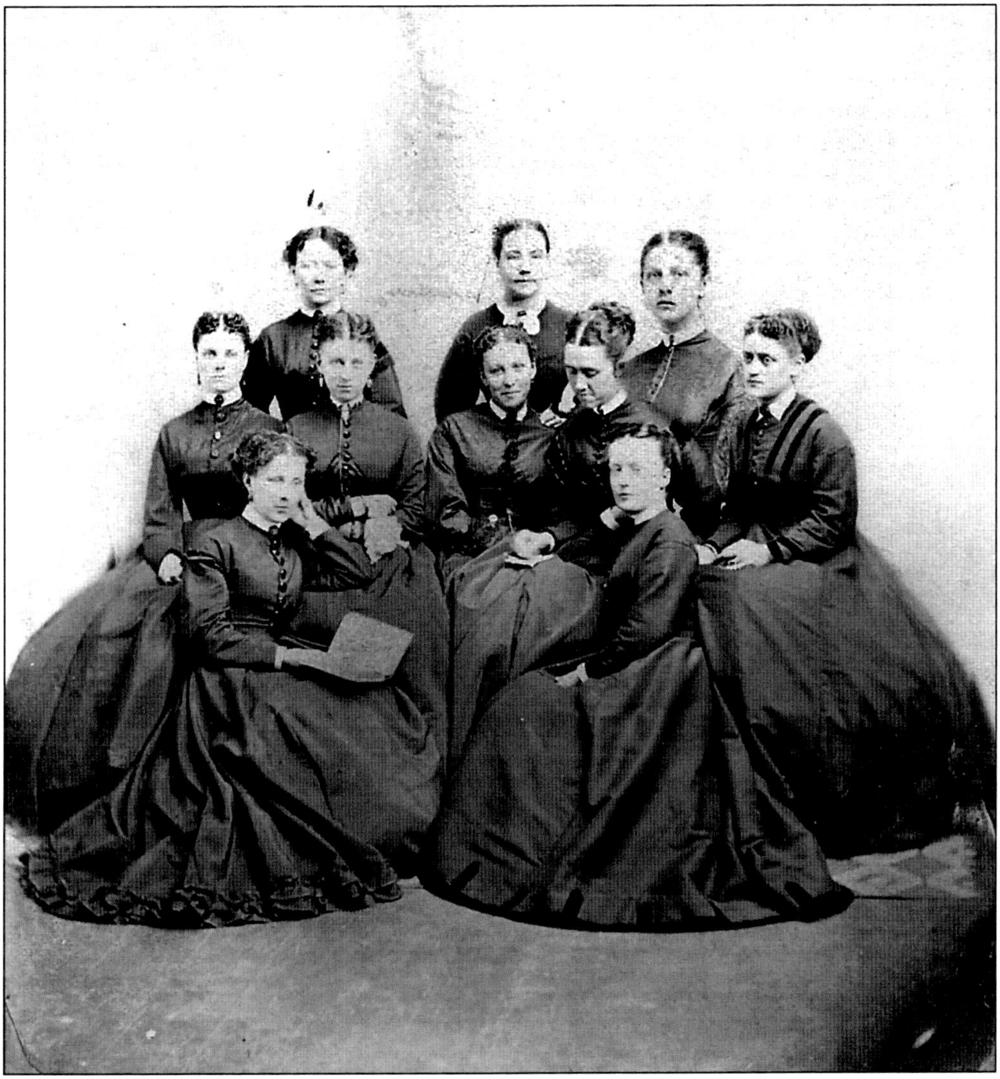

This photograph shows a group of educators in the City of Kankakee, *c.* 1870. They are members of the Teacher's Institute of Kankakee County, formed in 1856, which examined the qualifications of prospective teachers, selected text books, and approved the material taught in Kankakee classrooms. The woman standing at top left is Miss Nettie Sinclair, who was appointed Kankakee Superintendent of Schools in 1873. These women are also members of the Kankakee Ladies Library Association, formed in 1873. (Kankakee County Museum Photographic Collection, P0257.)

Opposite: The female instructors of the Saint Paul's Episcopal Church Sunday School gather for a group photograph taken on October 2, 1890, at one of their annual Harvest Home outdoor fund-raising events. Saint Paul's Episcopal operated both a grammar school and a Sunday school in the City of Kankakee from 1869. The smiling gentleman to the right in the photograph wearing a rather old fashioned (in 1890) "beaver" is the Reverend D.S. Phillips, the second rector of Saint Paul's, who arrived in Kankakee in 1867 and finally stepped down from his post 37 years later, in 1904. (Kankakee County Museum Photographic Collection, P0340.)

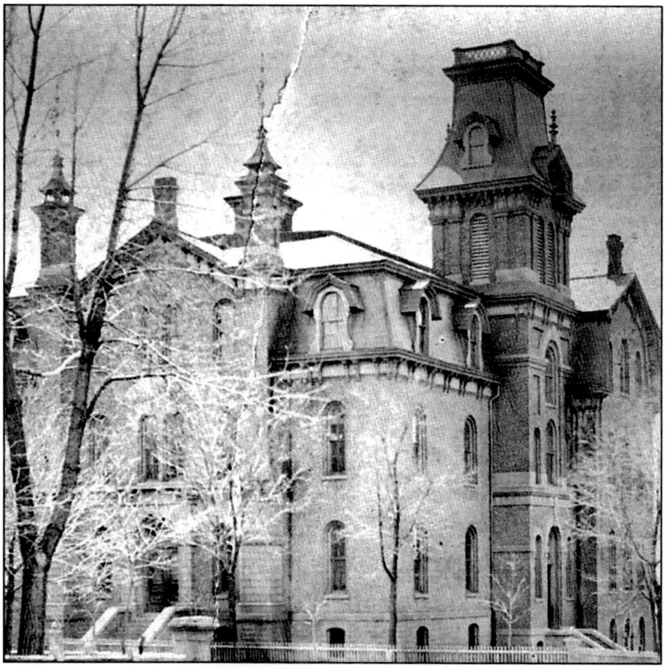

This structure is the imposing Central School, the first high school in the City of Kankakee, completed in 1869 and located at the southeast corner of East Merchant Street and South Indiana Avenue. The high school movement of the mid-19th century emphasized practical subjects over the traditional classical courses taught in antebellum private academies and subscription schools. The rather dour middle-Victorian architecture of Central School seems to suggest the seriousness of education. (Kankakee County Museum Photographic Collection, P0495.)

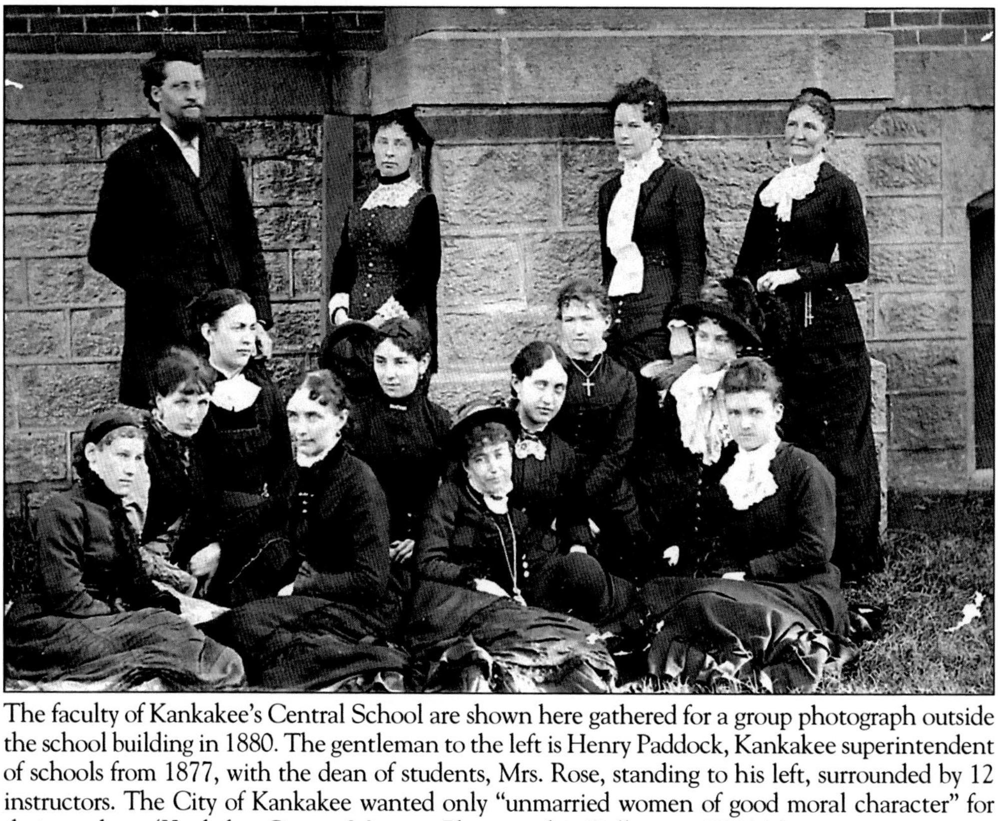

The faculty of Kankakee's Central School are shown here gathered for a group photograph outside the school building in 1880. The gentleman to the left is Henry Paddock, Kankakee superintendent of schools from 1877, with the dean of students, Mrs. Rose, standing to his left, surrounded by 12 instructors. The City of Kankakee wanted only "unmarried women of good moral character" for their teachers. (Kankakee County Museum Photographic Collection, P0214.)

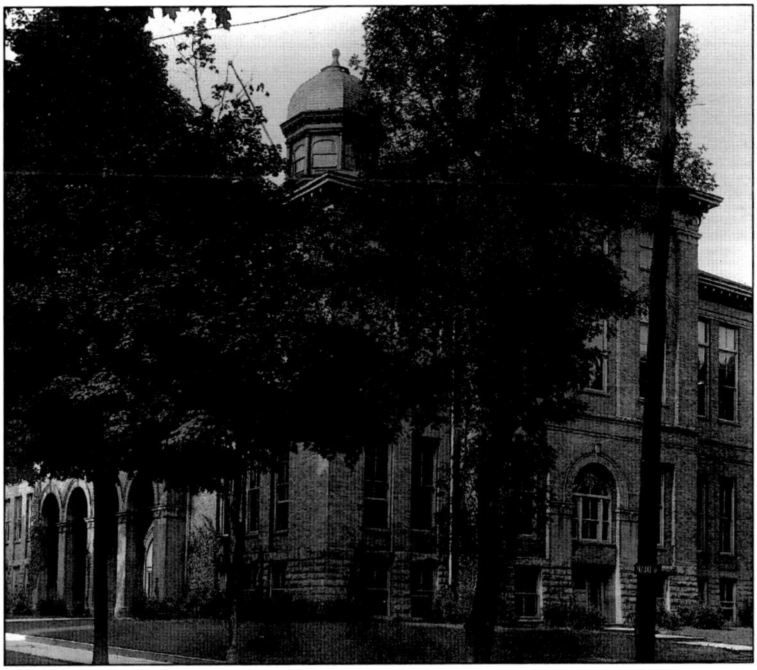

The "new" Kankakee High School, which was constructed between 1902 and 1905 at a cost of $100,000 is shown in this photograph, c. 1910. The first class to graduate from the Kankakee High School did so in June 1906. In 1923, it became a vocational school, until it was destroyed by fire shortly before World War II. (Kankakee County Museum Photographic Collection, P0315.)

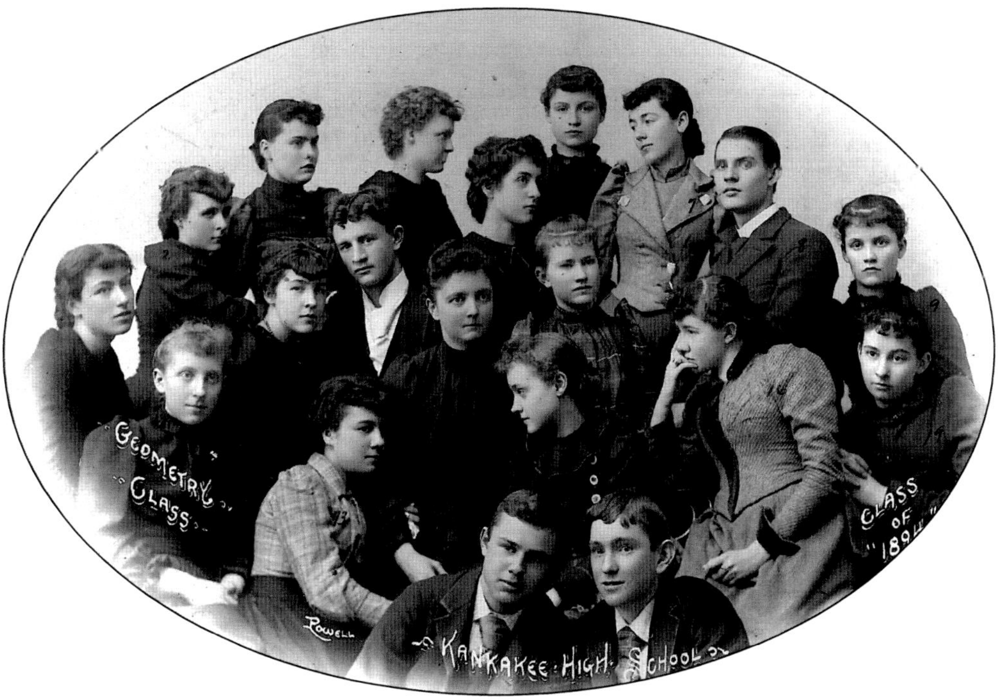

Members of a geometry class at the Kankakee High School pose for a group portrait in 1894. The gentleman in the upper right of the image (number eight) is Arthur Wilkens Deselm. Age 19 when the photograph was taken, he was the only male member of the 1894 graduating class. He would study law at the University of Michigan, become a prominent lawyer in the City of Kankakee, and Kankakee County Judge in 1902. (Kankakee County Museum Photographic Collection, P0432.)

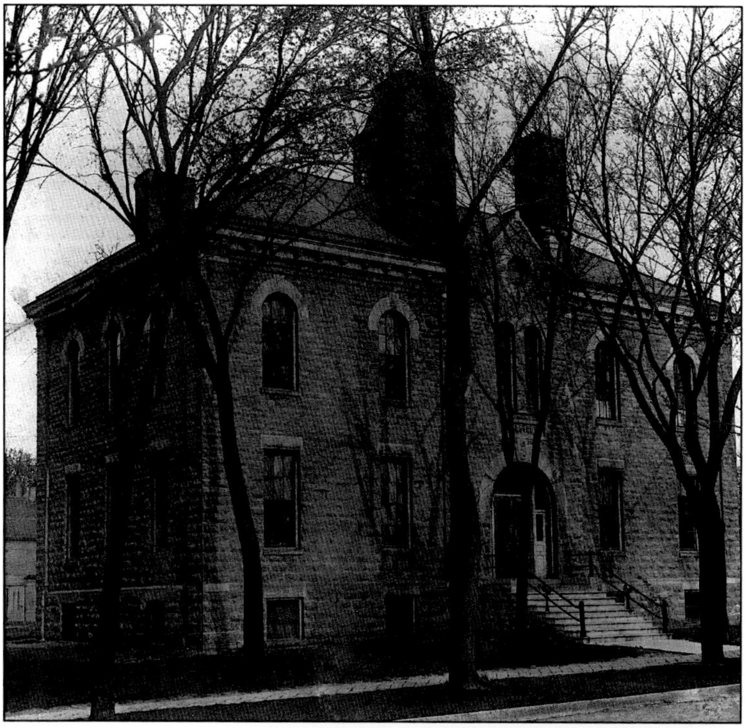

In the mid-19th century, the City of Kankakee built solid grammar schools, descendents of the earlier common schools, such as Lincoln School shown here, c. 1890. Lincoln School was built in 1863 and was located at the southeast corner of East Oak Street and North Dearborn Avenue. It was demolished after World War II. (Kankakee County Museum Photographic Collection, P0318.)

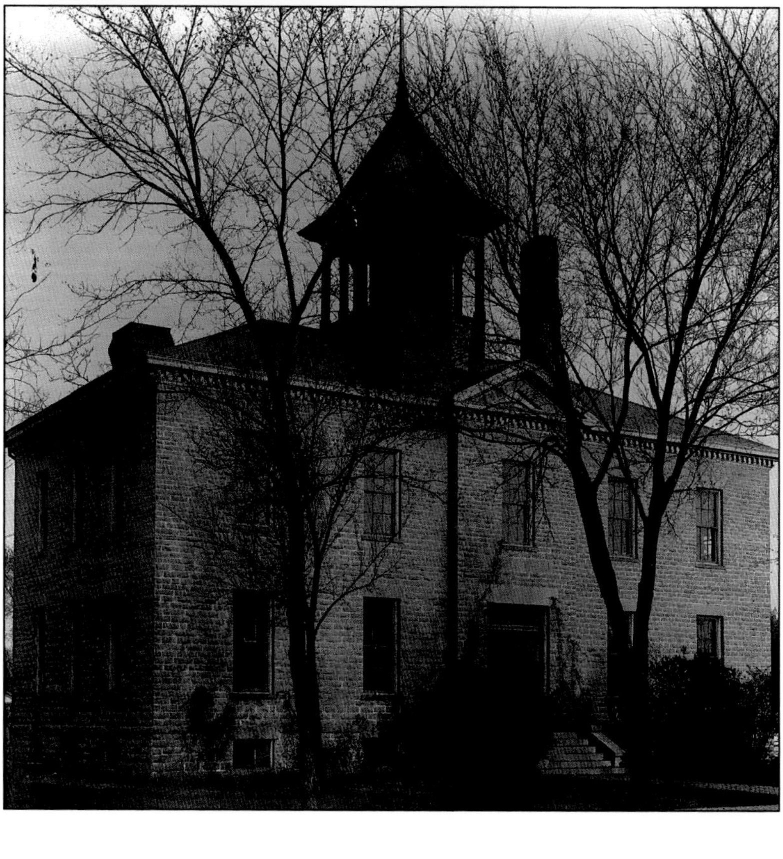

Another example of the City of Kankakee's 19th-century grammar schools is the Washington School, shown in this image c. 1900. The Washington School was erected in 1883 and was located on Fourth Avenue and Van Meter Street. It was enlarged in 1913 and again in 1950 and continued to function as a school as late as 1984. (Kankakee County Museum Photographic Collection, P0317.)

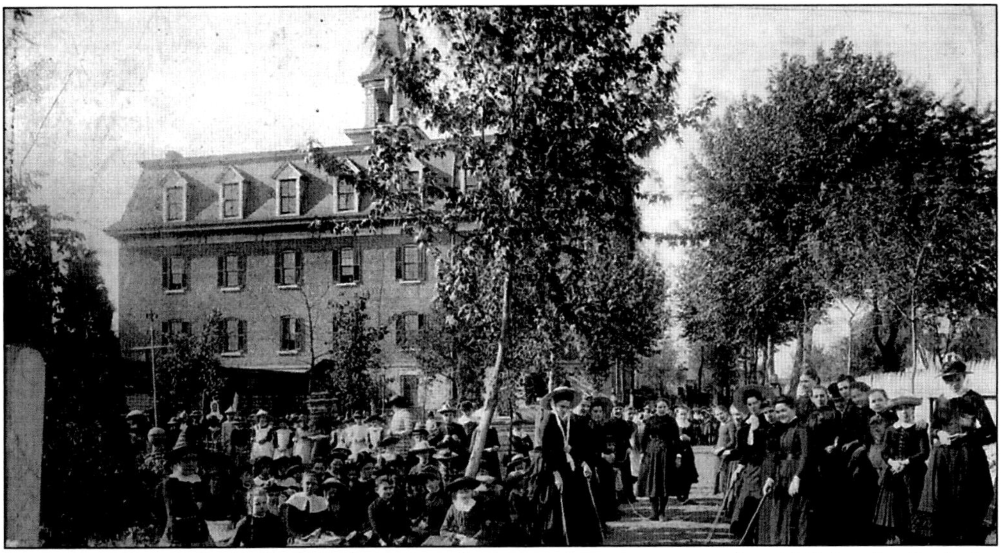

Saint Joseph Seminary, for the education of young ladies, commenced in 1865 by the Catholic Sisters of Notre Dame. In 1867, the Catholic Church erected a substantial building, located on West Merchant Street in the City of Kankakee, to house the school, which became the first operating high school in the Kankakee area. In the center of this image, c. 1875, some of the older girls are seen exercising with skip ropes, while to their right the younger girls are gathered to take the air and observe their elder's at play. (Kankakee County Museum Photographic Collection, P1337.)

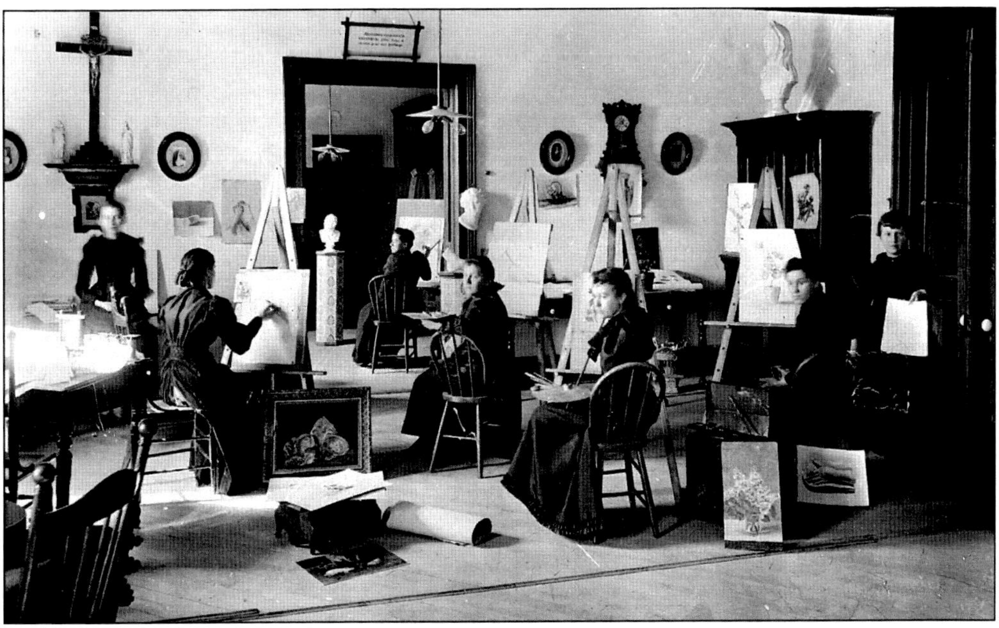

The young ladies attending Saint Joseph Seminary were expected to receive cultural development as well as study traditional subjects. The school's art studio, photographed here in 1890, could accommodate a large class where the girls were instructed in painting still life, landscapes, and portraits in watercolor and other medium. (Kankakee County Museum Photographic Collection, P3157.)

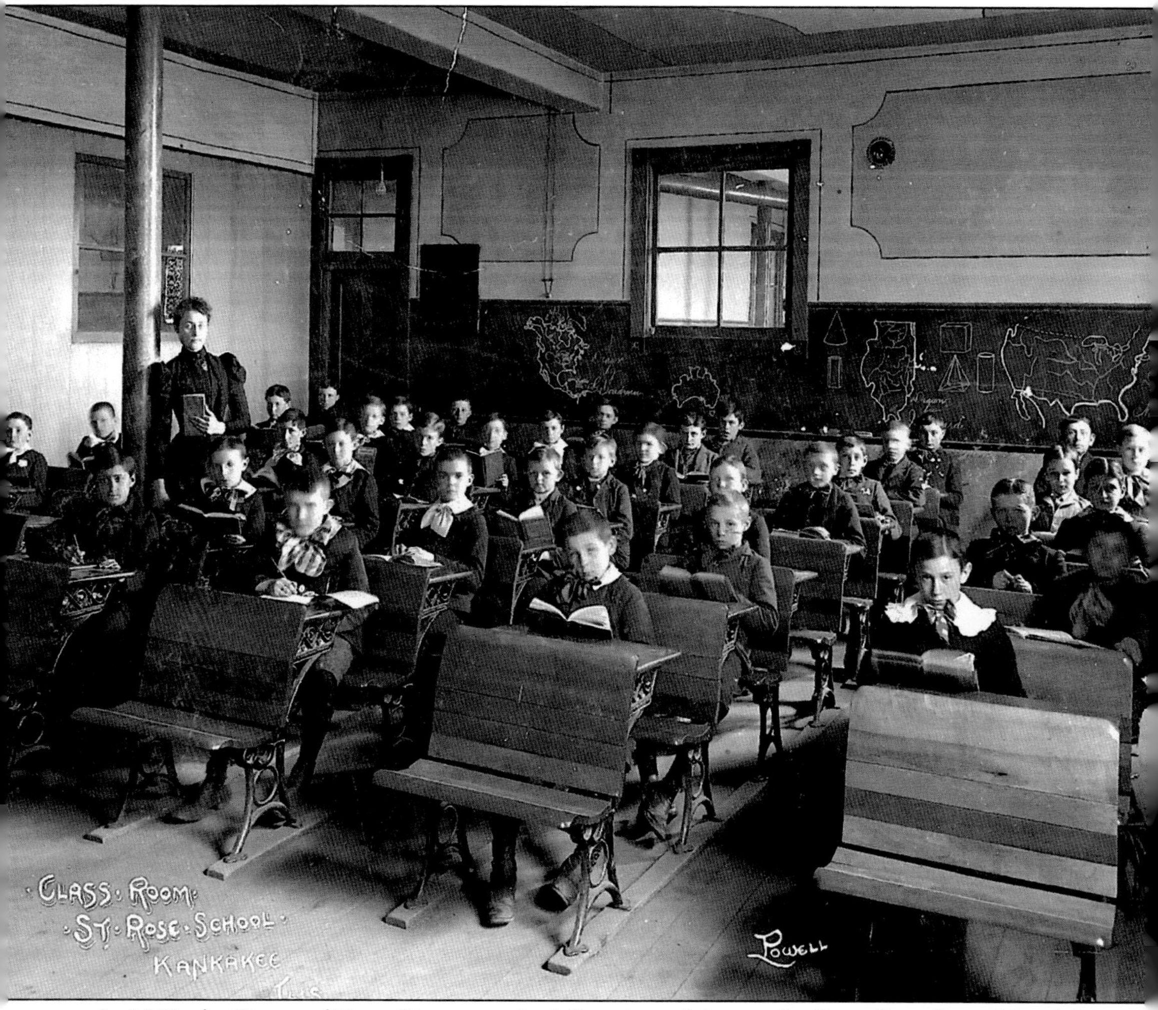

In 1882, the Sisters of Notre Dame acquired direction of the nearby Saint Rose Boys School (a grammar school), which had been operated by the Brothers of Saint Viator. This 1890 image shows the carefully dressed young men receiving their lessons from a "lay" instructor. Note the free-hand drawn maps and geometric shapes on the rear blackboard. (Kankakee County Museum Photographic Collection, P3156.)

Six

Residences

"Lovely and shady lanes abound here"

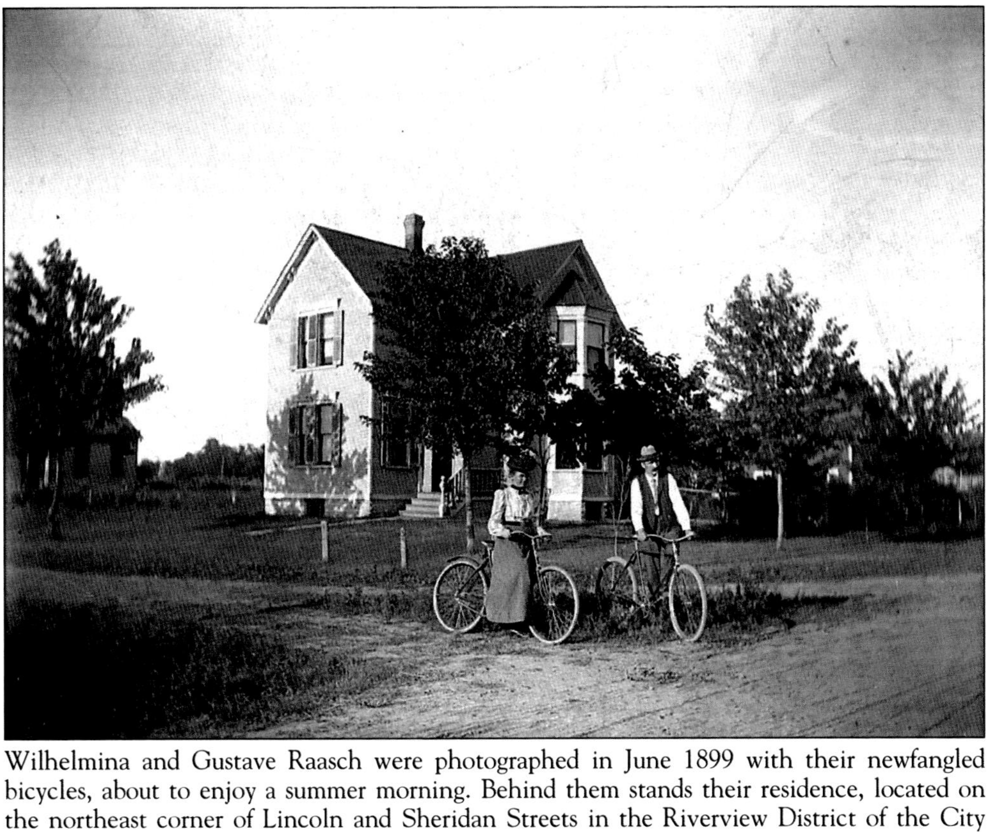

Wilhelmina and Gustave Raasch were photographed in June 1899 with their newfangled bicycles, about to enjoy a summer morning. Behind them stands their residence, located on the northeast corner of Lincoln and Sheridan Streets in the Riverview District of the City of Kankakee. Gustave Raasch was the owner and operator of the Sunnyside Greenhouse on Kankakee's East Maple Street. (Kankakee County Museum Photographic Collection, P5395.)

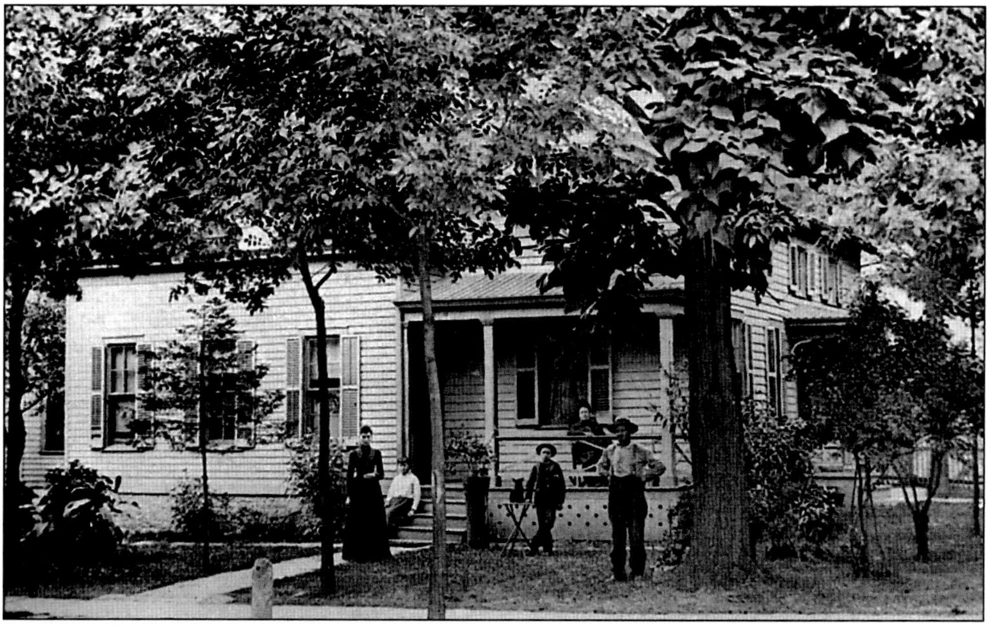

In 1890, the Kirchner family gathered before the side porch of their home, located at the northeast corner of Schuyler and East Oak Avenues for this photograph. The family dog appears in the center on the small folding table. The house lot, one of the first purchased in the City of Kankakee, was acquired by the Kirchners in 1859. The house was built in 1860 and 17 years later, in 1877, the property was assessed at $800. (Kankakee County Museum Photographic Collection, P3149.)

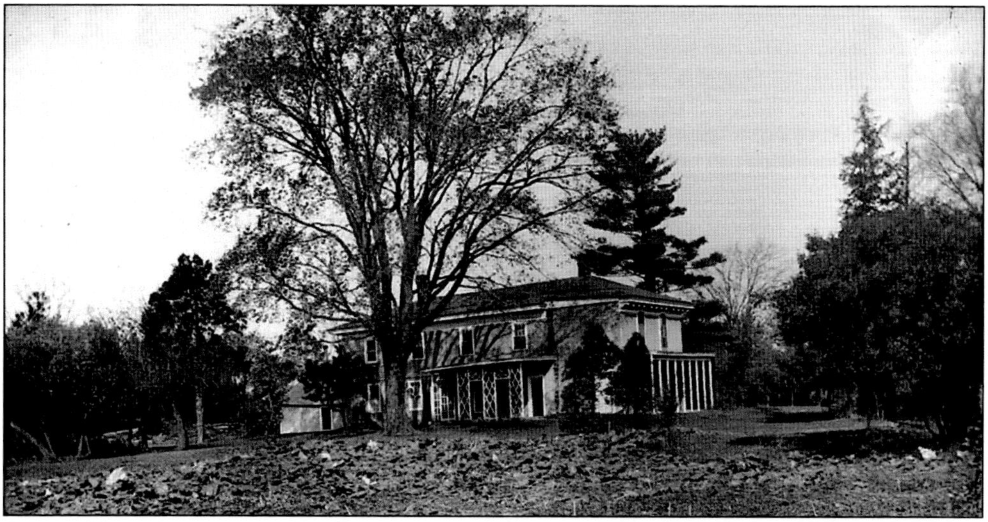

Doctor Abram Lennington Small came to Kankakee in 1850 to help fight a smallpox epidemic. In 1853, he purchased 47 acres of prairie land southwest of the center of the City of Kankakee and erected this house there in 1855. It was substantially enlarged between 1870 and 1875. By the turn of the 20th century, Dr. Small was one of Kankakee's most prominent professional men. The doctor became convinced of the medicinal value of rhubarb and by 1900 he had one of the largest private rhubarb farms in the nation. Part of his rhubarb fields can be seen in the photograph's foreground. (Kankakee County Museum Photographic Collection, P1396.)

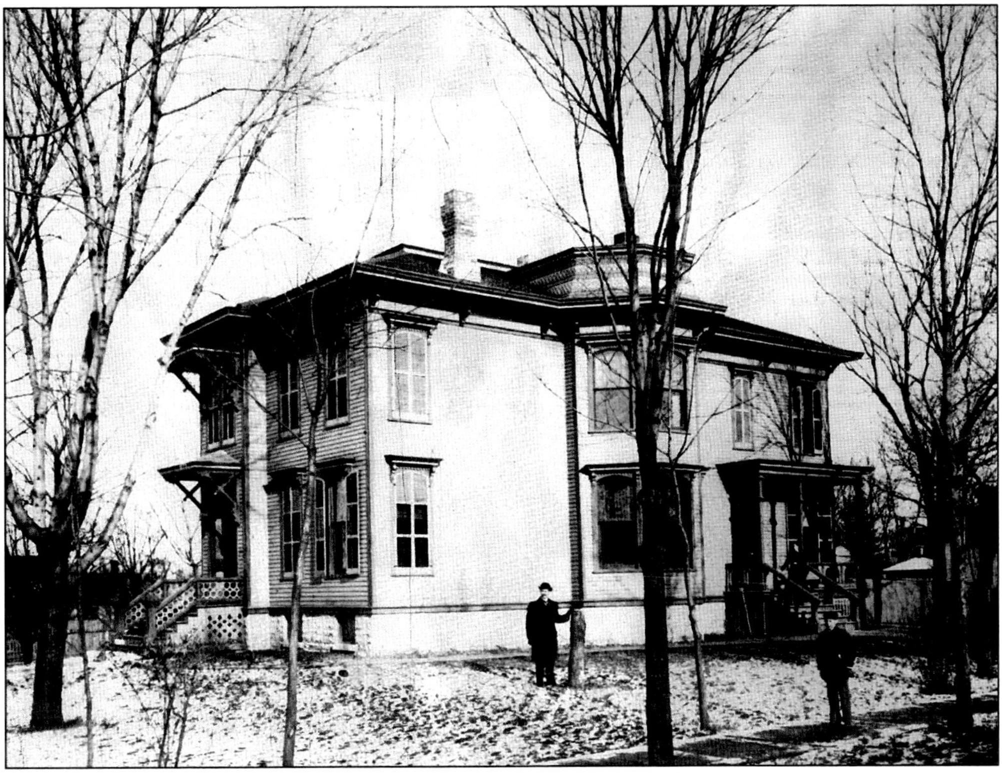

The residence of Hamilton Wheeler, located at the corner of Indiana and Oak Streets in the City of Kankakee, is shown in this image made in the winter of 1881. Hamilton Wheeler, who appears in the center of the photograph, his left hand on a tree stump, was an important lawyer in Kankakee who was employed by a number of railroads. His wife, Mrs. Mary Andrews Storrs Wheeler, stands on the side porch to her husband's left rear. (Kankakee County Museum Photographic Collection, P0553.)

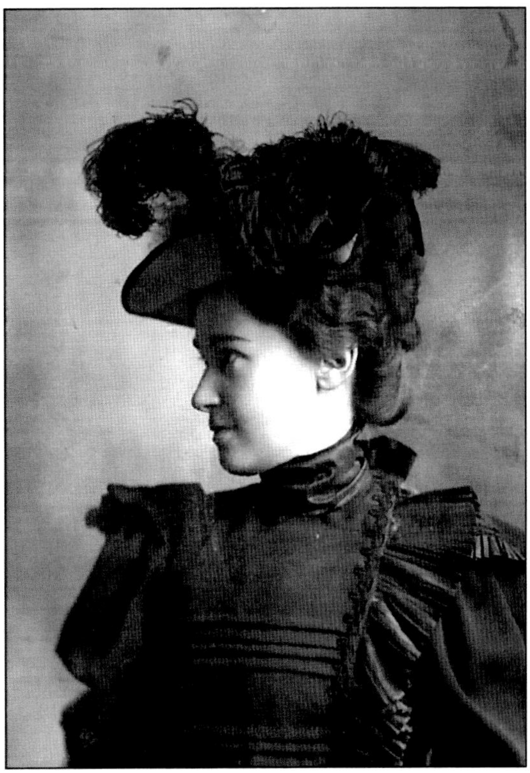

Dr. Abram Lennington Small and his wife Calista Currier Small had six children in their Kankakee home. Their fifth child, Mrs. Calista Small Humrichhauser, appears in this portrait dressed for travel, *c.* 1890. Their fourth child, Lennington Small, born in their Kankakee home in 1862, would serve as governor of Illinois between 1921 and 1929. (Kankakee County Museum Photographic Collection, P2373.)

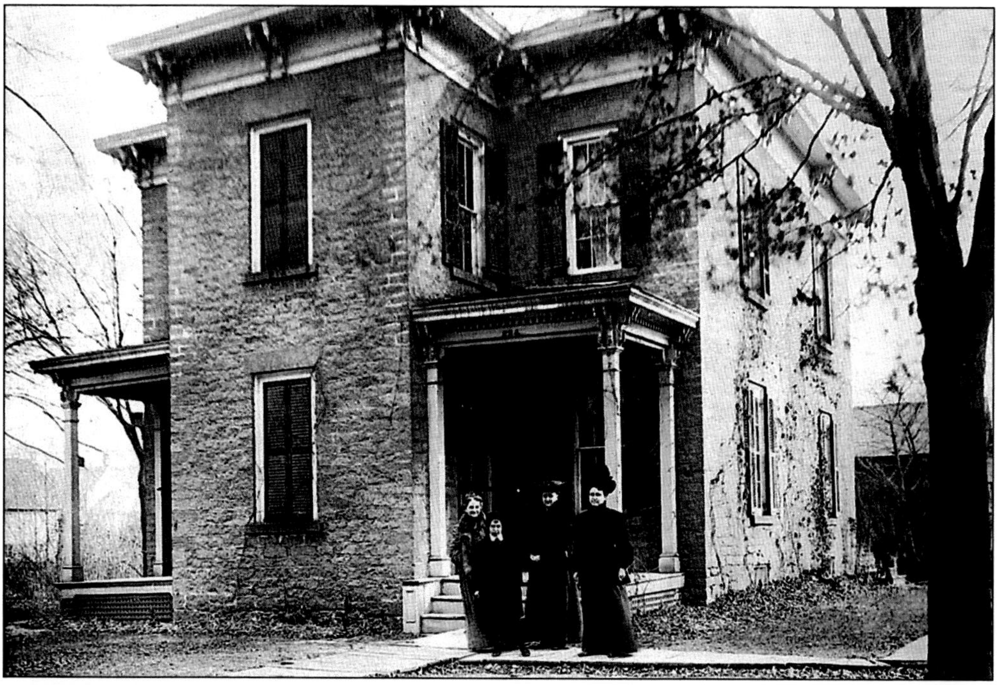

The Bonfield House, built in 1867, is shown in this photograph, *c.* 1890. The owner, Thomas Philip Bonfield was one of the City of Kankakee's earliest and most prominent citizens. Bonfield was a lawyer and one of the first judges in Kankakee County. He was an ardent advocate of civic growth, encouraging the railroad and lobbying for the new insane asylum. In the photograph, standing in front of the house (from left to right) is his wife Maria Eastman Bonfield, daughters Annie Bonfield and Mrs. Alice Bonfield Hemstreet, and the Hemstreet's daughter Bonfield. (Kankakee County Museum Photographic Collection, P5394.)

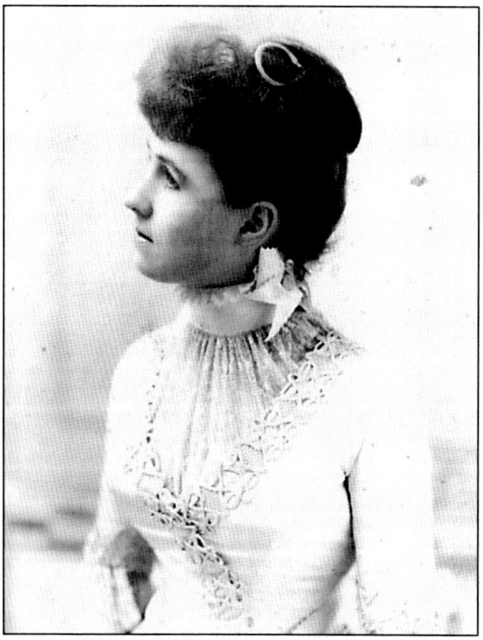

An undoubted visitor to the Bonfield House would have been Miss Edith Bonfield, who appears in this studio portrait, *c.* 1900. Miss Bonfield was the daughter (one of six children) of Dr. Wesley Bonfield and his wife, Emma Dixon Bonfield. Dr. Bonfield had been employed by the Illinois Central Railroad since 1852 as a surgeon for the railroad workers until 1862, when encouraged by his brother Thomas Philip Bonfield, he decided to permanently relocate to the City of Kankakee to start a drug store. (Kankakee County Museum Photographic Collection, P0281.)

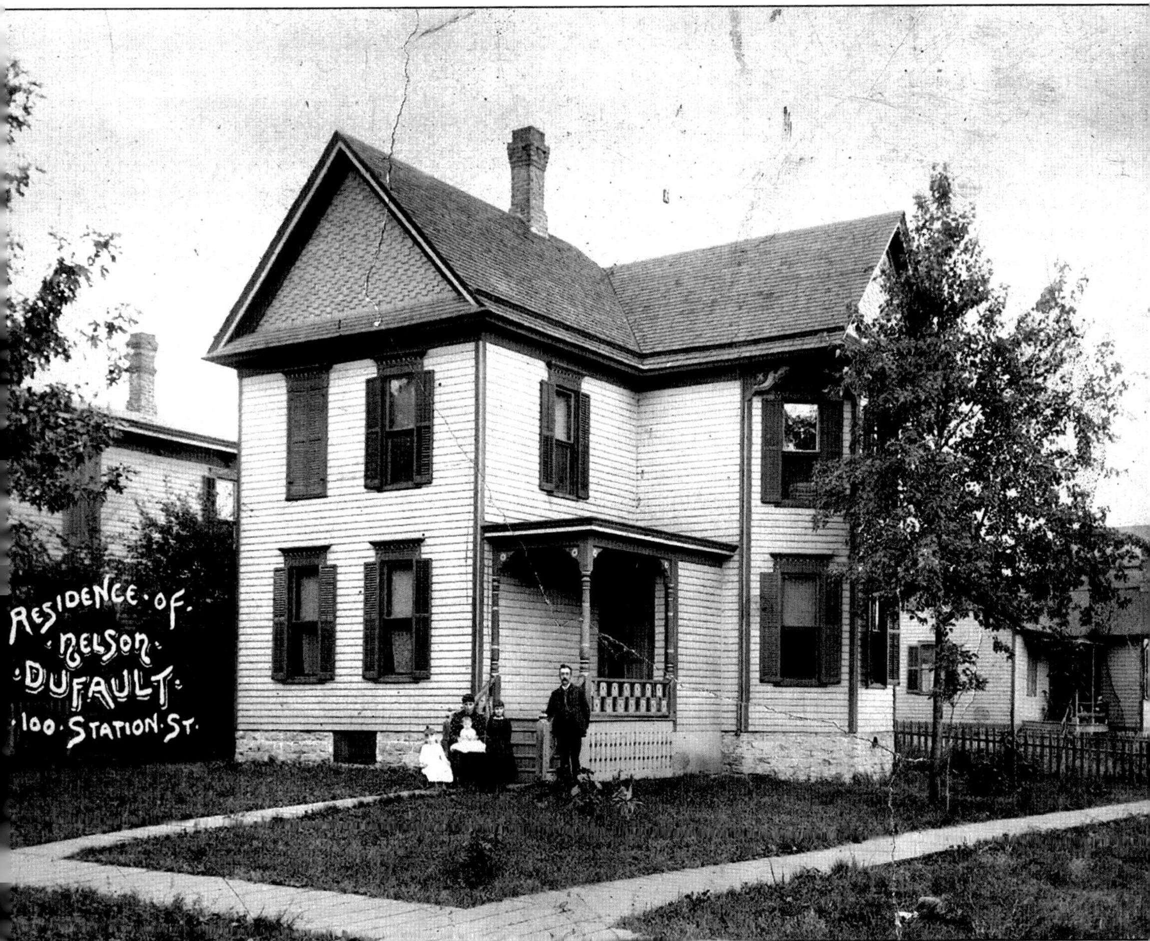

Nelson Dufault poses with his wife Judith Lord Dufault and their children Adell, Henry, and Rosalie, c. 1890. Their house was located on Station Street in the City of Kankakee. Nelson Dufault was a prominent building contractor. He operated a cement and concrete factory, which provided masonry material for numerous Kankakee buildings. (Kankakee County Museum Photographic Collection, P5357.)

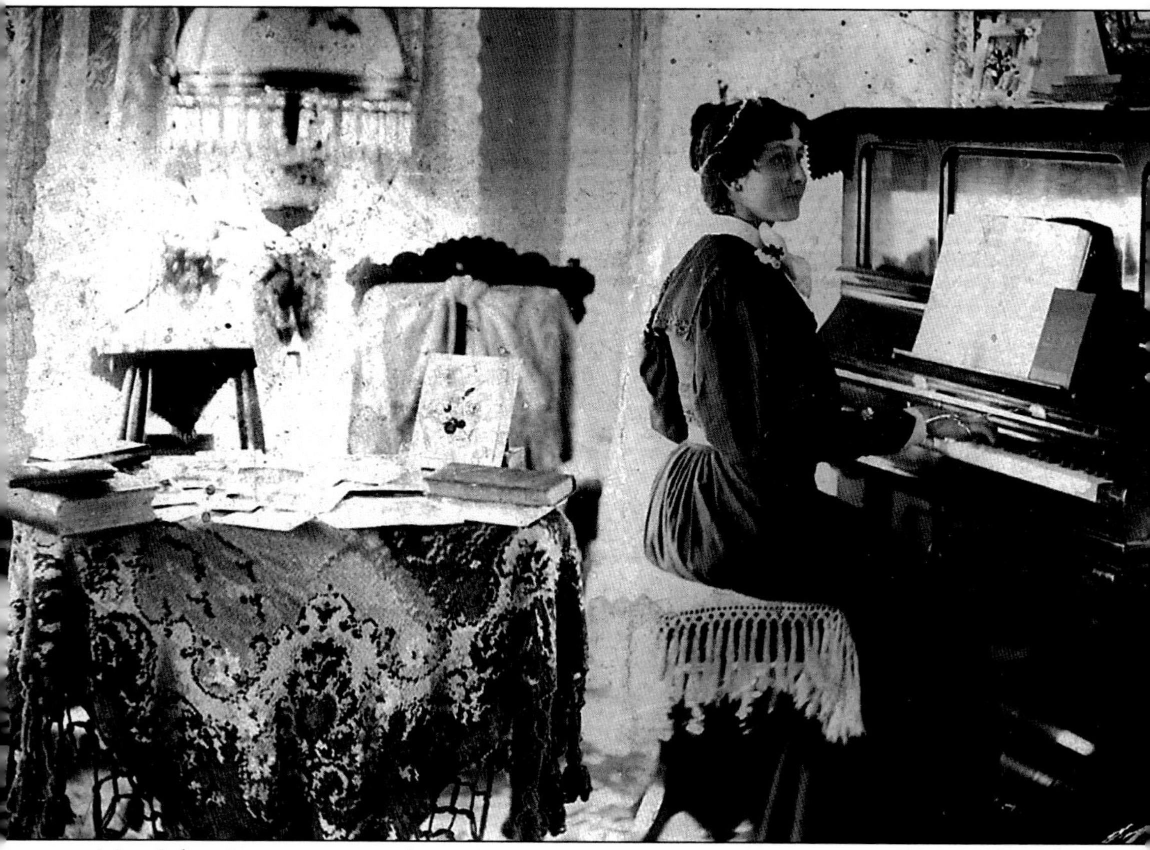

Miss Sylvia Tetreuse is seen here playing the piano on October 1, 1895. She is doing so in the formal parlor of her father's house, helping to celebrate the 22nd birthday of her family friend Armand Pallissard, a Kankakee French-Canadian farmer. (Kankakee County Museum Photographic Collection, P8164.)

Opposite, top: The impressive Briggs-Lillie House, located at the corner of River Street and Harrison Avenue in the City of Kankakee, is seen in this image, c. 1910. The house was constructed in 1868 by Kankakee architect James Lillie for J. Smith Briggs, who made a fortune in Colorado coal and silver mining. In 1884, Lillie bought it from Briggs. The Lillie home quickly became the centerpiece of fashionable Kankakee society. (Kankakee County Museum Photographic Collection, P0064B.)

Opposite, bottom: The South Harrison Avenue entrance to the Lillie House is seen in this photograph taken in the fall of 1885. Note the children sitting on the veranda railing and the ladies prepared to take a Sunday drive. The homeowner, architect James Lillie, built many important buildings in Kankakee, such as the Arcade Building, the Hotel Riverview, and the main structures of the Illinois Eastern Hospital for the Insane. (Kankakee County Museum Photographic Collection, P0064A.)

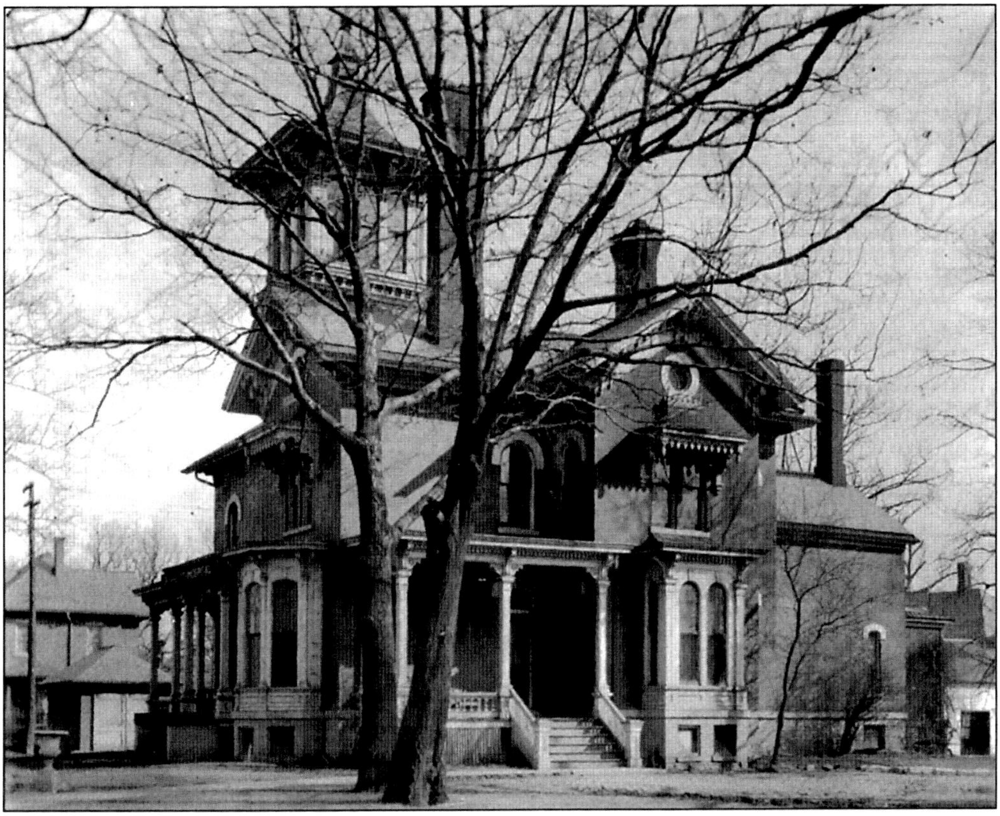

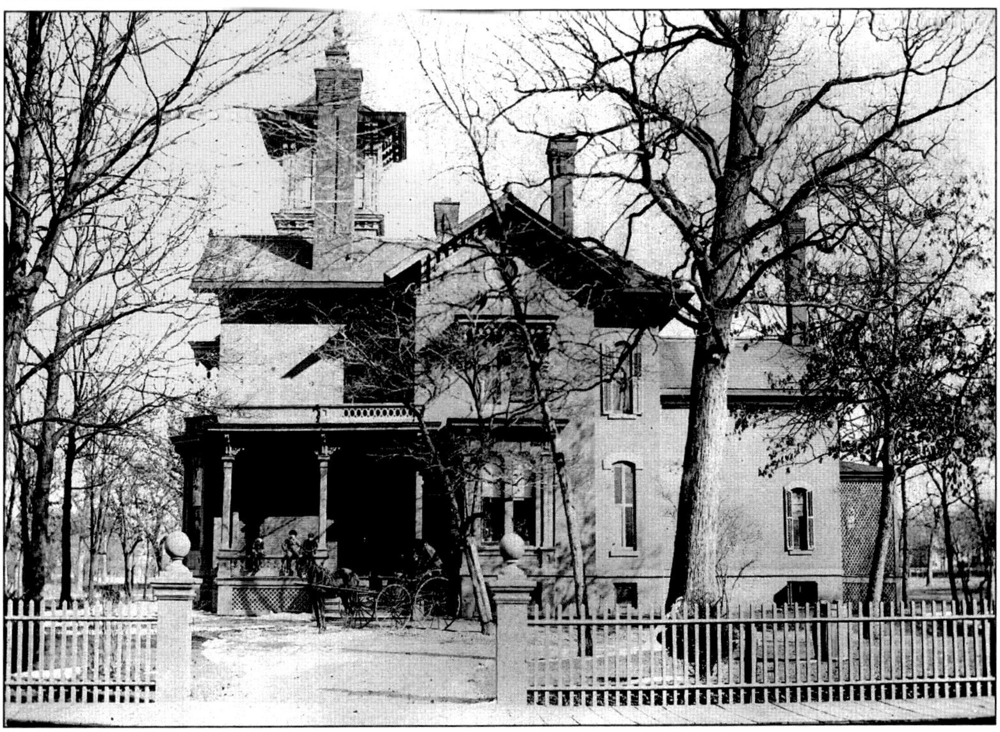

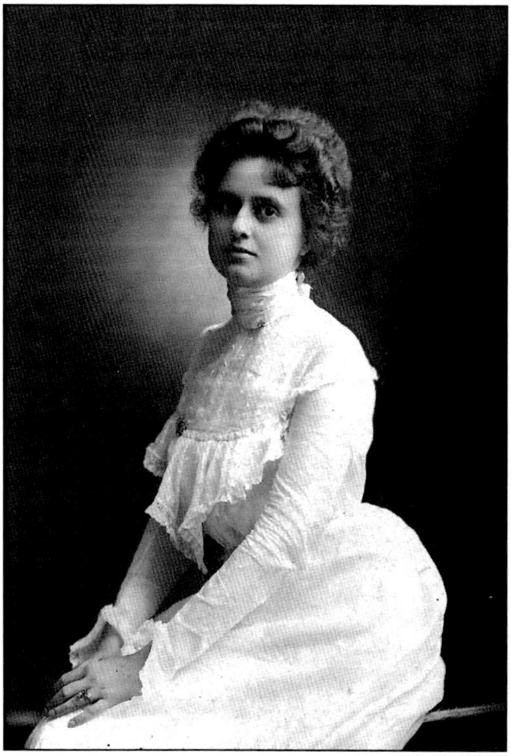

No doubt, on occasion the elegant Miss Louise Hotchkiss visited the Lillie House. This formal studio portrait of her was made in 1902 by her father Eugene Hotchkiss, who operated a photography store in the City of Kankakee. (Kankakee County Museum Photographic Collection, P0455.)

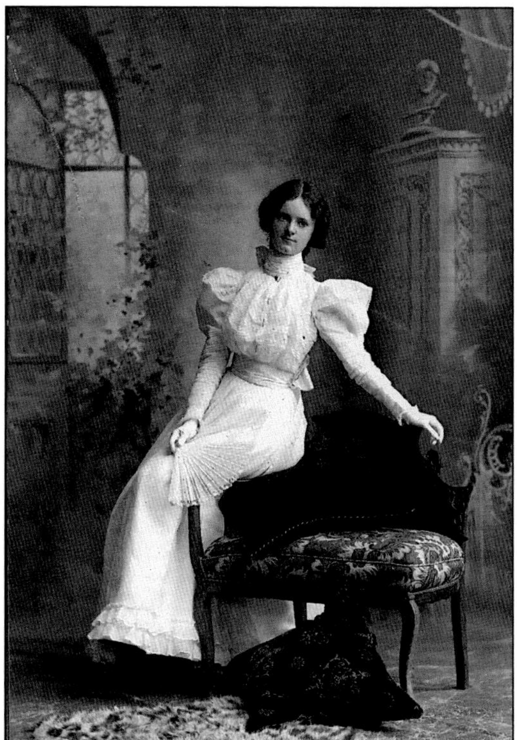

The beautiful Miss Anna Livingston, also appearing in a formal studio portrait taken on June 2, 1898, certainly made formal calls at the Lillie House. Her father was Charles Livingston, operator of a printing business and a prominent newspaper man in the City of Kankakee. He owned the *Kankakee Daily Times* from 1885. (Kankakee County Museum Photographic Collection, P1358.)

In the late 19th century, polished young women were supposed to be able to play some musical instrument in order to entertain company. Miss Mary Campbell Gelino is shown here with her violin in this photograph taken in 1897. Her father, Joseph Gelino, a well-known Kankakee merchant, went into business with Joseph Lecour in 1867. (Kankakee County Museum Photographic Collection, P9014.)

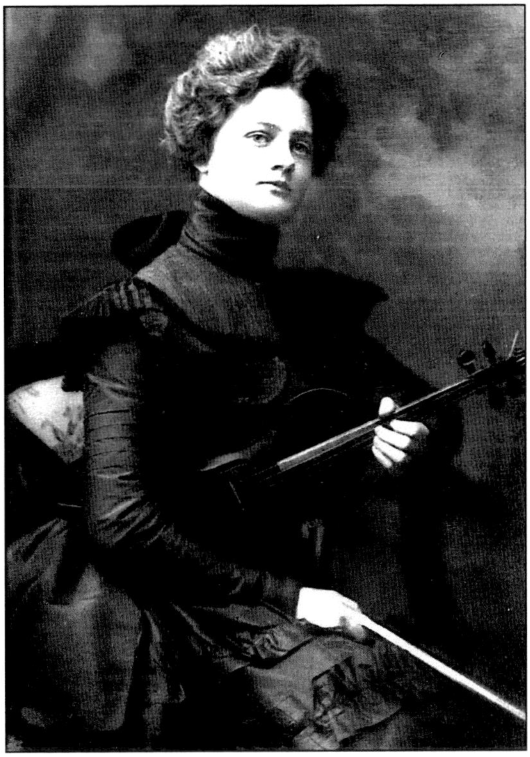

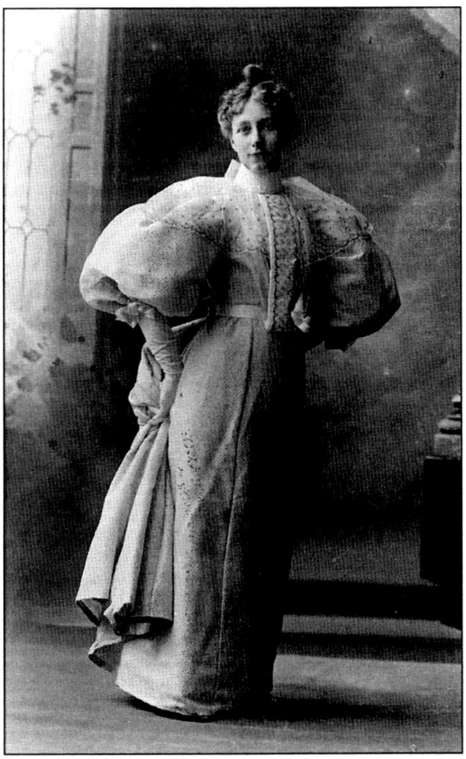

The elegant Mrs. Lura Lowe Hannigan posed for this formal portrait on February 18, 1896. Her father, Peter Lowe, who arrived in the Kankakee area in 1835, was one of the region's first settlers. He became a prosperous farmer. The fashionable Mrs. Hannigan would undoubtedly have visited the best homes in Kankakee. (Kankakee County Museum Photographic Collection, P3972.)

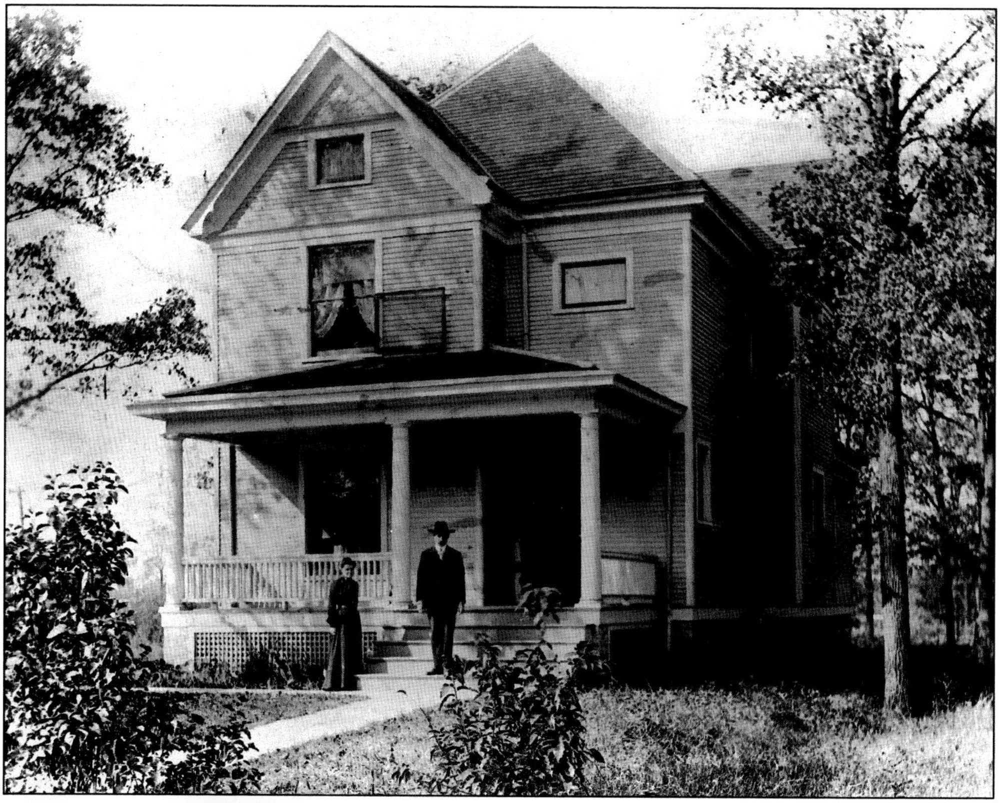

The dreaded annual ritual of spring cleaning has arrived at the Mang residence, located on Greenwood Avenue in the City of Kankakee. In this 1900 photograph, Mrs. Minnie Beckman Mang seems to be ushering her husband, William Mang, off to work and thus out of the way, so that full-scale cleaning operations can commence. (Kankakee County Museum Photographic Collection, P8688.)

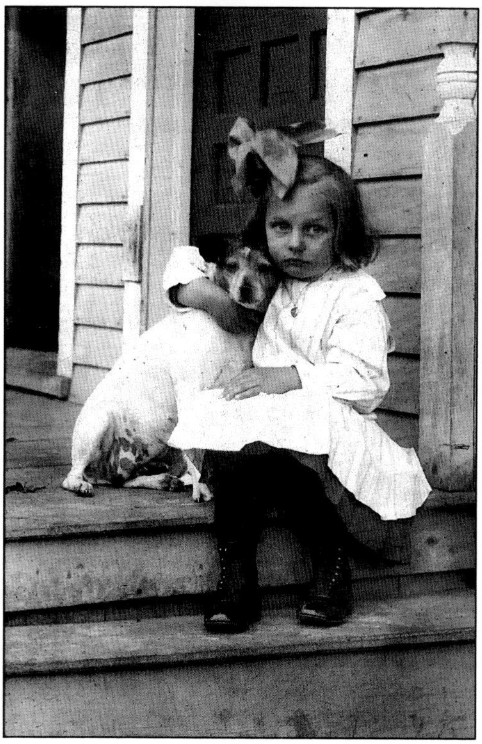

Young Miss Perry Weably and her beloved companion Washington were captured in this delightful image made in the late spring of 1904. Hopefully, they enjoyed their summer at the turn of the 20th century, participating in Kankakee's recreational activities. (Kankakee County Museum Photographic Collection, P8399.)

Seven

ENTERTAINMENT

"Our social pleasures were different in those days"

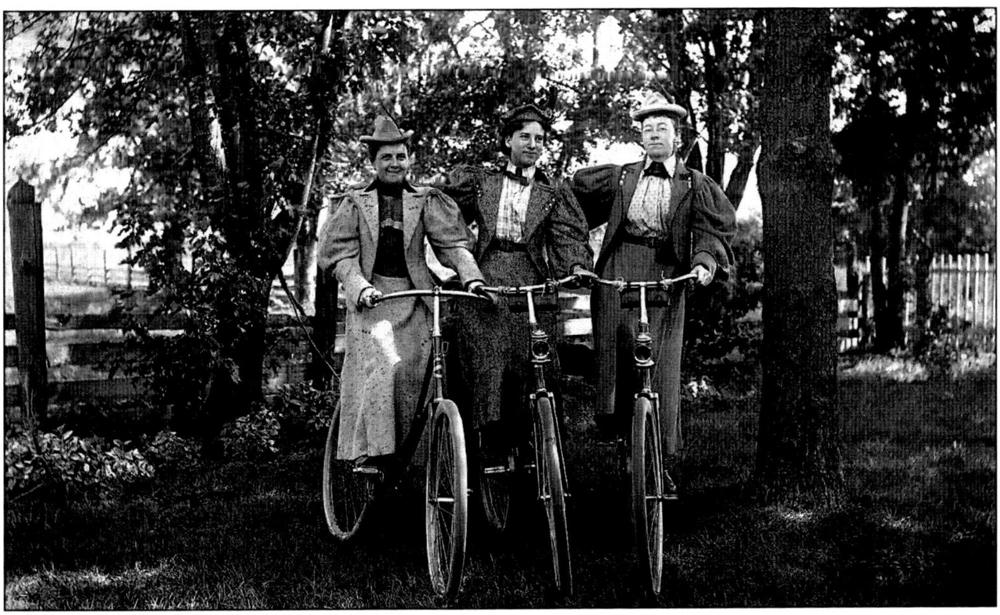

In 1884, John Kemp Stanley invented the safety bicycle, very much like the modern type with a version for women available by 1887, and in another year models with pneumatic tires, enclosed gears, and coasting brakes. In 1888, over 50,000 Americans pedaled for pleasure, such as these three ladies at Kankakee. Miss Laster in the middle, an unidentified woman to the right, and to the left Mrs. Minnie Burt, whose husband was the superintendent of Chicago's Hahnemann Hospital. (Kankakee County Museum Photographic Collection, P1404.)

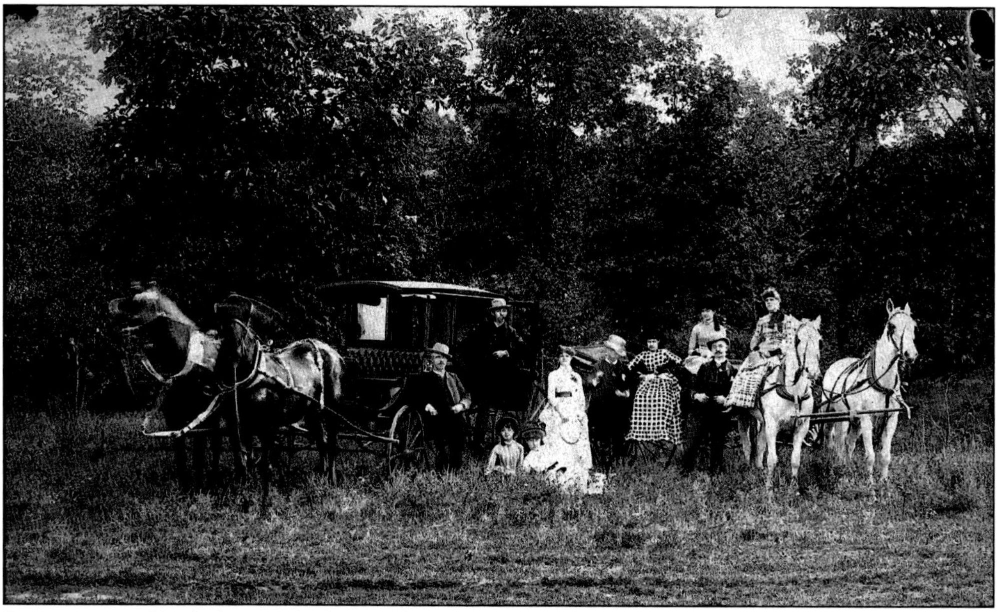

Recreation in Kankakee in the late 19th century often involved a simple drive into the country, such as this picnic party, photographed in 1889. The gentleman leaning on the carriage wheel to the left is Edward Lecour and his brother Louis Lecour appears in the carriage's open door. The Lecour brothers were in partnership with their father Joseph Lecour and were among the most prominent merchants in the City of Kankakee. (Kankakee County Museum Photographic Collection, P0793.)

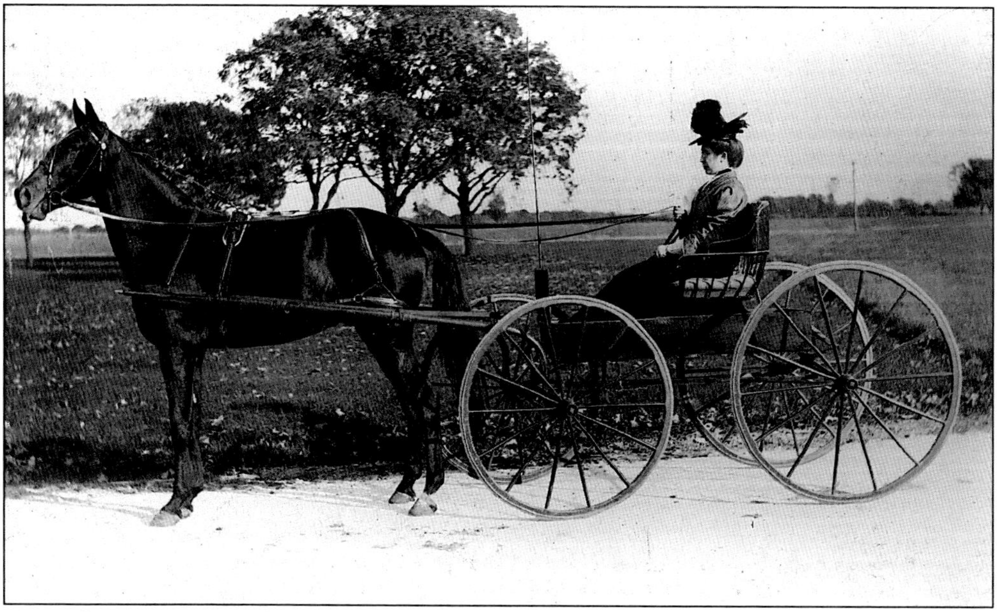

Miss Alberta Martin is shown here taking a solitary recreational ride through the Kankakee area. She was photographed in September 1906, with her horse Ceylon. Miss Alberta's father, Edward Martin, had been a farmer in Kankakee since 1880. (Kankakee County Museum Photographic Collection, P8400A.)

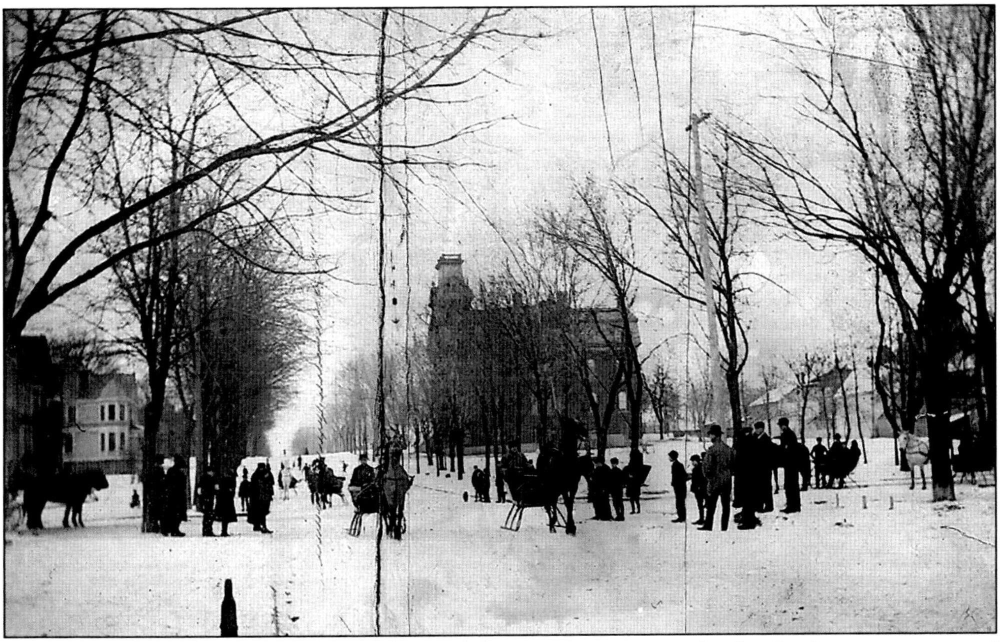

In the late 19th century, winter recreational driving meant using sleighs. In this image a crowd can be seen, gathered to watch cutter races on South Indiana Avenue in the City of Kankakee, c. 1900. In the background, the Central School can be seen. (Kankakee County Museum Photographic Collection, P0015.)

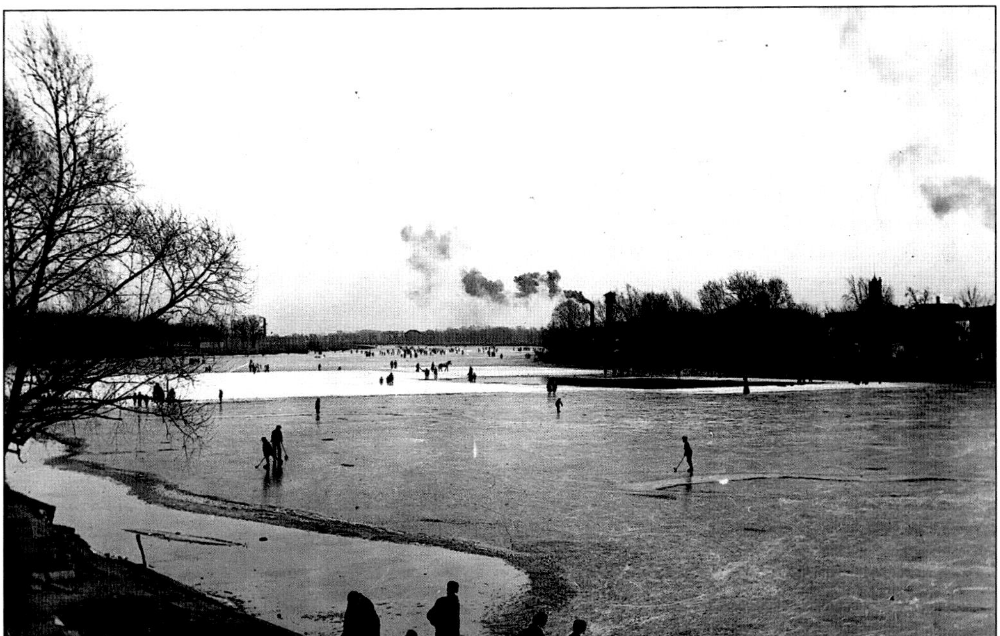

This photograph shows people enjoying the iced over Kankakee River in 1890. Some boys are curling—playing an old Scottish game on the ice. To the right, on the south bank of the Kankakee, buildings of the Illinois Eastern Hospital for the Insane can be seen. (Kankakee County Museum Photographic Collection, P5465.)

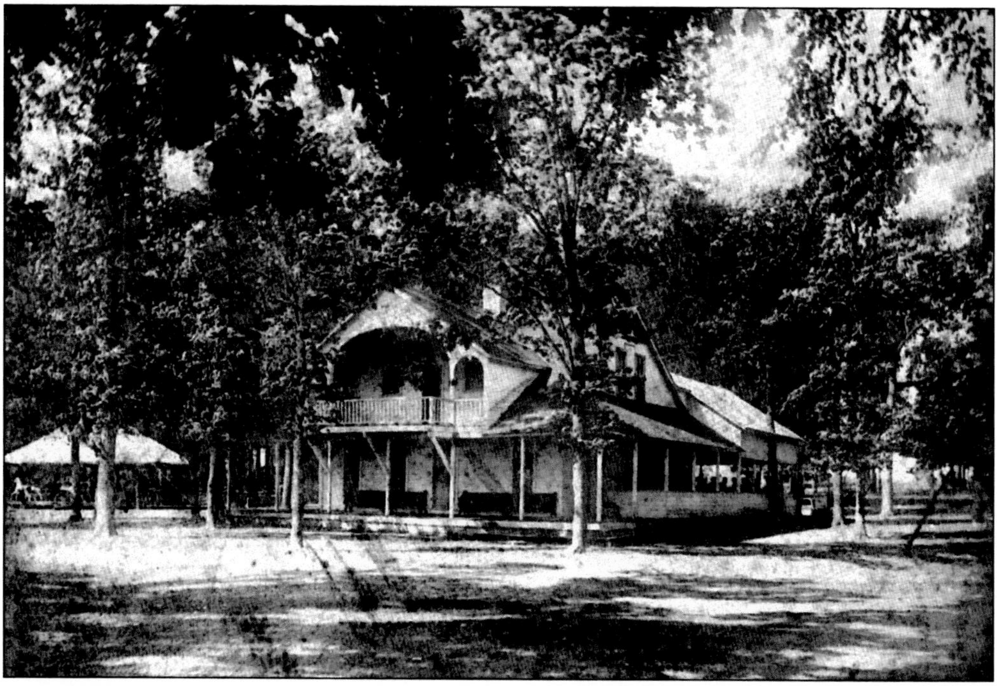

Gougar Grove's main pavilion, about five miles north of the center of the City of Kankakee, was photographed here in 1910. Staring in 1883, the steamer *Minnie Lillie* would take people up the Kankakee River to picnic and relax in the country atmosphere. (Kankakee County Museum Photographic Collection, P0556.)

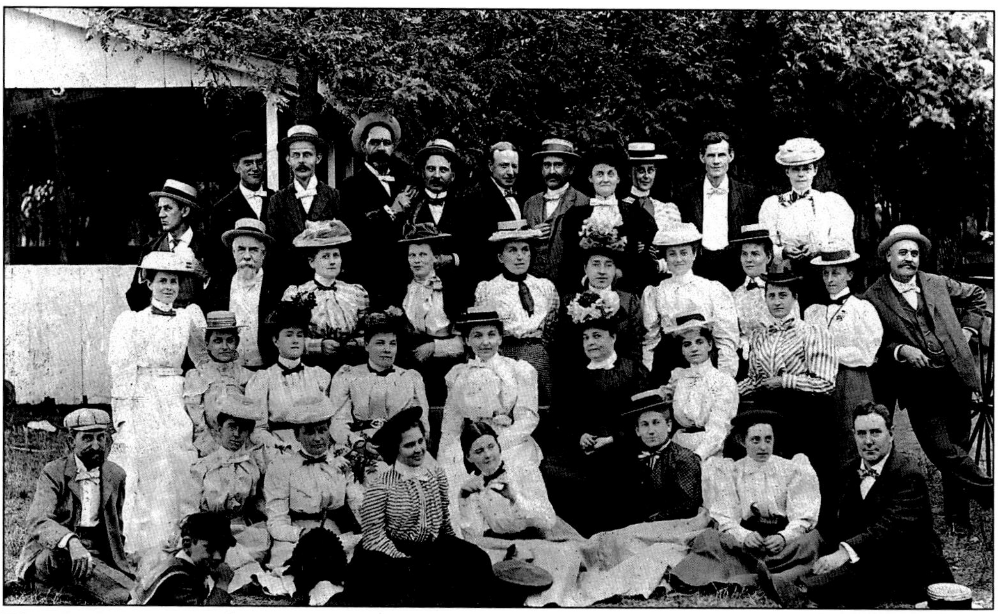

This group picture of a picnic party at Gougar Grove on the Kankakee River was made in 1902. The facility offered summer cabins for overnight campers and as another attraction there was the nearby pony farm operated by S.L. Harnit. (Kankakee County Museum Photographic Collection, P0256.)

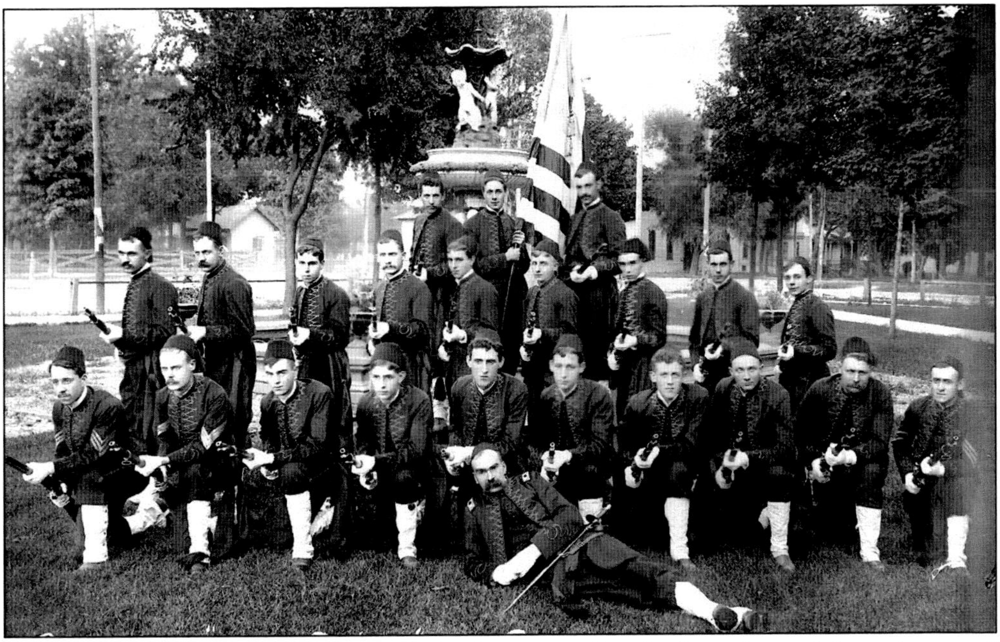

Captain Charles F. Whitmore poses with his Riverview Guards, formed up at "charge bayonets" (minus the bayonets) around the fountain on the City of Kankakee's court house lawn, *c.* 1890. The guards represented the City of Kankakee at the opening ceremonies of the 1893 Chicago World Fair, the Columbian Exposition meant to celebrate the 400-year anniversary of Christopher Columbus' voyage of discovery. (Kankakee County Museum Photographic Collection, P0705.)

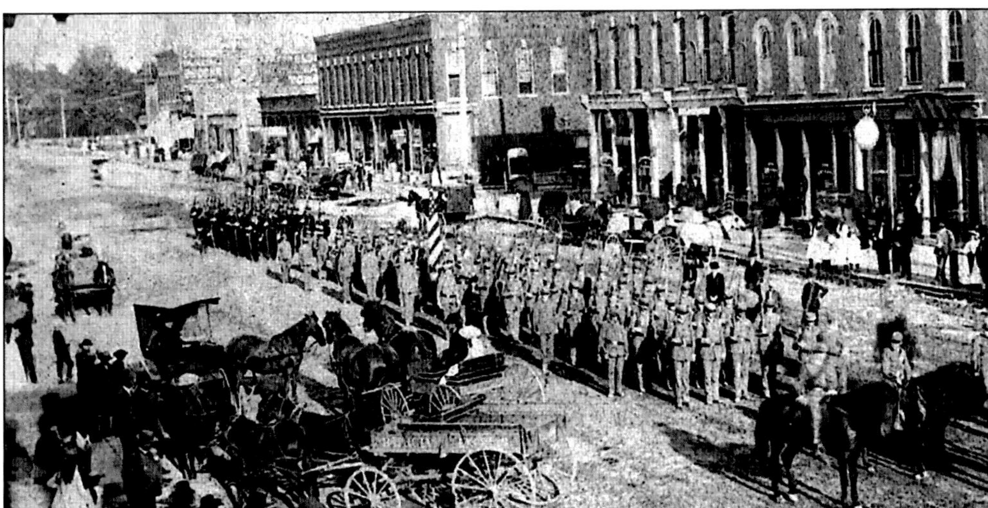

The Saint Viateurs (or St. Viator) Corps of Cadets were captured in this image, as they participate in a City of Kankakee Fourth of July parade held in 1885. They were photographed in East Court Street, between Schuyler and Dearborn Avenues. The smaller contingent to their rear, uniformed in blue, is Company H/4th Illinois National Guard, a Kankakee area formation. The College of Saint Viator was founded in 1868. Located in nearby Bourbonnais, by 1874 its impressive buildings served 250 students. Unfortunately, all its structures, with the exception of the gymnasium, were destroyed by fire in 1906. (Kankakee County Museum Photographic Collection, P0874.)

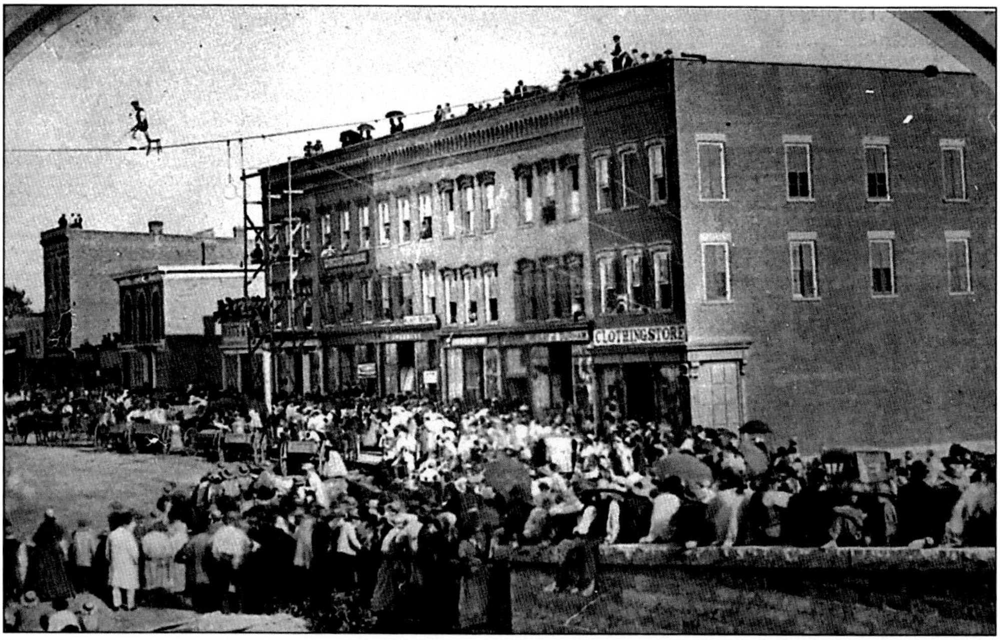

Exciting entertainment was provided in the center of Kankakee by a tight-rope performance over East Court Street, viewed here from the viaduct, in a photograph taken on July 4, 1868. The "professor" is resting on the back of a chair, halfway across. (Kankakee County Museum Photographic Collection, P1275.)

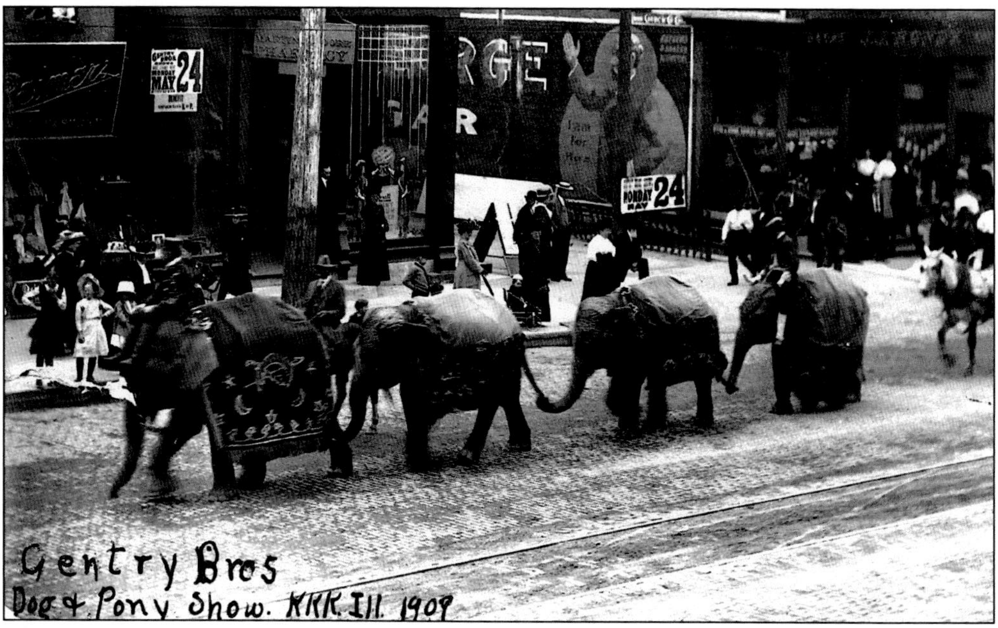

The circus comes to town in 1909. The elephants of the Gentry Brothers Dog and Pony Show are seen here parading through Kankakee's Court Street. Kankakee had always been something of a circus town, since one of the Midwest's biggest circuses, the Yankee Robinson Show, wintered in Kankakee from 1857 to 1876. (Kankakee County Museum Photographic Collection, P5721.)

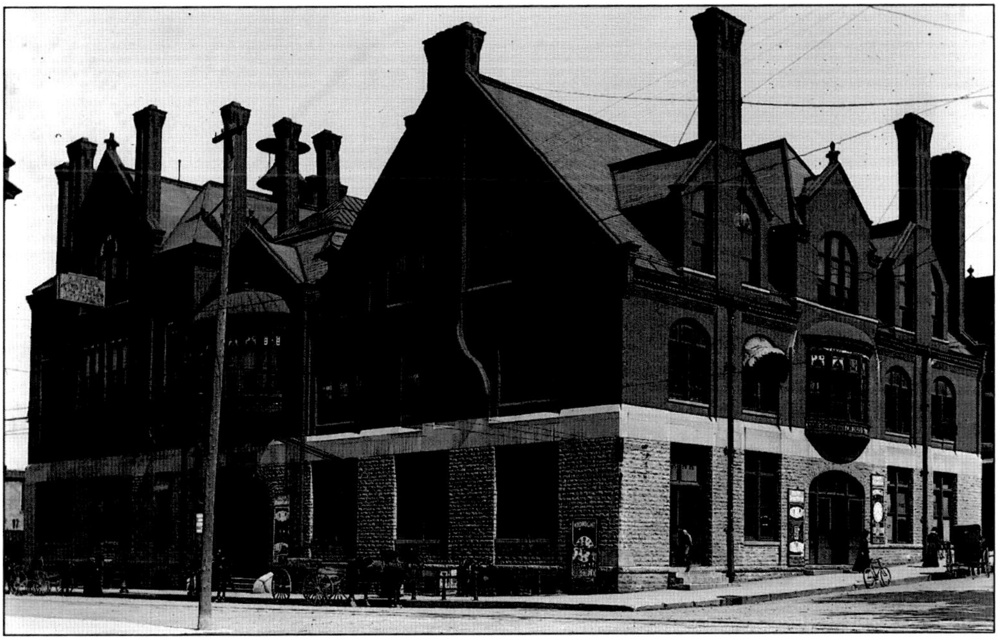

The entire western half of the Arcade Building, built in 1882 and located at Schuyler Avenue and Merchant Street in the City of Kankakee, was occupied by an opera house, offering all types of theater, which opened for its first performance on November 14, 1884. This photograph was taken on June 2, 1900, and around the building can be seen advertisements for the current production, "Midnight in China Town." (Kankakee County Museum Photographic Collection, P9594.)

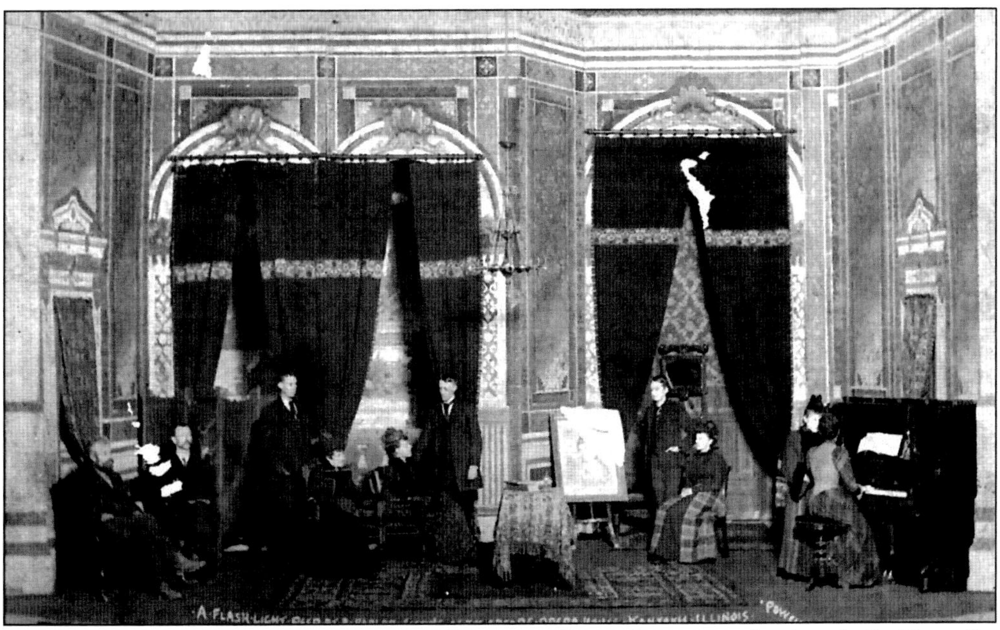

This photograph shows an interior image of the opera house, located in the Arcade Building. On stage is the local talent cast of an amateur production, c. 1890. At the piano, to the right with her back to the camera, is Mrs. Mattie Bernier, who generally played the piano at the opera house for all kinds of performances. (Kankakee County Museum Photographic Collection, P0008.)

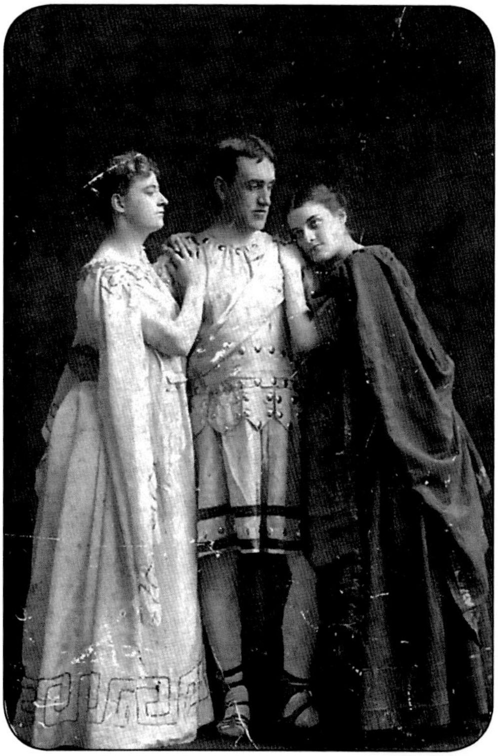

In the spring of 1895, a local theater group gave a performance of *Ben Hur: A Tale of Christ*, at Kankakee's Saint Paul's Episcopal Church. To the right of the image is Miss Laura La Parle Hickox, playing Ben Hur's sister, and to the left is Mrs. Lucia Paddock Cobb, playing Ben Hur's mother. In the center is Charles Haven Cobb (superintendent of the Kankakee Water Works) appearing in the starring role as Ben Hur. (Kankakee County Museum Photographic Collection, P2681.)

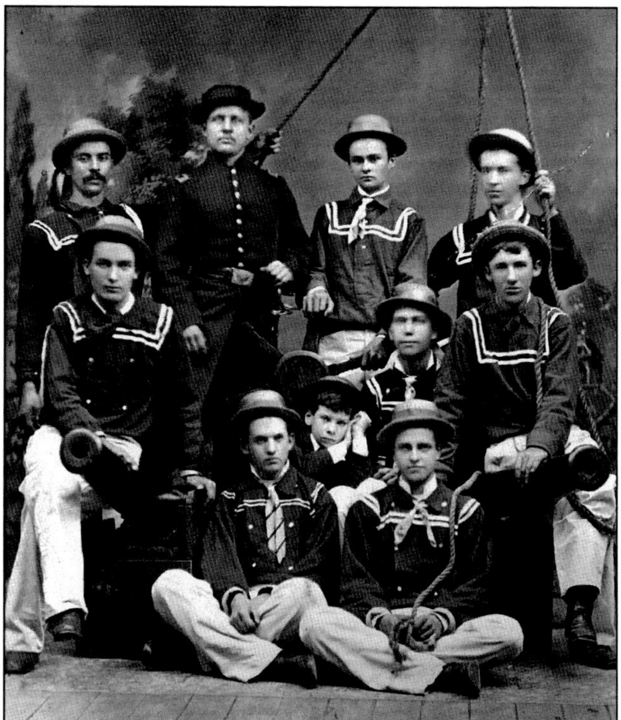

The cast of the new operatic farce by Gilbert and Sullivan, *H.M.S. Pinafore*, were photographed at Kankakee in 1885. "As the balls whistle free over the briny blue sea, we stand to our guns all day..." They were performing at Kankakee's Opera House, located in the Arcade Building, during the theater's second season. (Kankakee County Museum Photographic Collection, P0329.)

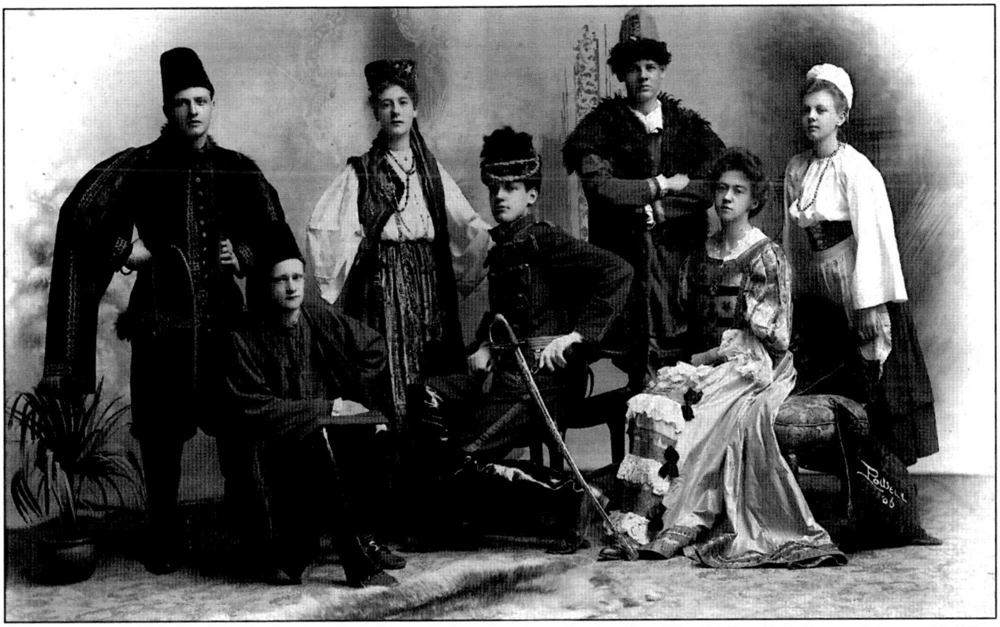

The Kankakee High School's 1906 Senior Play was performed at Kankakee's "Opera House." The play was evidently set in Hungary, or at least somewhere in Eastern Europe, as evidenced by the costumes worn by the cast in this group photograph. (Kankakee County Museum Photographic Collection, P4587.)

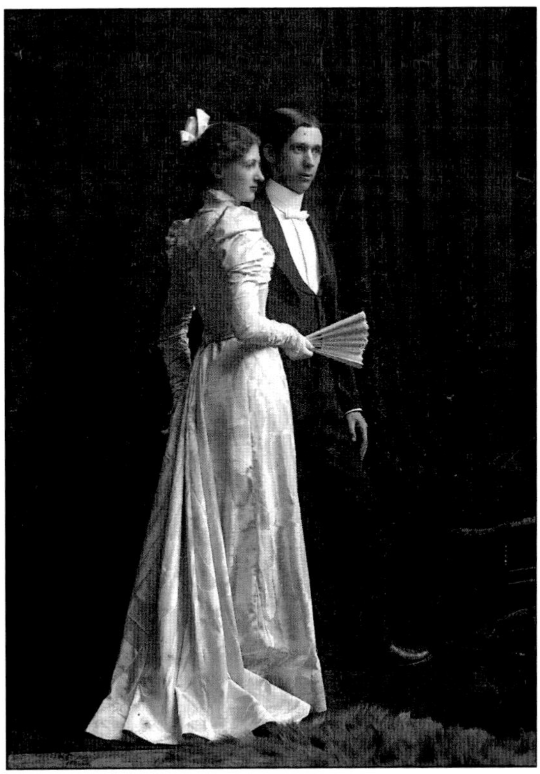

Interest in amateur theatrics appeared at many levels in late-nineteenth century Kankakee. Eben Gowers appears in this photogrpah taken in 1900, with his wife Mar Florence Gray Gower, when they appeared together in a play performed at Kankakee's "Opera House." Eben Gowe was a lawyer and prominent judge in Kankakee. (Kankakee County Museum Photographic Collection, P2856.)

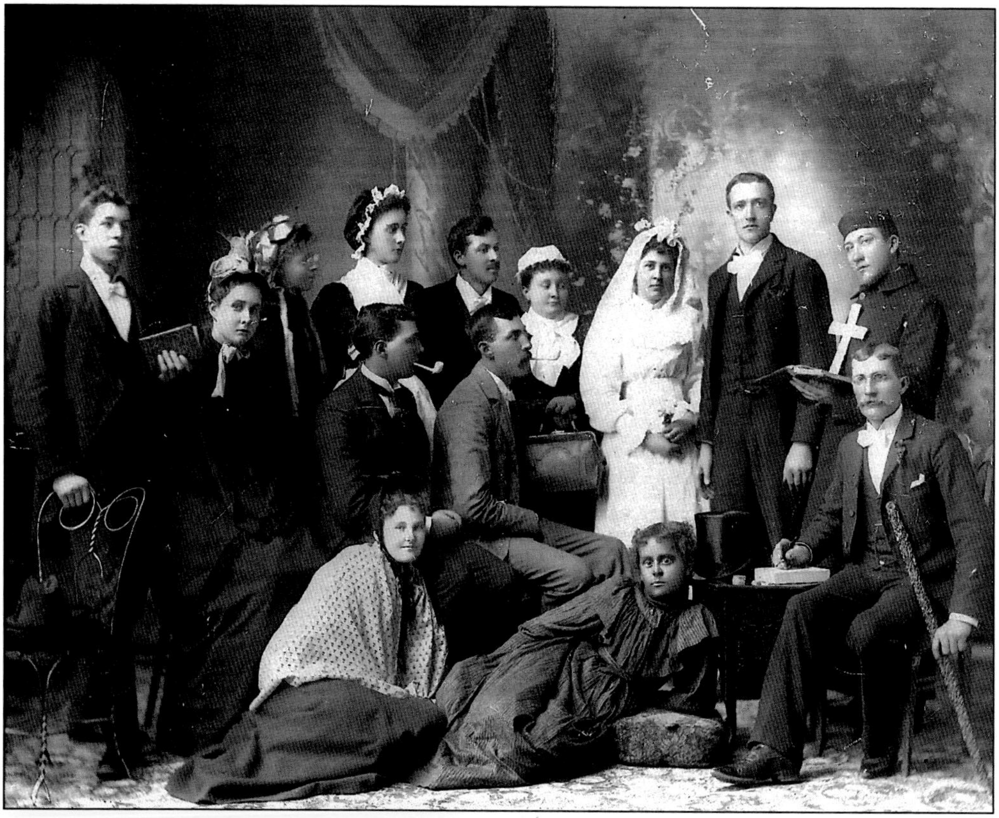

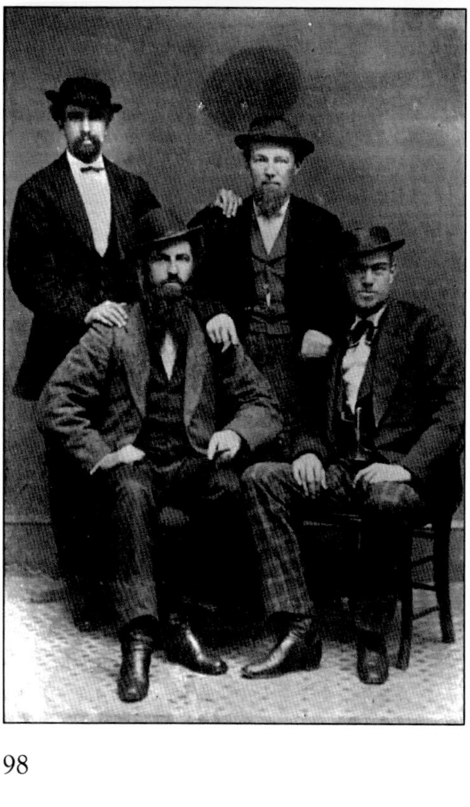

This group photograph shows the cast of an unknown theatrical production that played at the Kankakee "Opera House," c. 1900. The players are local amateur talent. The young lady sitting on the floor leaning on a cushion appears to be in black face. (Kankakee County Museum Photographic Collection, P8808.)

The members of Kanakee's Aneid Society, a rather small and informal group bemused and apparently ready for a night on the town, were photographed in 1874. Standing at left is Alphonsus Robert La Parle and standing at right is Andrew Kerr, a tinner and hardware store owner. Seated at left is William Gougar, who operated steam paddle boats on the Kankakee River, and seated to the right, sporting his bold trousers, is Julius Taylor. (Kankakee County Museum Photographic Collection, P0084.)

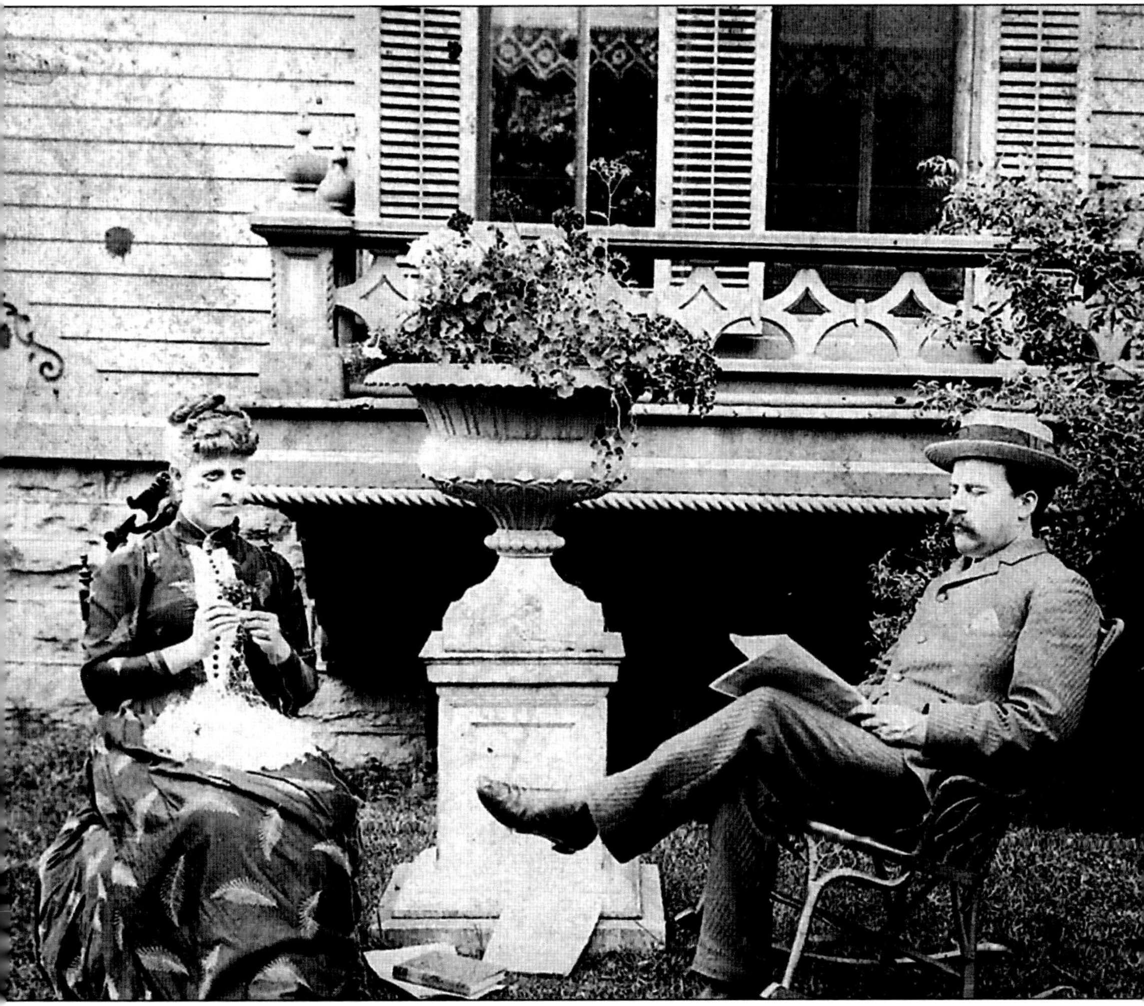

The Paddocks are shown here enjoying a lazy summer afternoon in 1887. Wearing a summer boater, James Paddock reads the evening paper while his wife, Mary Louisa Crawford Paddock, works on a domestic project. Home entertainment was simple. (Kankakee County Museum Photographic Collection, P2555.)

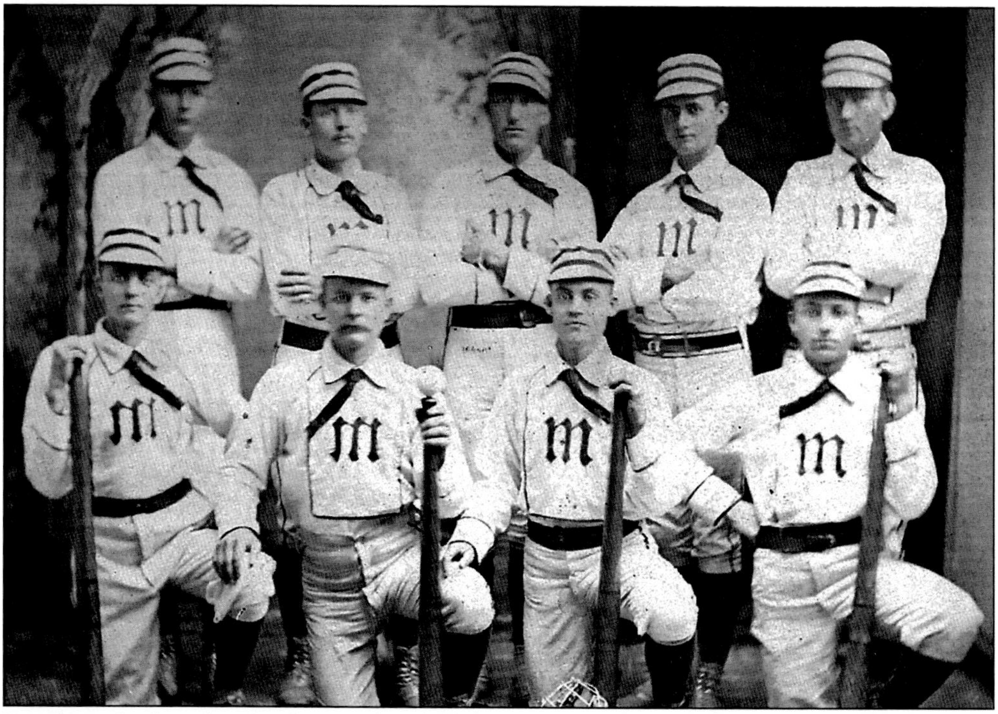

Popularized after the Civil War, baseball became a national craze, particularly after the Cincinnati Red Stockings toured the country in 1869, meeting all challengers without loosing a game. Early teams usually fielded a nine, such as the Momence Hurlers, an area team that was photographed in 1882, when they came to play the Kankakee Nine. (Kankakee County Museum Photographic Collection, P0739.)

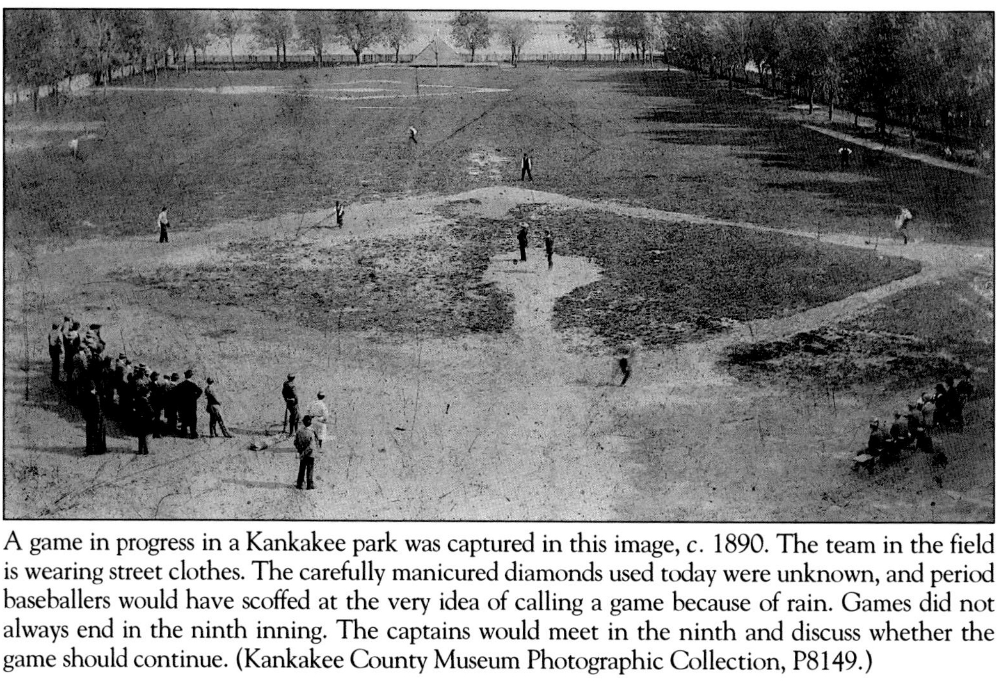

A game in progress in a Kankakee park was captured in this image, *c.* 1890. The team in the field is wearing street clothes. The carefully manicured diamonds used today were unknown, and period baseballers would have scoffed at the very idea of calling a game because of rain. Games did not always end in the ninth inning. The captains would meet in the ninth and discuss whether the game should continue. (Kankakee County Museum Photographic Collection, P8149.)

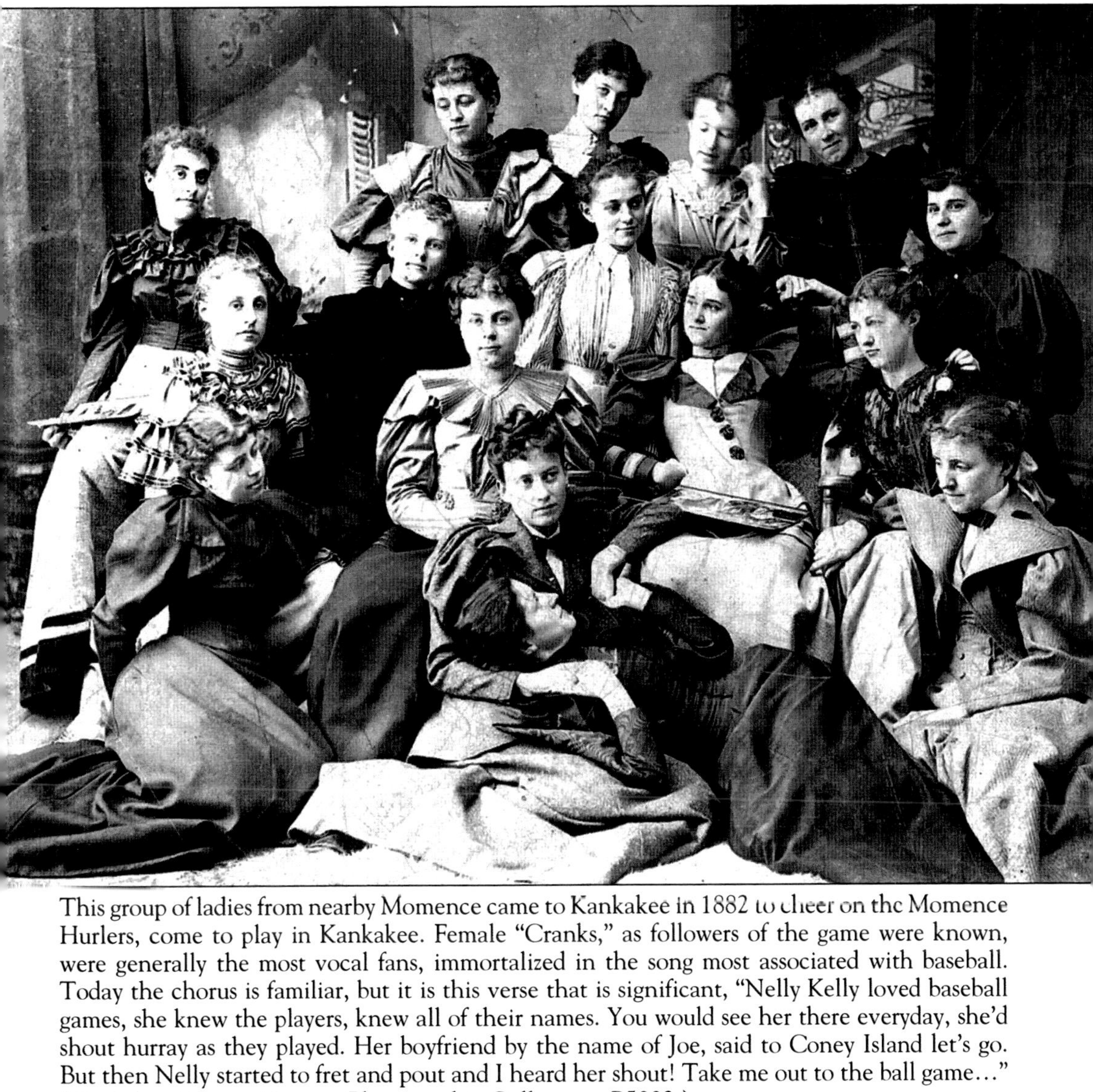

This group of ladies from nearby Momence came to Kankakee in 1882 to cheer on the Momence Hurlers, come to play in Kankakee. Female "Cranks," as followers of the game were known, were generally the most vocal fans, immortalized in the song most associated with baseball. Today the chorus is familiar, but it is this verse that is significant, "Nelly Kelly loved baseball games, she knew the players, knew all of their names. You would see her there everyday, she'd shout hurray as they played. Her boyfriend by the name of Joe, said to Coney Island let's go. But then Nelly started to fret and pout and I heard her shout! Take me out to the ball game..." (Kankakee County Museum Photographic Collection, P5003.)

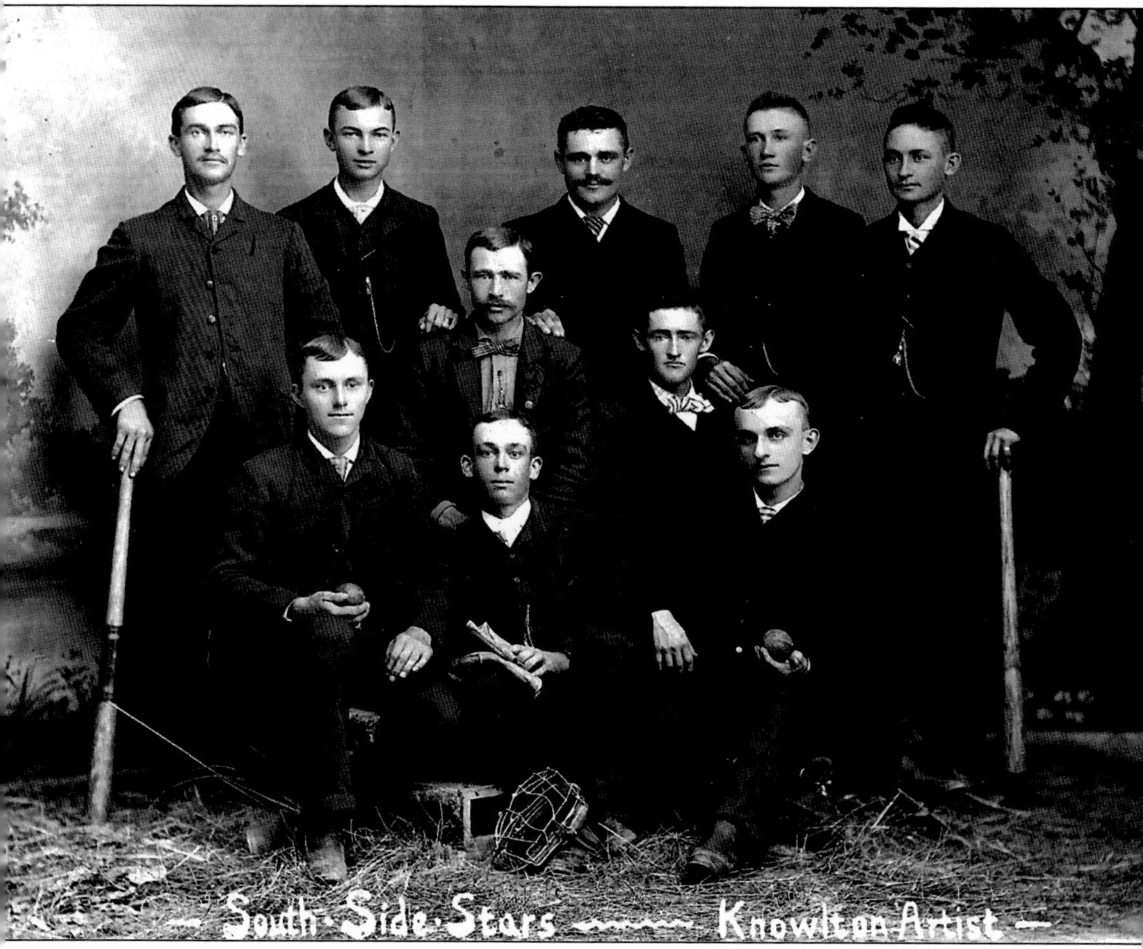

The gentlemanly City of Kankakee South Side Stars pose for their team portrait taken in 1897. At this time, fielding was done with bare hands and as result scores of over a hundred were not uncommon. The Stars are shown with a catcher's mask, a new innovation, regarded as a feminine affectation by purists of the game. (Kankakee County Museum Photographic Collection, P0476.)

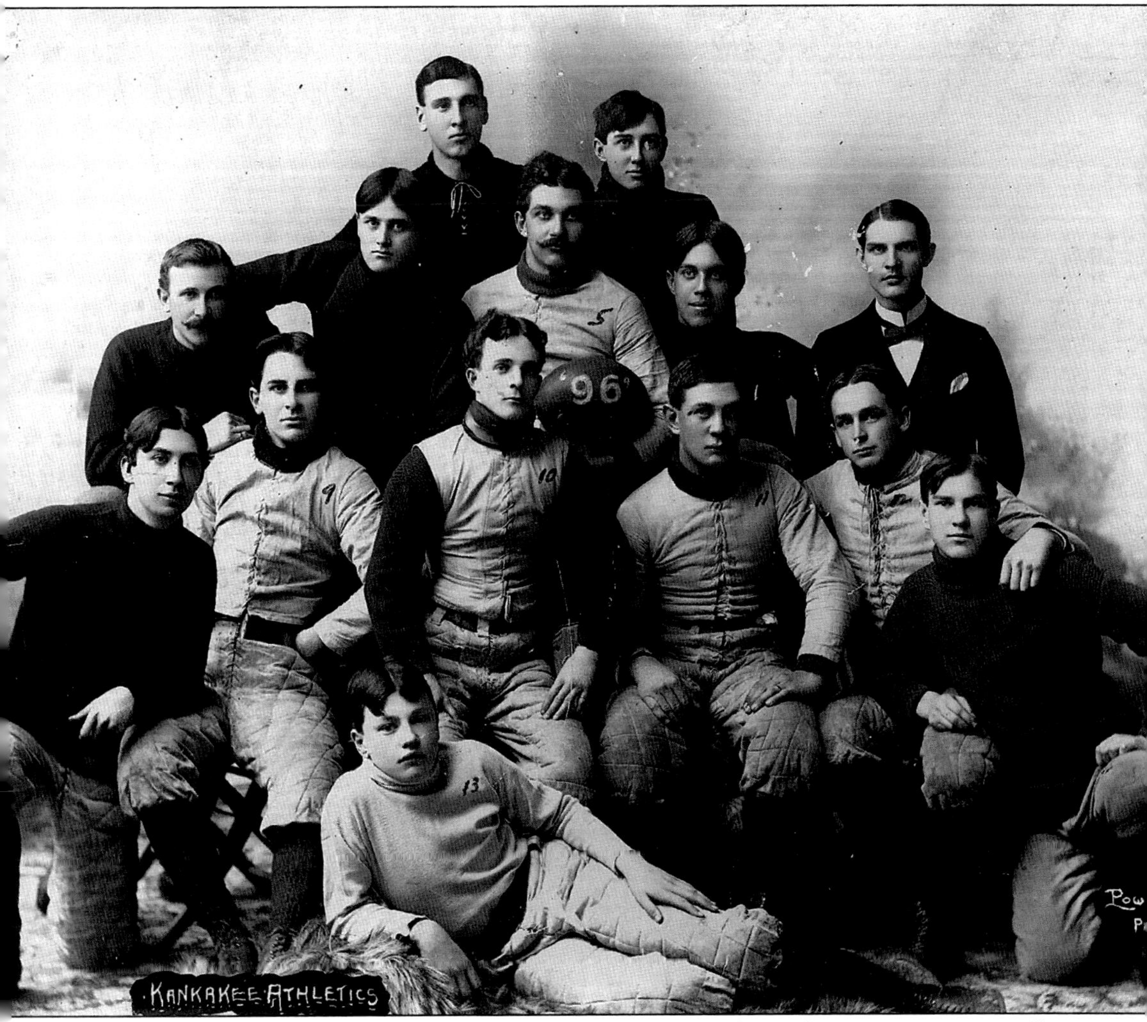

American Football became increasingly popular after 1870. The early teams were generally clubsthat played purely as amateurs. Shown here is the first football team organized in Kankakee, the Kankakee "Athletics," in their 1896 teaam portrait. (Kankakee County Museum Photographic Collection, P0429.)

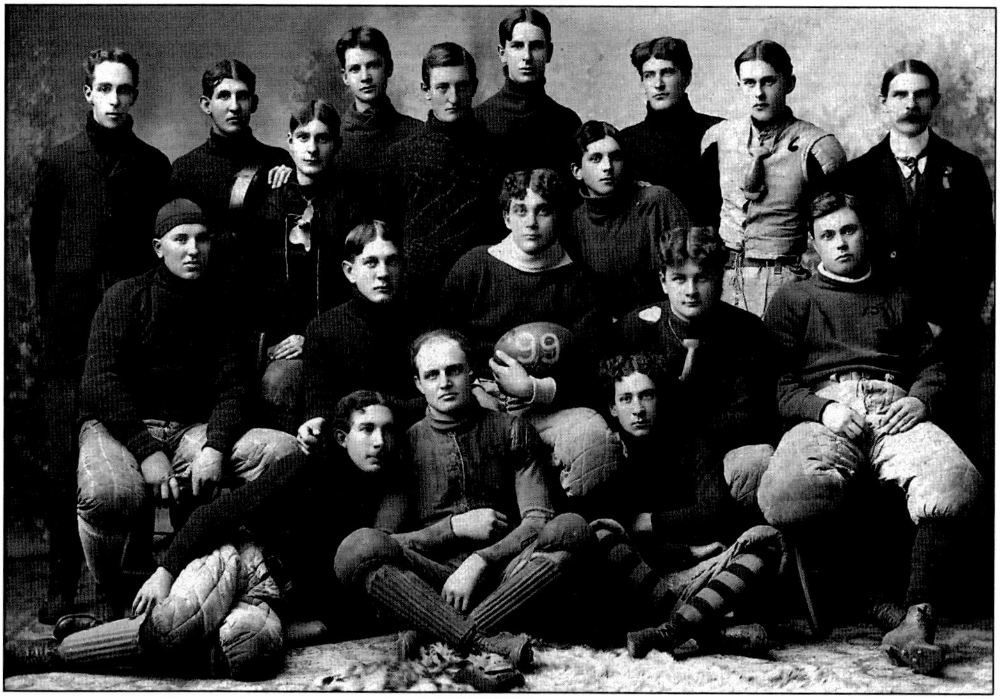

Staring defiantly at the camera, the 1899 Kankakee Athletics squad is seemingly grimly determined to create a "winning season." The forward pass was not yet invented and footballers relied on a punishing and very physical ground game. The rules of the game were not well codified, or even agreed upon. (Kankakee County Museum Photographic Collection, P0431.)

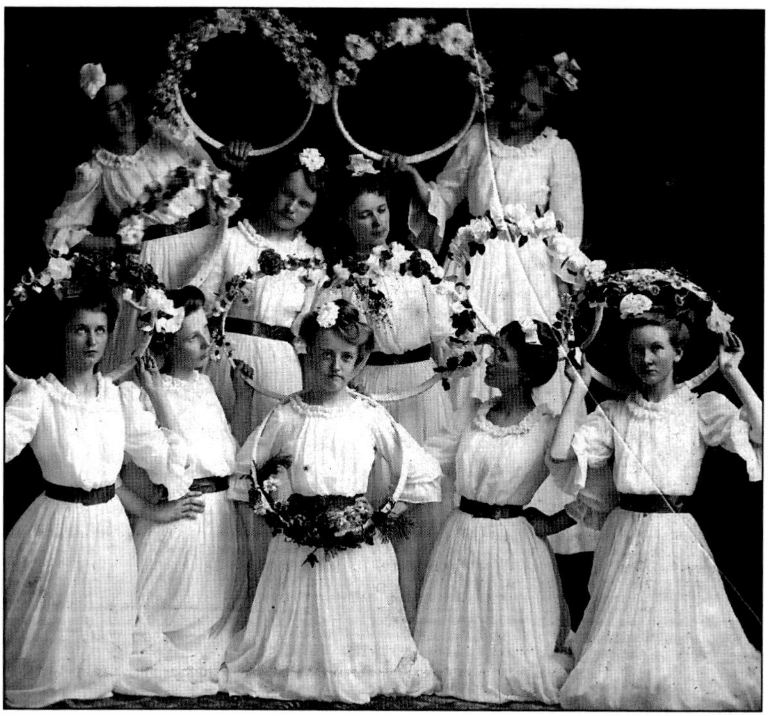

Somewhat more gentile and innocent entertainment could be found in Kankakee's grammar schools, such as might have been seen at a spring school production, photographed here c. 1890. Concern for physical fitness and internal cleanliness became a perfect mania in late 19th-century America. (Kankakee County Museum Photographic Collection, P6365.)

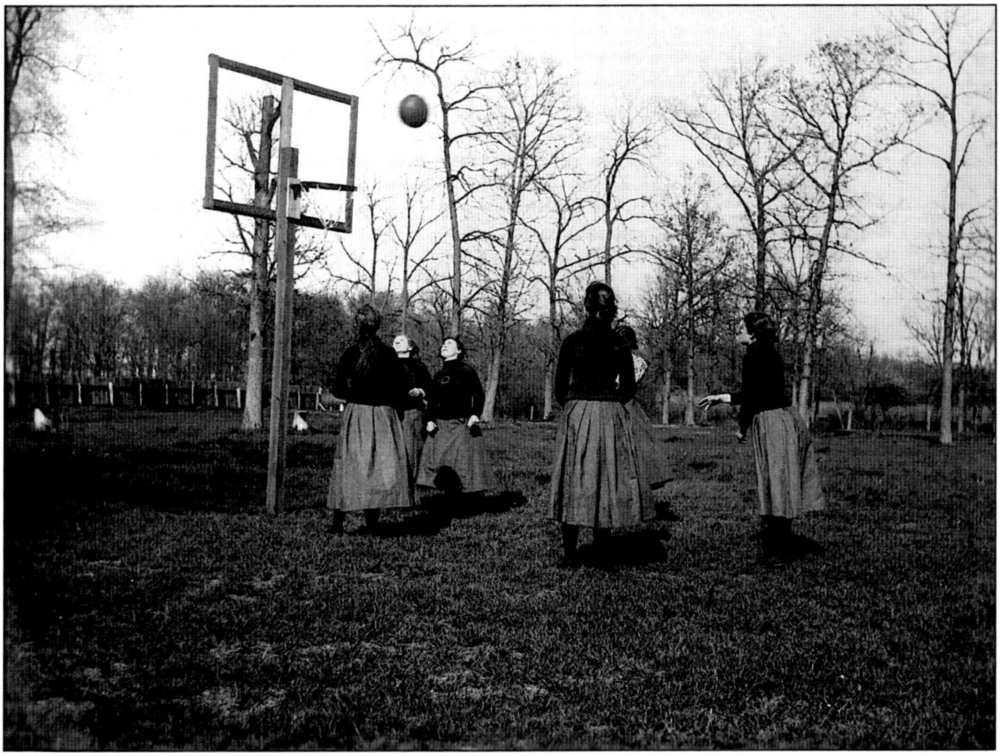

Americans were urged to adopt the strenuous life, improve their eating habits, and indulge in good and healthy sport. Young ladies attending the Kankakee High School are shown here playing "baskets" in October 1897. (Kankakee County Museum Photographic Collection, P0053.)

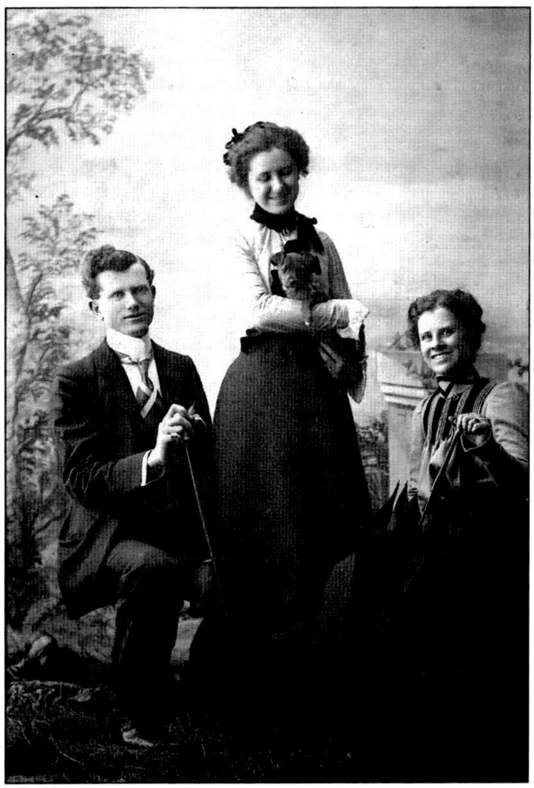

Summer recreation in Kankakee toward the end of the 19th century might simply mean companionship and the light hearted fun to be found in photography, becoming more commonly available with the introduction of the Kodak camera in 1888. The Kodak came with a roll of film containing 100 exposures. You returned the entire camera and got back the same camera with a new roll of film and 100 photos developed and mounted. This young Kankakee gallant was photographed with identical twin sisters, the one in the middle holding their puppy, c. 1890. (Kankakee County Museum Photographic Collection, P9711.)

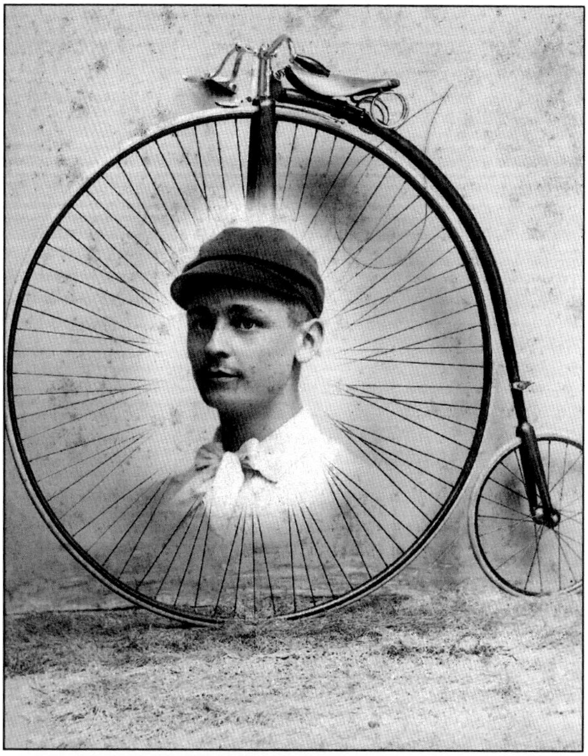

The high wheeler bicycle appeared about 1870. Riding it took balance, skill, and physical strength. It was regarded as a manly activity and wheeler clubs appeared all around Illinois. Intrepid "Wheelman" Nathan Halsey, who was an accountant and the city treasurer of Kankakee, had this portrait made in 1882. (Kankakee County Museum Photographic Collection, P0054.)

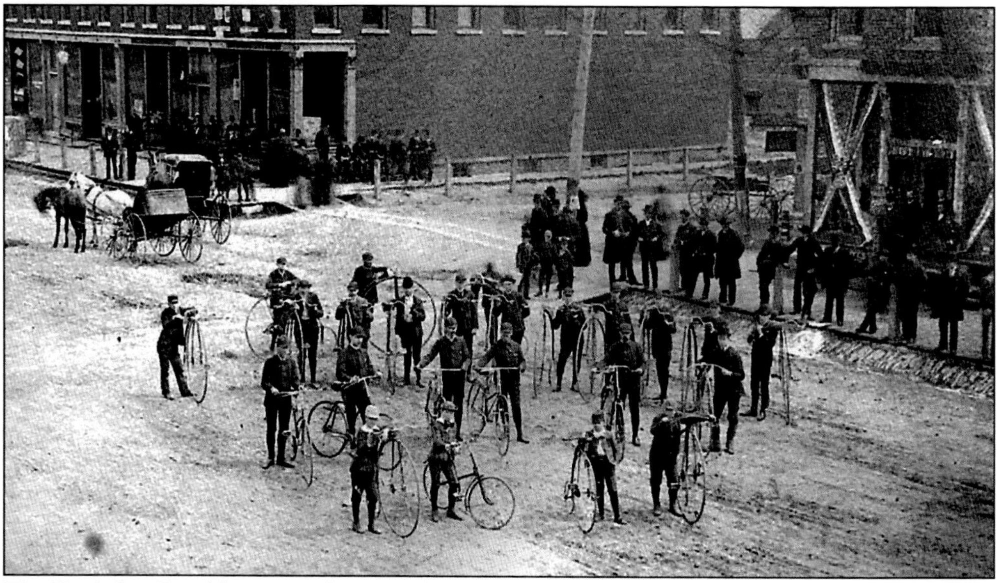

The Kankakee Ramblers were photographed on Kankakee's Court Street in 1889. The Ramblers mapped out numerous cross country runs and on Memorial Day in 1895 they held races before 1,000 spectators at the Kankakee County Fairgrounds. A contemporary newspaper recorded, "femininity stood upon tiptoe of expectation to see the bare legged and athletic riders as they nerved themselves for their rapid wheel of the track. They swooned as their heroes were lifted from their mounts and carried into the dressing tent to recover from the rigors of their manly exercise." (Kankakee County Museum Photographic Collection, P0168.)

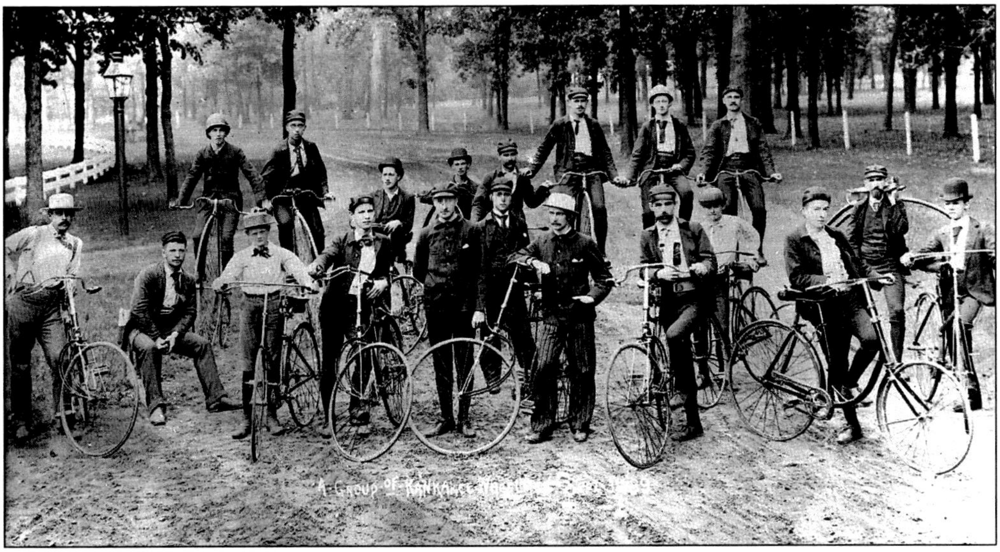

The Kankakee Ramblers appear in this group image, taken on September 3, 1889. Some of their wheelmen, in the rear of the picture, are aboard their high wheelers and some of the Ramblers in front are displaying their brand new Stanley Safety Bicycles. They had been invented only two years before. By 1888, over fifty thousand Americans pedaled alone or with organized groups like the Ramblers. (Kankakee County Museum Photographic Collection, P0351.)

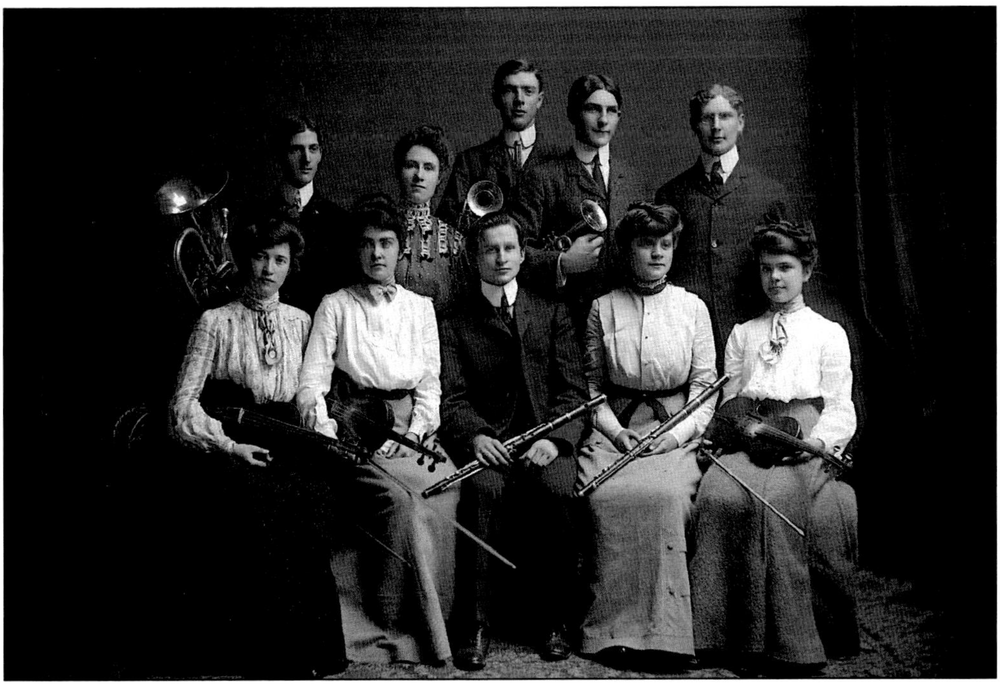

Music was an important part of recreation in Kankakee. It was an era of gazebos and outdoor summer concerts. Every town seemed to have its marching brass band and in every town people gathered to make music, like this Kankakee amateur orchestral group did. They were photographed together with their instruments in 1906. (Kankakee County Museum Photographic Collection, P3050.)

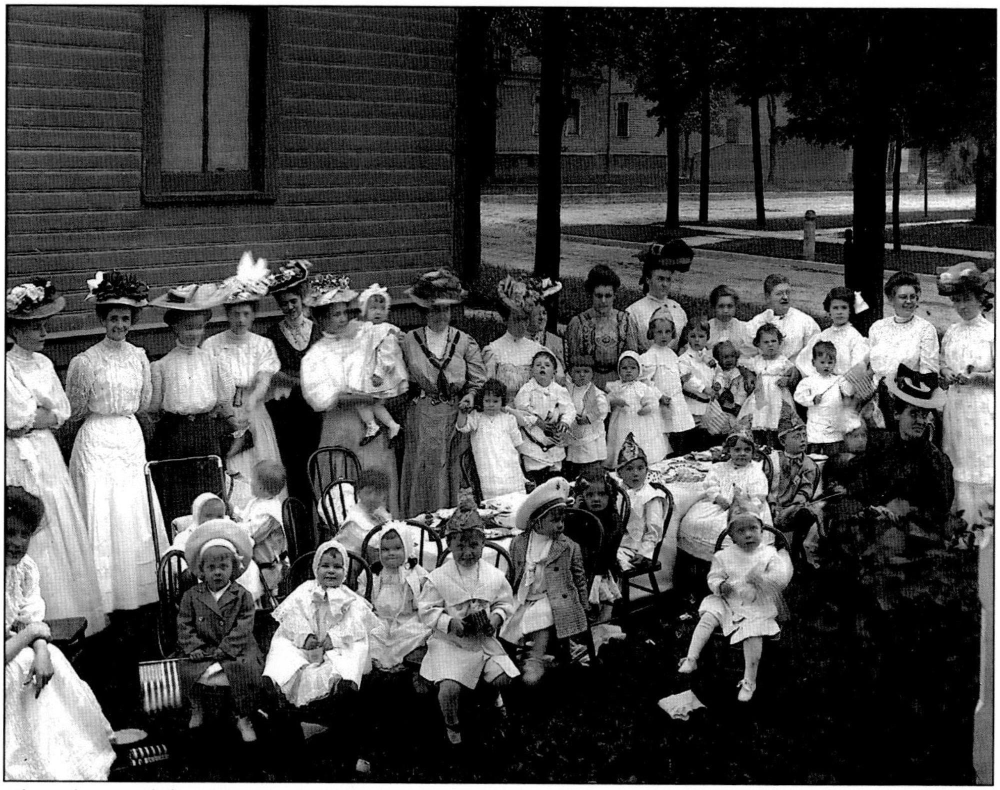

The advent of the American Century, coming after the successful Spanish-American War in 1899, at the turn of the 20th century filled Americans with pride. These confident Kankakee mothers are no exception, as they surround their children at a Fourth of July Party held in 1908. Kankakee would face an increasingly different America. (Kankakee County Museum Photographic Collection, P1972.)

Opposite: At the turn of the 20th century, the City of Kankakee and America would enter the world stage, commencing what historians are beginning to term the American Century. It was the Spanish-American War in 1898 that started the nation down the path toward becoming a world power and within a decade Americans discovered their nation a very different place than it had been before the conflict with Spain. These men were participants in that change. This photograph of Company L/3rd Regiment Illinois National Guard was taken after their return from overseas deployment at Springfield, Illinois, in 1900. Company L was recruited exclusively in Kankakee. On May 12, 1898, Company L was sent to Camp Thomas at the Chickamauga Georgia National Battlefield Park, where they spent nine weeks training before joining the campaign against Spanish-held Puerto Rico. These Kankakee guardsmen were in several skirmishes and during the major battle on Puerto Rico, the engagement at Guayama on August 13, 1898, Company L had the extreme right of the American line. These officers and soldiers, along with their two animal comrades, their dog mascot, and the kitty that joined them in Puerto Rico, witnessed events leading to momentous alterations in the fabric of American life. (Kankakee County Museum Photographic Collection, P0711.)

Eight

FROM THE SPANISH-AMERICAN WAR INTO A NEW CENTURY

"There has been a hot time in old Santiago town, and as a result, it seems that things are rather different now"

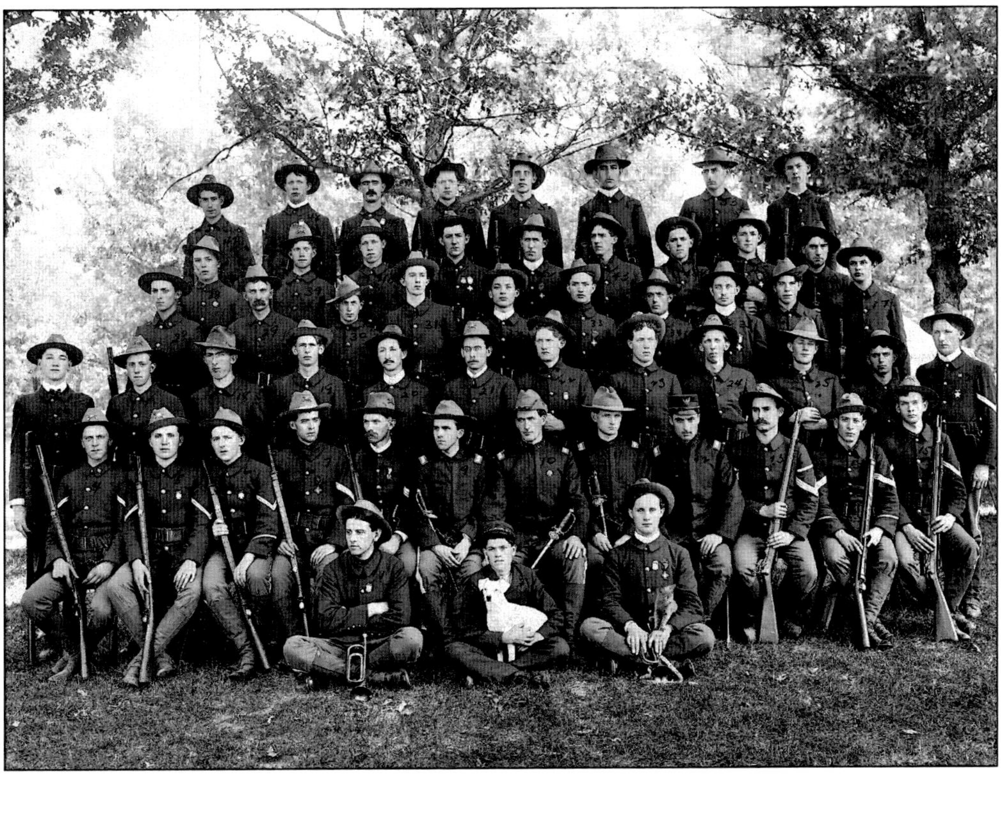

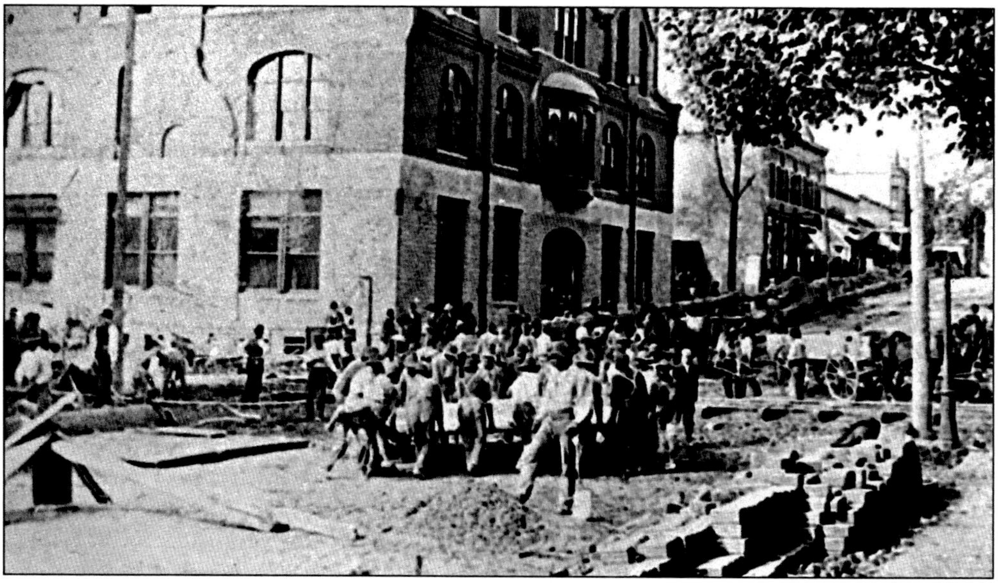

Toward the end of the 19th century, the City of Kankakee began to undertake serious civic improvements, demonstrating that Kankakee enjoyed a vibrant economy. In this 1896 image, workmen are shown laying paving stones just near the intersection of Merchant Street and Schuyler Avenue. The structure to the left is the Arcade Building, with the Railroad Depot further to the left down Merchant Street (out of the photograph). Note the temporary track used to haul heavy building materials to the site. (Kankakee County Museum Photographic Collection, P0722.)

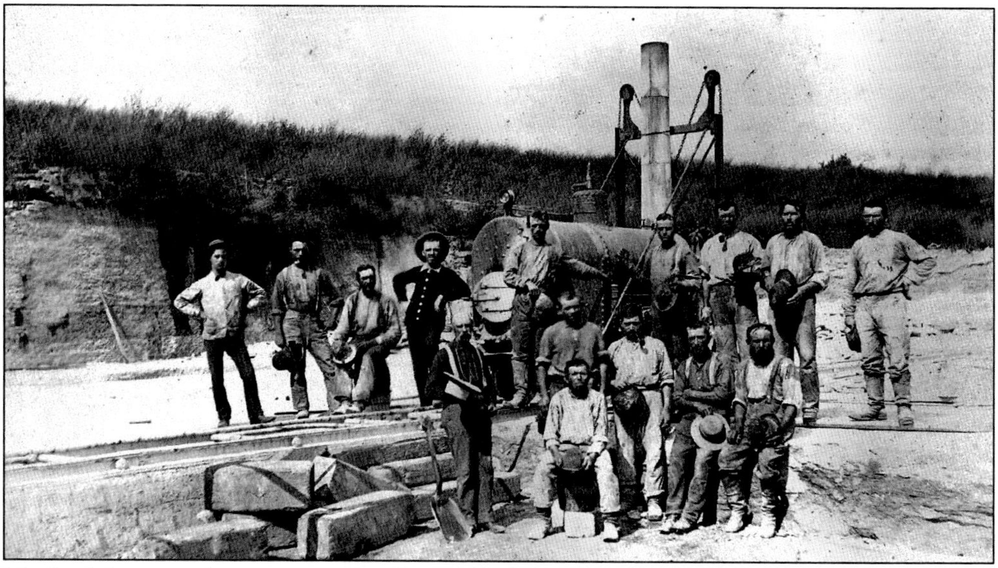

Much of the stone for improving the City of Kankakee's streets would have come from Knight's Quarry, owned and operated by Solon Knight's Kankakee Stone and Lime Company since 1867. In this photograph, taken in 1895, Knight's workers are shown near the quarry's east entrance with their new mechanical stone crusher. The stone found in Knight's Quarry, Niagara Limestone, was considered excellent material for heavy work. (Kankakee County Museum Photographic Collection, P1343.)

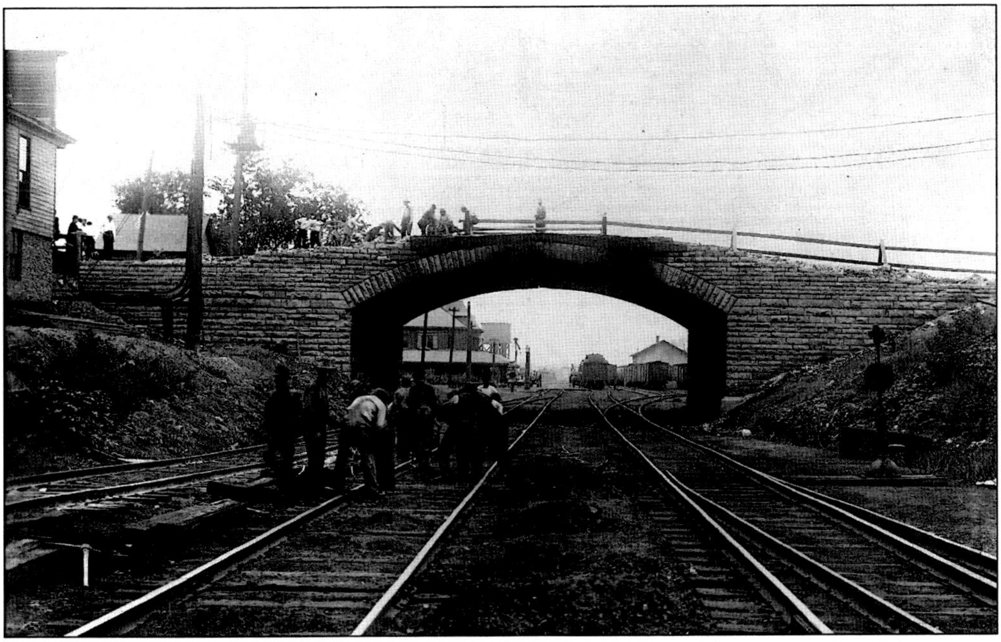

The railroad remained an important part of Kankakee's economic life through the 19th century and well into the 20th century. In this image, c. 1900, workers can be seen finishing the stonework over the Illinois Central's viaduct spanning their tracks, where workmen can also be seen repairing the rails. Beyond the viaduct's arch, the Illinois Central's new depot building can be seen, finished in January 1898. (Kankakee County Museum Photographic Collection, P3035.)

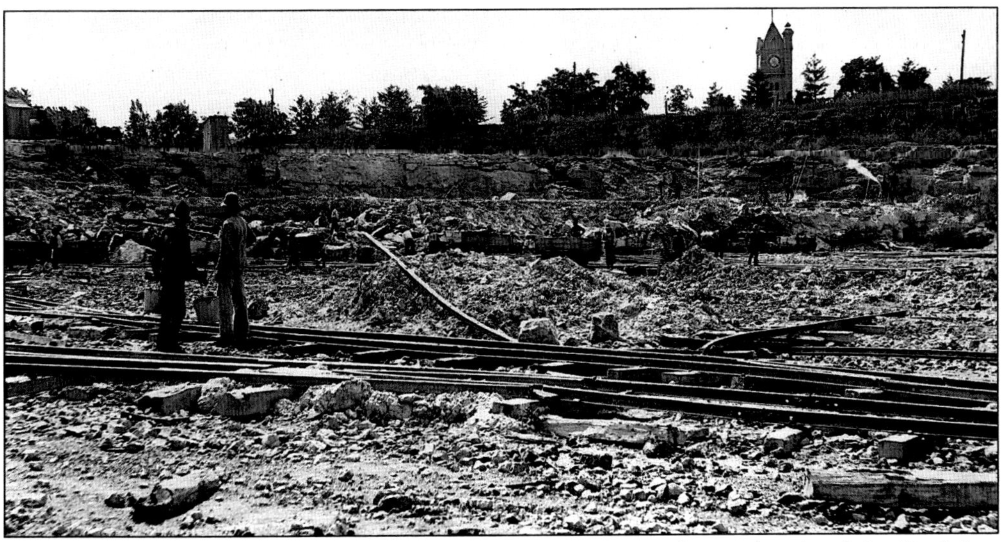

This image shows workers engaged in quarrying operations on the south side of the Kankakee River in 1900. The site was owned and operated by Donald Sinclair, a mason who came to the United States from Scotland in 1887. The Sinclair Construction Company commenced operation in Kankakee in 1891, initially to supply stone to the Illinois Central Railroad. For years, Sinclair's workers supplied stone building material to the Illinois Eastern Hospital for the Insane, whose distinctive clock tower can be seen in the upper right of the photograph, rising from the opposite bank of the Kankakee River. (Kankakee County Museum Photographic Collection, P1249.)

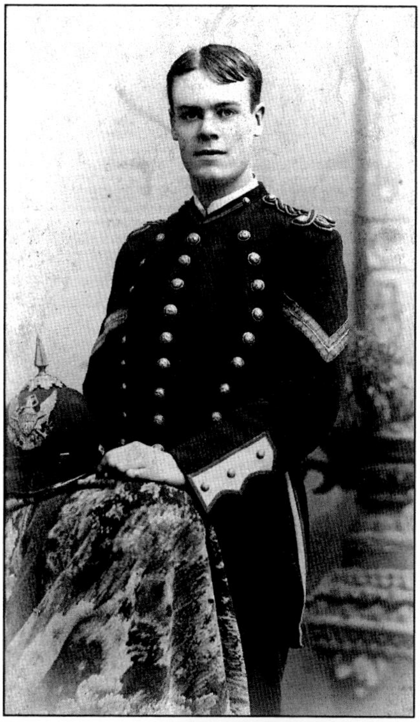

In the last quarter of the 19th century, some Kankakee citizens developed an interest in military affairs. This formal portrait of Charles Livingston was taken in 1896. He is wearing the dress uniform of a corporal in the 4th Regiment Illinois National Guard. Note the 1872 model dress infantry shako sitting on the table, with its decidedly Prussian appearance. (The Army of the United States adopted it following Prussian military victory in the Franco-Prussian War of 1870, when it stopped affecting French military fashions.) Charles Livingston was a reporter for the *Chicago Tribune*. He was following in his father's, Charles Prentice Livingston, footsteps, who had participated in 20 battles during the Civil War with the 100th New York Volunteers, and who in 1868 became the third owner and publisher of the *Kankakee Gazette*. (Kankakee County Museum Photographic Collection, P1346.)

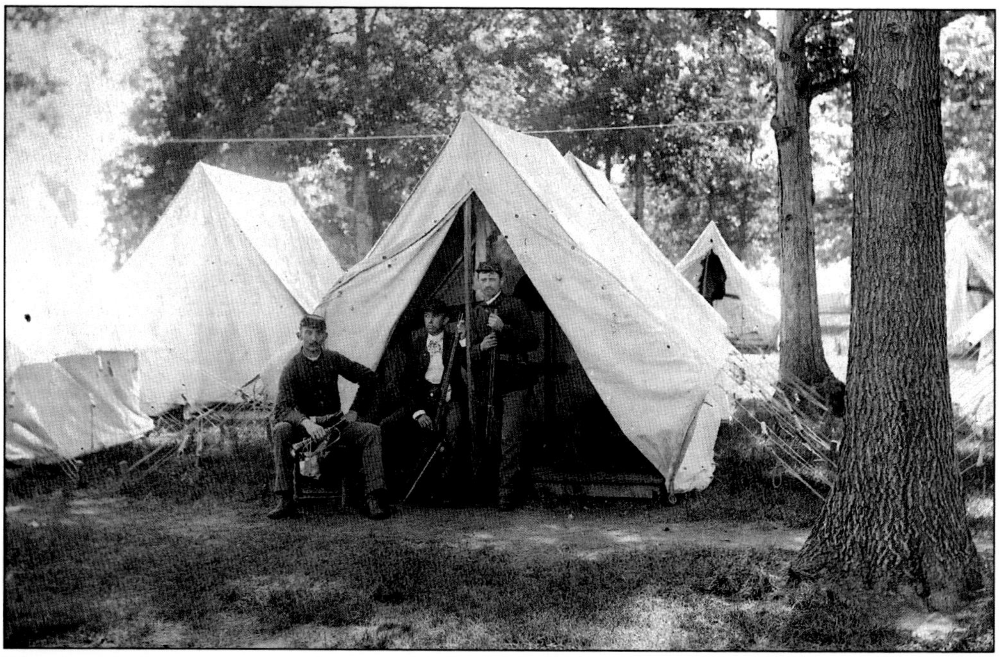

This image shows some gentlemen rankers from Kankakee in 1878. They are members of Company H/4th Regiment Illinois National Guard, photographed during a training exercise held at the Kankakee Fairgrounds. They are wearing undress uniforms similar to those worn during the Civil War by Federal infantry. They are armed with the army's first general service breechloader, the 1873 model trapdoor Springfield Rifled Musket. (Kankakee County Museum Photographic Collection, P0474.)

That the appearance of United States infantry had changed little in 20 years is illustrated by this photograph of Thomas Walters taken at Camp Tanner, near Springfield, Illinois, in 1897. This native of Kankakee is shown at parade rest, with his 1873 trapdoor Springfield Rifled Musket. A member of Company L/3rd Regiment Illinois National Guard, Private Walters returned to Camp Tanner the following year in May 1898 and from there eventually went to participate in the Puerto Rican Campaign. (Kankakee County Museum Photographic Collection, P3719.)

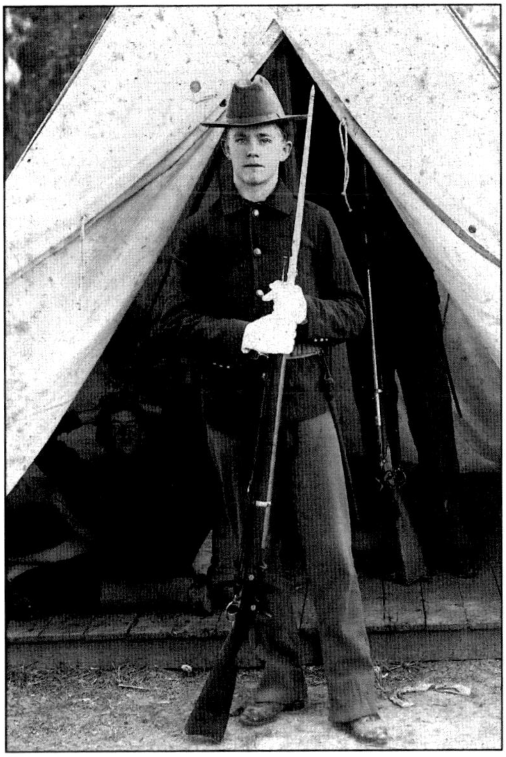

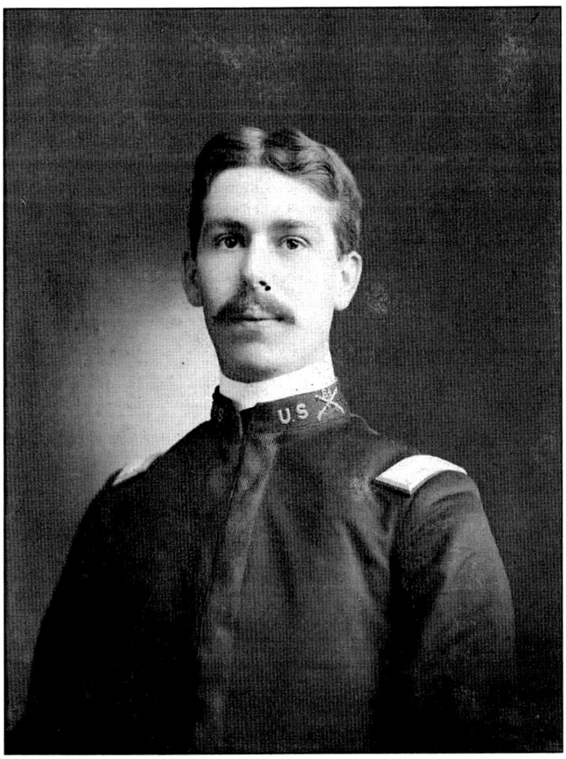

Another Kankakee participant in the Spanish-American War was Robert Edward Frith, 2nd Lieutenant/24th United States Infantry. He sat for his portrait in August 1898, just after returning from the campaign against Santiago de Cuba. His regiment was one of four in the regular army composed of African-American soldiers and Caucasian officers. (Kankakee County Museum Photographic Collection, P0094.)

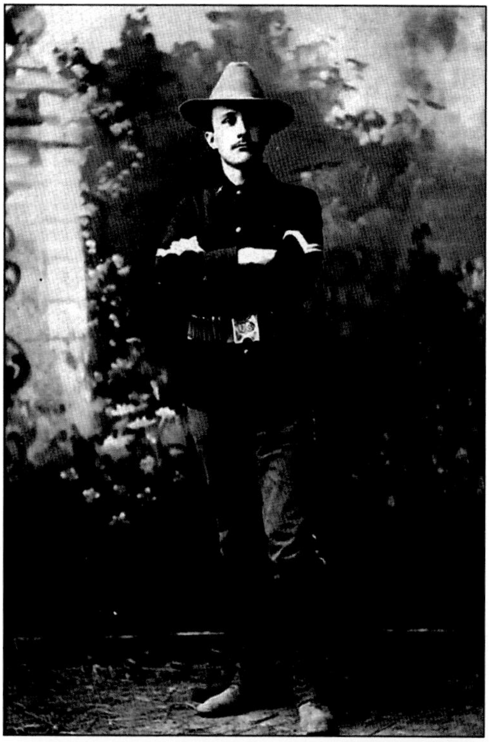

Corporal Frank Joseph Cartier strikes a martial pose in January 1899, shortly after returning from the Puerto Rican campaign, where he served with Company L/3rd Regiment Illinois National Guard. Note the marksmanship badge worn on his right collar, his campaign hat, and canvas web belt. Following service in the Spanish-American War, Cartier went to work as a house painter for his father Rufus Boselice Cartier, who was the director of the Illinois Eastern Hospital for the Insane's painting crew. (Kankakee County Museum Photographic Collection, P0578.)

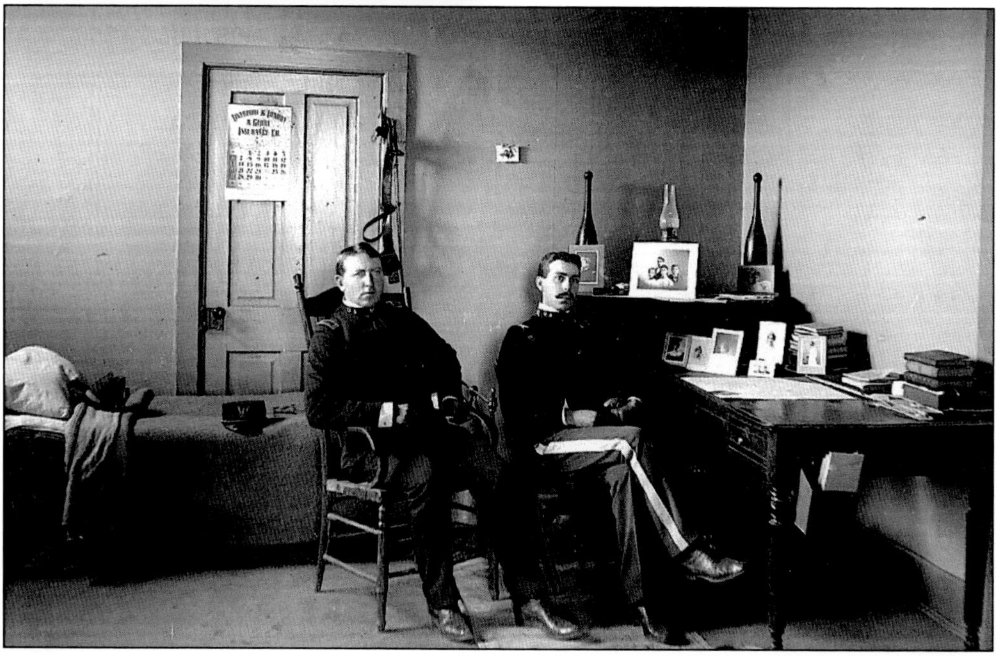

Following active duty in the field during the Spanish-American War, Lt. Robert Edward Frith resumed more mundane garrison duties with his regiment, the 24th United States Infantry (made up of African-American soldiers), which was sent to Texas. He is pictured here in his quarters receiving a visit from an unidentified officer, a 1st Lieutenant and Assistant Surgeon. (Kankakee County Museum Photographic Collection, P0189.)

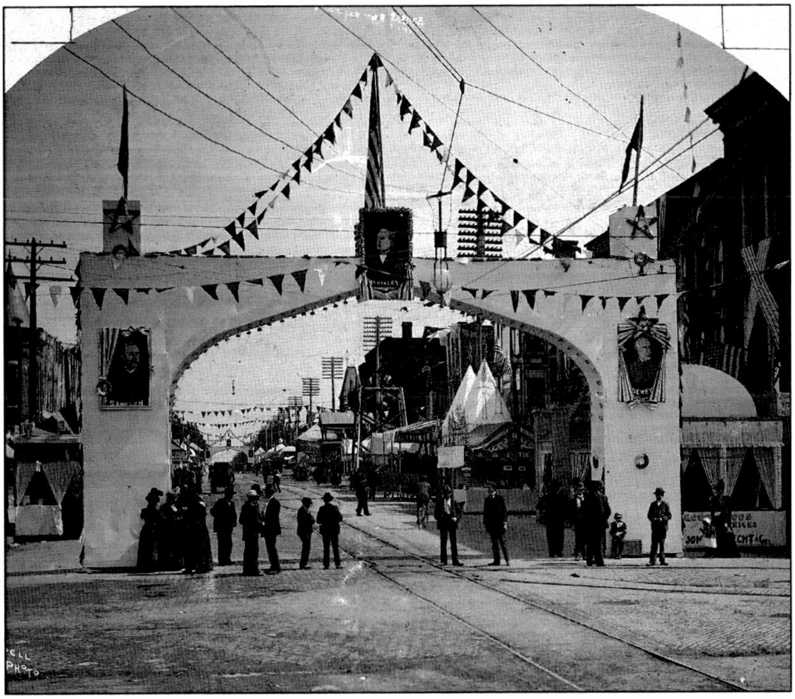

Patriotic Americans were proud of their nation's successes in the "Splendid Little War," as the Spanish-American War came to be called. Kankakee was no exception, as is shown by this photograph of a temporary celebratory arch erected across Court Street in August 1898. At the top center of the arch is an image of President William McKinley, flanked by images of his two successful naval commanders, Rear Adm. William Sampson, whose fleet destroyed a Spanish squadron attempting to break out of Santiago de Cuba on July 3, 1898, and Comdr. George Dewey, whose Asiatic Squadron had earlier destroyed the Spanish Philippine Squadron at Manila Bay on May 1, 1898. (Kankakee County Museum Photographic Collection, P0548.)

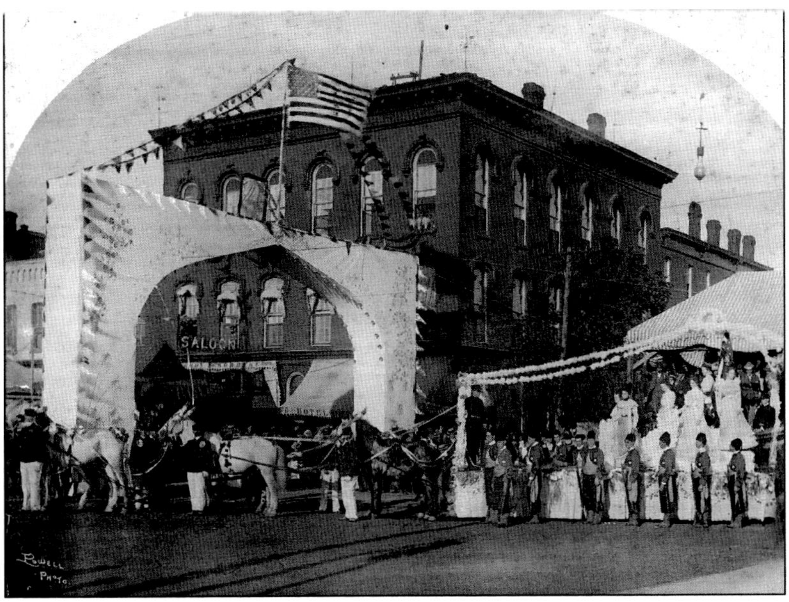

This image shows the rear of Kankakee's 1898 celebratory arch, built to commemorate American victories in the Spanish-American War. The building in the center of the photograph is the Commercial Hotel, located at the northeast corner of East Avenue and Station Street. The float about to pass through the arch, bearing several Kankakee belles, is escorted by a detachment of Kankakee's Riverview Guards. (Kankakee County Museum Photographic Collection, P0304.)

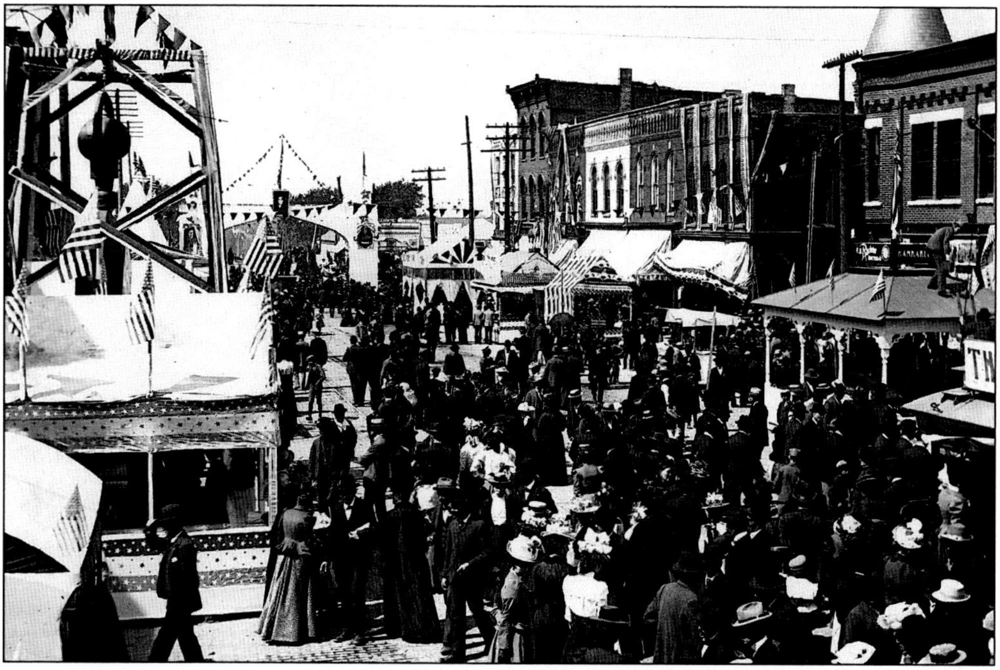

As is demonstrated in this photograph, Kankakee's 1898 street fair was well attended. This is a view taken looking down Court Street. The intersection of Court Street and Schuyler Avenue can be seen just beyond the pavilion with the three small American flags on the roof. In the City of Kankakee this event combined a growing sense of community with the brassy patriotism common in America during this era. (Kankakee County Museum Photographic Collection, P1326.)

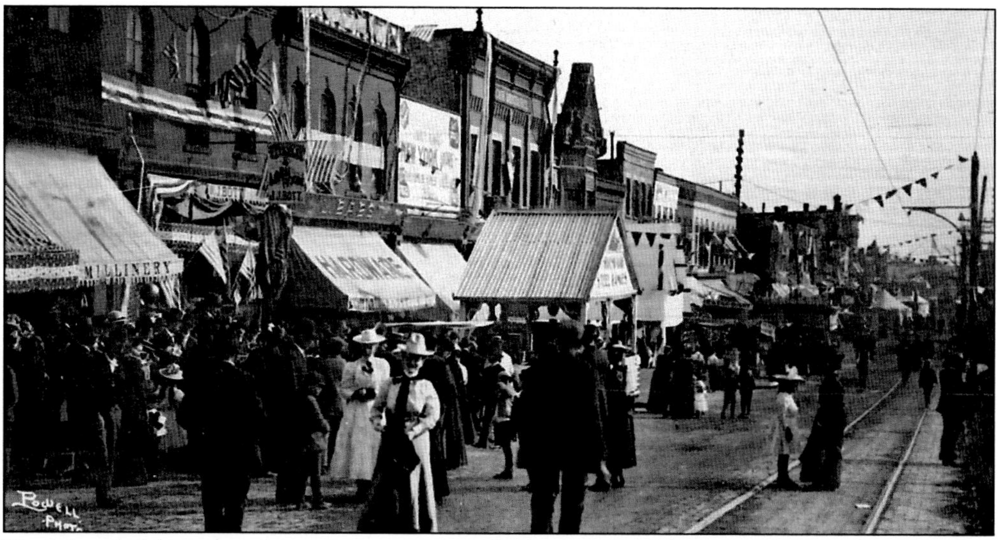

Kankakee held a street fair in association with the city's celebration of American Spanish-American War successes. This image shows the street fair along East Avenue. Area businesses like L. Babst Hardware are showing their products, while local eateries, including J. Bott's Lunch Room, are open and available to strolling patrons. In the distance, to the left in the photograph beyond the electric street car rails and overhead telephone wires, Kankakee's 1898 celebratory arch can be seen. (Kankakee County Museum Photographic Collection, P0546.)

As in the Civil War, which had ended 33 years before, at the conclusion of the Spanish-American War Kankakee veterans came home to resume their lives. Charles Hotchkiss learned a skill during his army service. He is shown here in November 1898 as a noncommissioned officer with the Signal Corps, where he learned photography, not quite yet readily available to the general public. Following the war, he went to work as a photographer for Kankakee's Powell Photography Studio with his brother Eugene. (Kankakee County Museum Photographic Collection, P1329.)

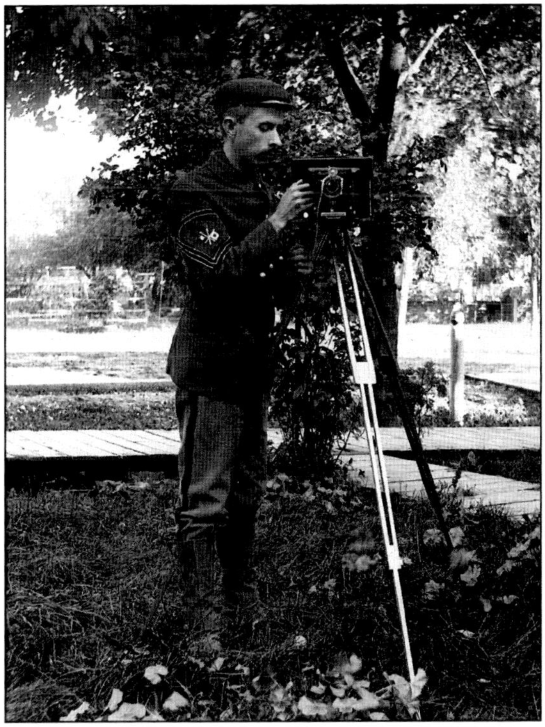

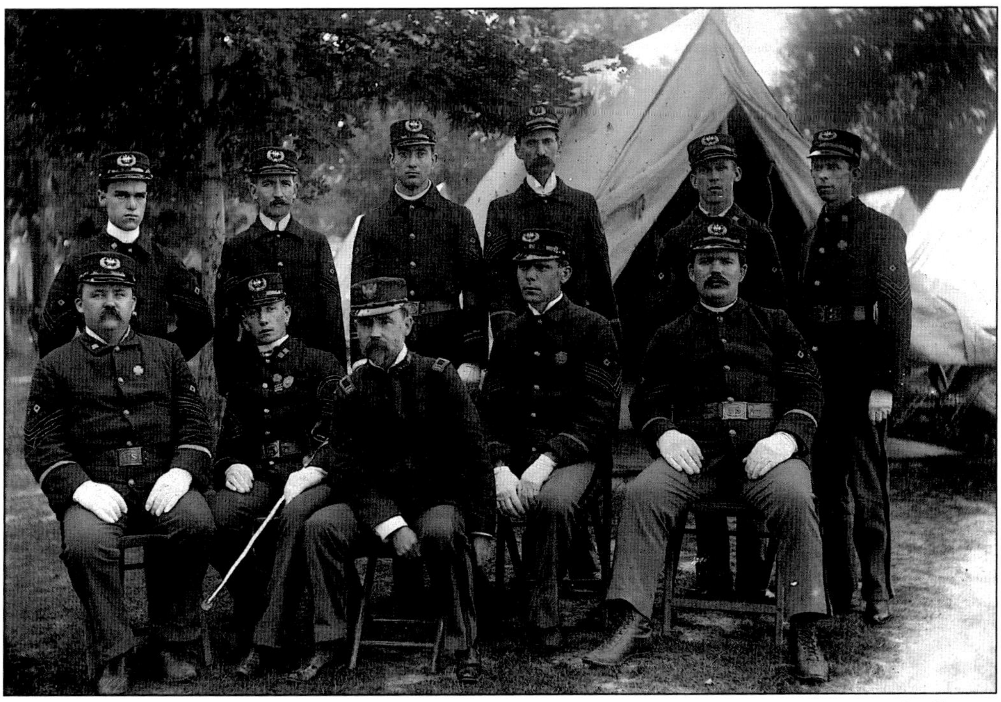

Sergeant Charles Hotchkiss poses here with his captain and fellow noncommissioned officers, who served with him in a Signal Corps detachment during the Spanish-American War. Hotchkiss stands in the back row, third from the right in the photograph. (Kankakee County Museum Photographic Collection, P3701.)

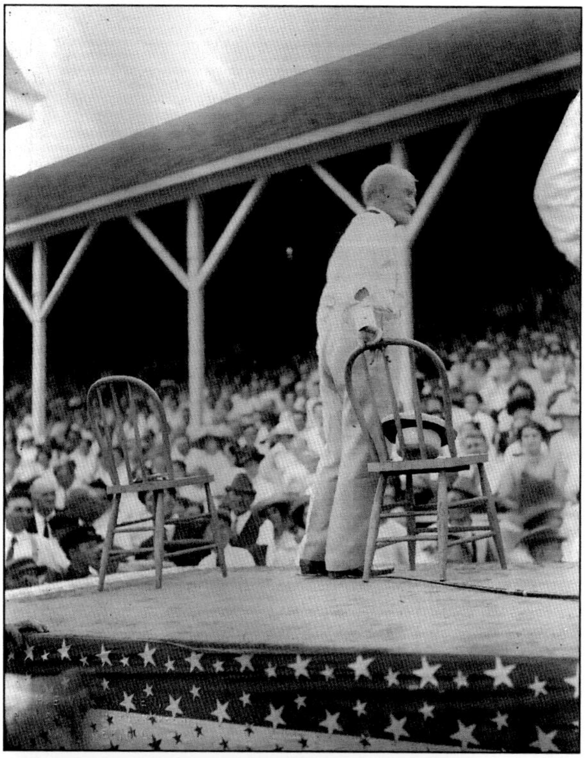

In July 1901, the Chautauqua Speaking Association, a national organization becoming increasingly popular in middle America, started a series of summer public lectures in Kankakee. Demonstrating an increasing awareness of America's new position in world affairs the first speaker invited was William Jennings Bryan, who had been the Democratic Party presidential candidate in the elections of 1896 and 1900. Staying at Kankakee's Lafayette Hotel, Bryan quipped to his Kankakee admirers, "I am a private citizen now and Republican papers will tell you that I have an excellent prospect of remaining one." This image shows the dynamic Bryan giving his lecture, "A Conquering Nation," which supported American expansionism in the far East. (Kankakee County Museum Photographic Collection, P9715.)

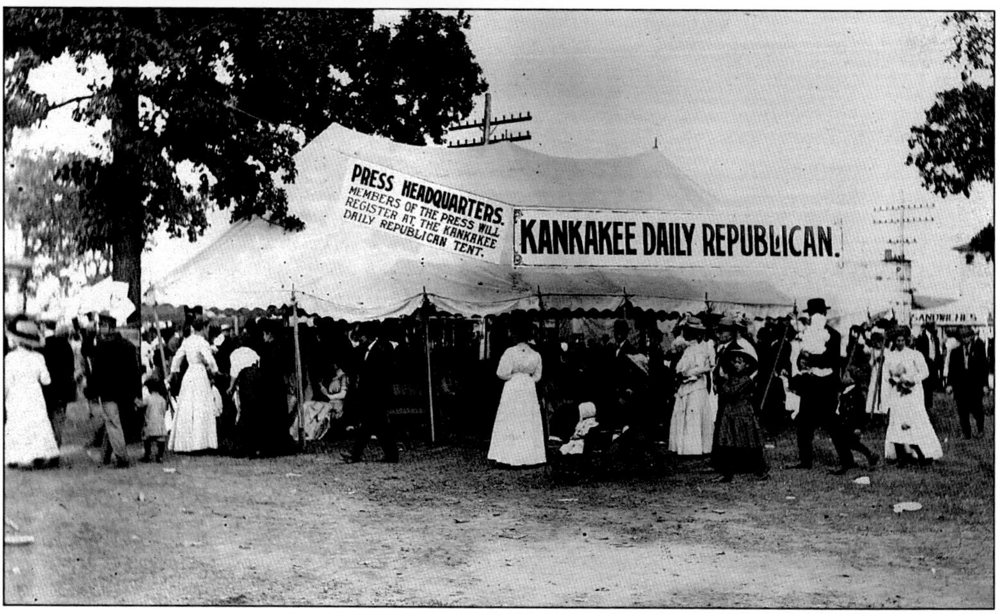

In this image the crowd can be seen moving toward the speaker's stand to hear William Jennings Bryan, who is about to give his oration. Bryan would urge his Kankakee audience to "remember their place in the new American order of things" and he advocated firmer American measures to end the current "Philippine Insurrection." In the center is the tent of the Kankakee *Daily Republican*, no doubt hostile to the sentiments of the Democratic Party's Bryan, sheltering the headquarters of the press. (Kankakee County Museum Photographic Collection, P6047.)

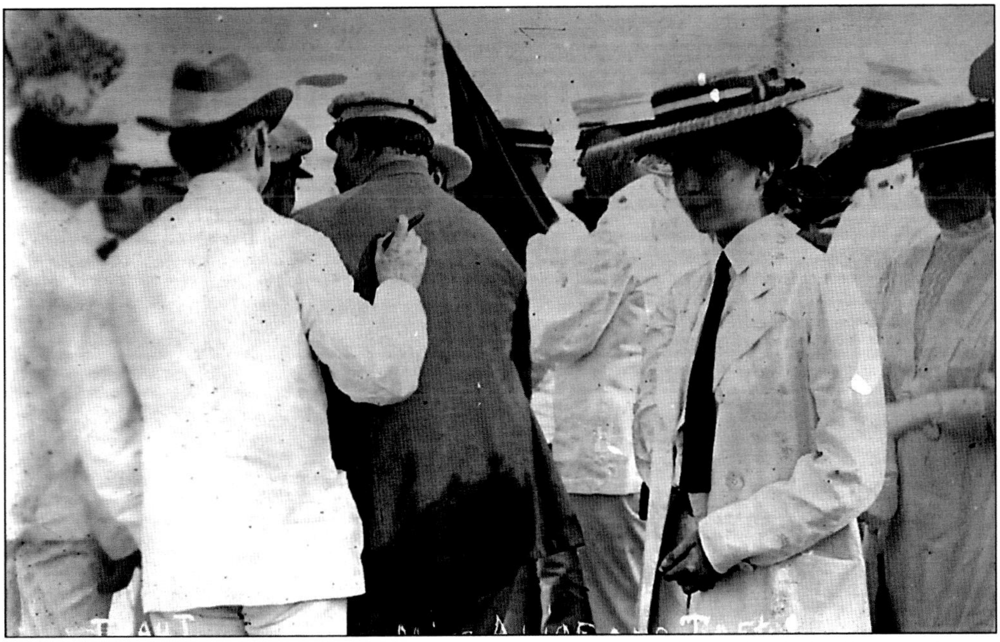

A boating party enjoying the Kankakee River was photographed in July 1909. The gentleman wearing the dark suit and white yachting cap, with his back to the camera is the President of the United States, William Howard Taft. To his left, two army officers wearing undress summer whites can be seen. Always good newspaper copy, the woman wearing a straw boater and tie (second from the right in the photograph) is Miss Alice Roosevelt, outspoken daughter of former President Theodore Roosevelt. (Kankakee County Museum Photographic Collection, P6363.)

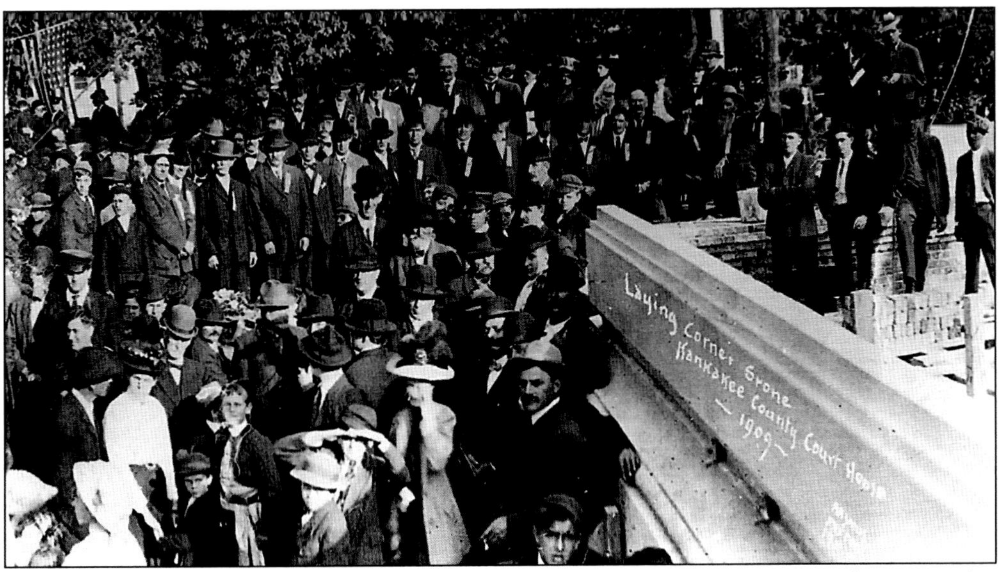

Participating in the American Century, Kankakee continued to develop. Shown in this photograph is part of the 20,000 spectators that gathered on October 2, 1909 at the Court House Square to witness the laying of the cornerstone for the third and present Kankakee County Court House. The structure, built at a cost of $250,000, would be formally opened for county business on July 2, 1909. (Kankakee County Museum Photographic Collection, P3210.)

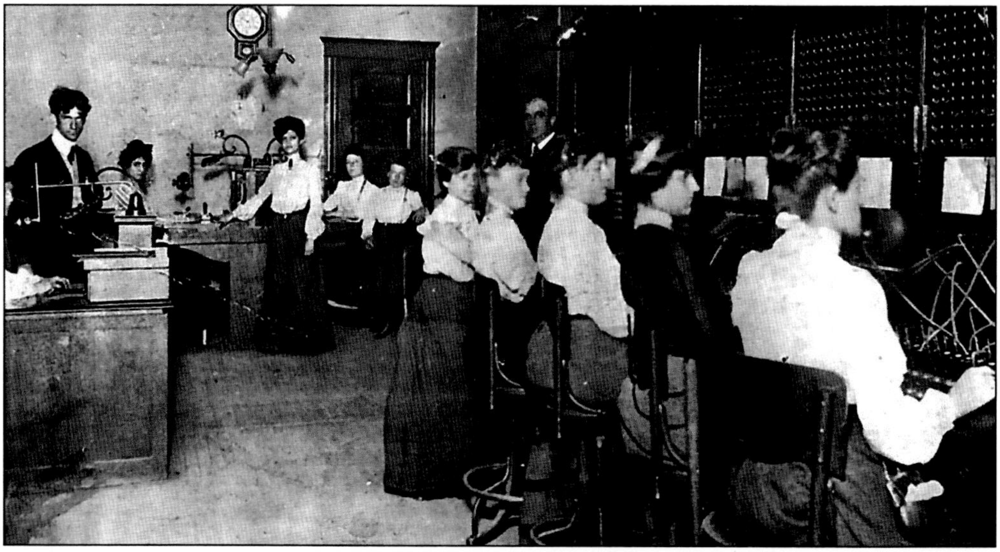

A measure of progress in Kankakee's movement into the early 20th century was the profusion of telephone lines and increased telephone service throughout the community. Invented in 1876, it was not until about 1900 that the telephone became a common fixture in middle class Kankakee homes. This photograph shows the "hello girls" with other staff and supervisors of Kankakee's Central Union Telephone Company in 1902. "Unmarried and attractive women," were wanted by Central Union, who advertised for young ladies with "pleasant voices and engaging personalities." (Kankakee County Museum Photographic Collection, P0761.)

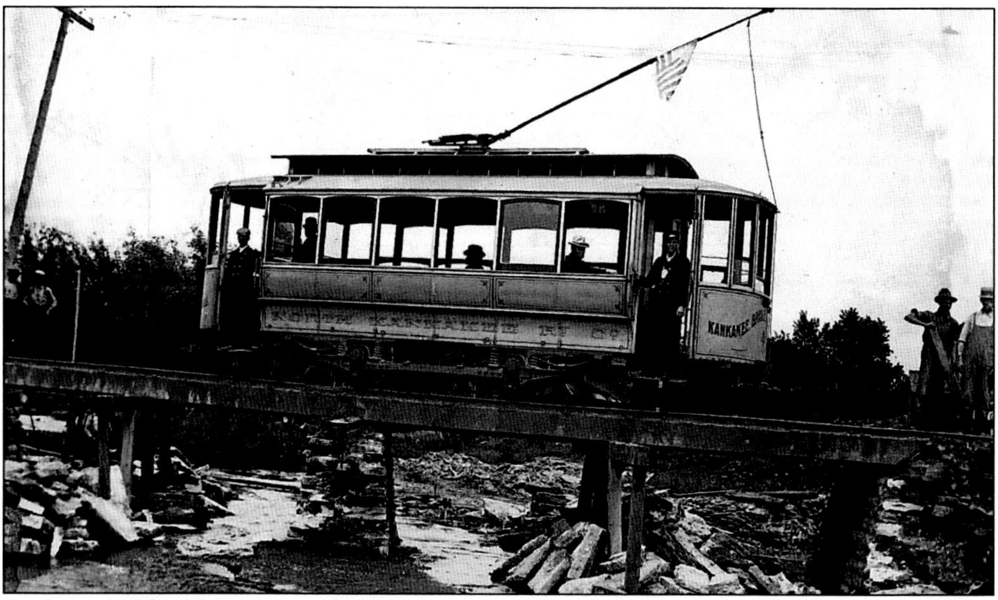

At the end of the 19th century, electric street cars made their appearance in Kankakee. The North Kankakee Street Railway Company was formed in 1892. It ran tracks from the intersection of Kankakee's Court Street and Schuyler Avenue, through the villages of Bradley and Bourbonnais, with side lines leading to the county fairgrounds and to local baseball fields. This 1900 image shows their car no. 4. Frank Miller is the conductor standing in the car's doorway at the right of the photograph. (Kankakee County Museum Photographic Collection, P1247.)

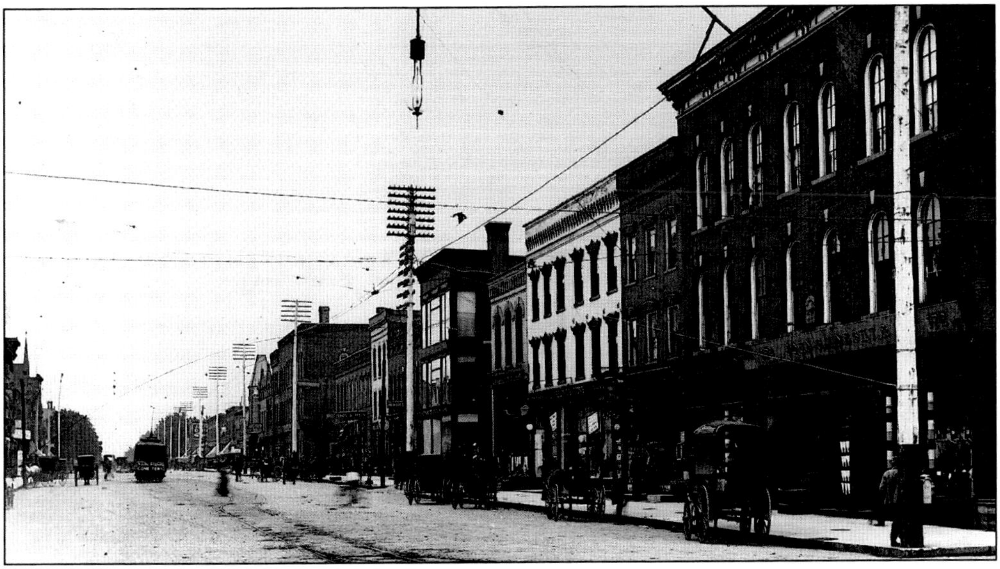

The overhead wires and tracks laid in the center of city streets necessary to run electric street cars changed the look of Kankakee. This photograph taken in 1905 from East Avenue focuses on the south side of Court Street. Elaborate telephone poles are now a part of Kankakee's landscape. One of the North Kankakee Railway Company's electric street cars can be seen in the lower left of the photograph heading east. (Kankakee County Museum Photographic Collection, P2792.)

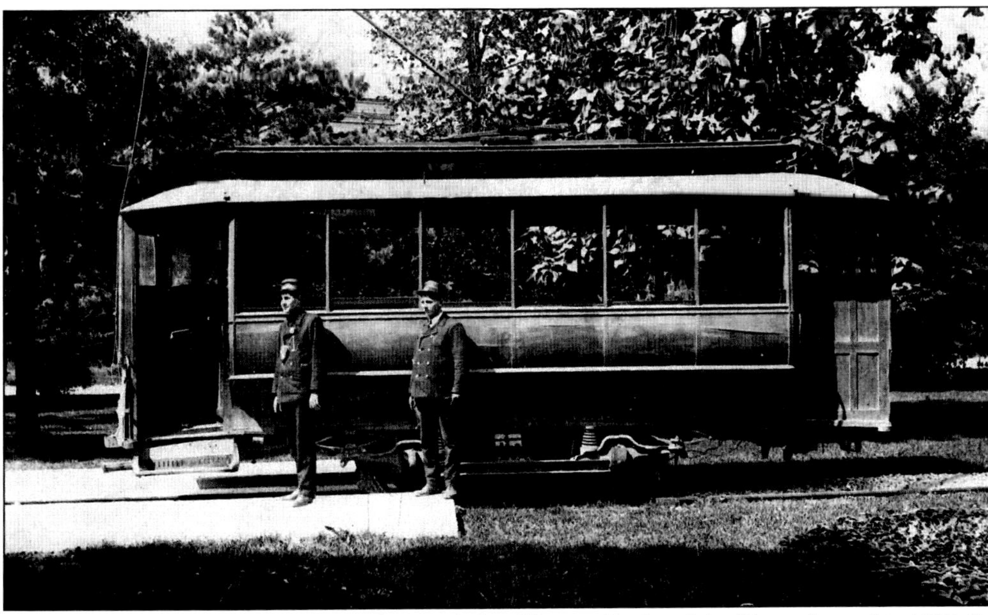

A rival electric street car company, the Kankakee Electric Railroad, had been formed in 1891. Its tracks largely served the area's residential districts, from East Court Street through the Riverview area, with connections to all depots, the hospital, and cemeteries. This photograph depicts a Kankakee electric railroad car in 1907. Kankakee's electric street cars were all manufactured by the St. Louis Car Company, located in St. Louis, Missouri. (Kankakee County Museum Photographic Collection, P0561.)

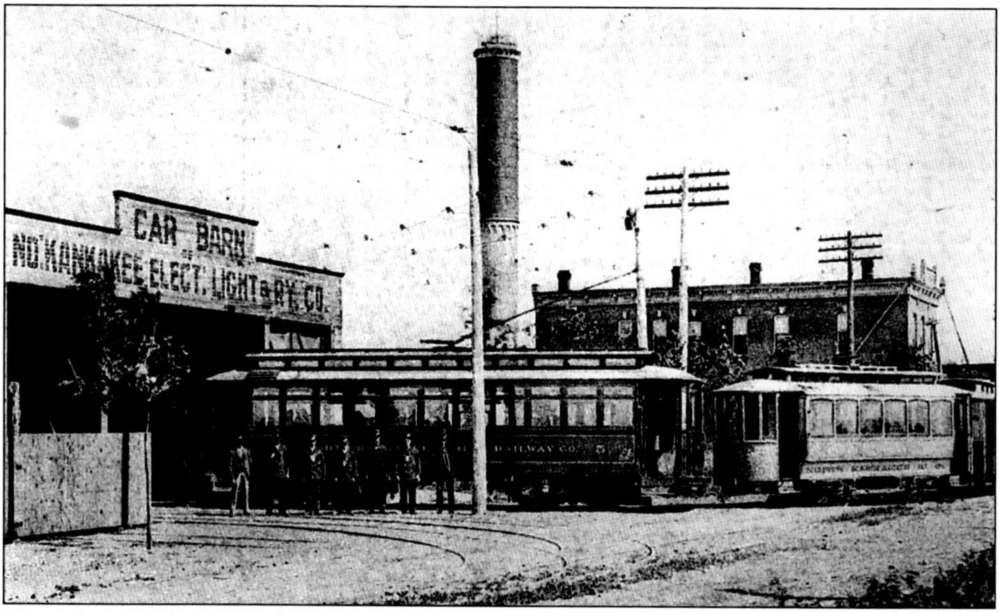

This photograph shows the end of the line for the North Kankakee Street Railway, who maintained their electric car barn at the northern terminus of their track in the village of Bradley. The North Kankakee Street Railway Company operated five cars on four miles of track. Seven of their conductors can be seen standing in front of car no. 5. (Kankakee County Museum Photographic Collection, P3222.)

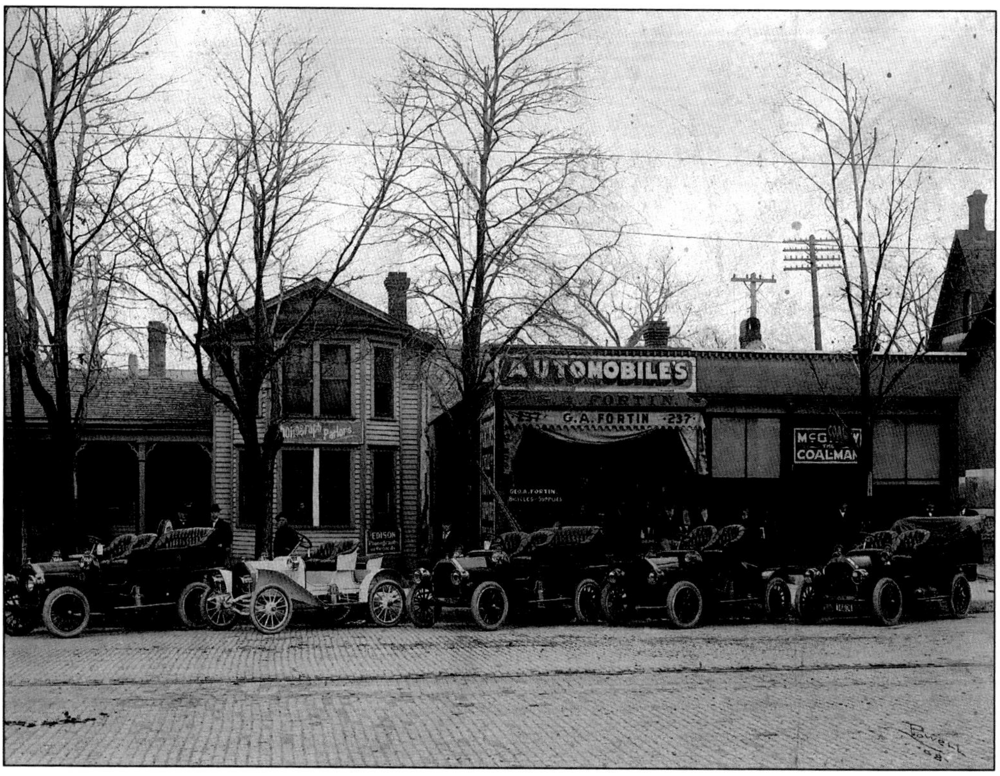

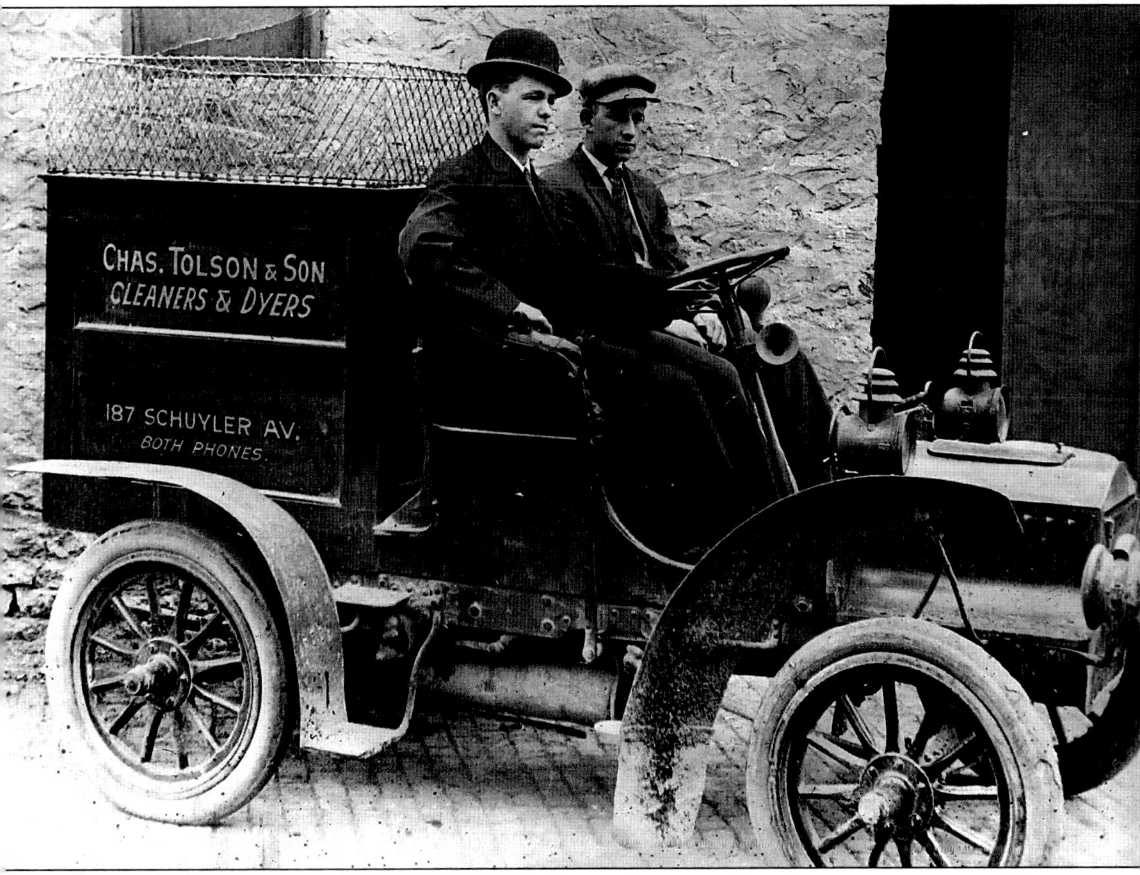

The automobile would soon be employed for commercial use as well as for private recreation. This photograph taken in 1912, shows the first automobile delivery truck operating in Kankakee. The 1904 one-cylinder Cadillac truck was owned by Charles Tolson and used to make deliveries for his cleaning establishment. The fellow wearing the derby is Charles Engel and his comrade in the cap is Herman Ramien. (Kankakee County Museum Photographic Collection, P3231.)

Opposite: The automobile would become an icon of American culture during the first quarter of the 20th century. The first gasoline fueled automobile sold to a private citizen was purchased on April 1, 1898. There were six privately owned automobiles in the City of Kankakee in 1902. The following year, in March 1903, Kankakee's auto pilots organized themselves into the Kankakee Auto Club. The first automobile was built in Kankakee in 1909 by the Worth Auto Company. These five early cars were photographed on East Court Street in 1910. Note the sign advertising "Edison phonographs and records," appearing just above the white roadster. (Kankakee County Museum Photographic Collection, P2618.)

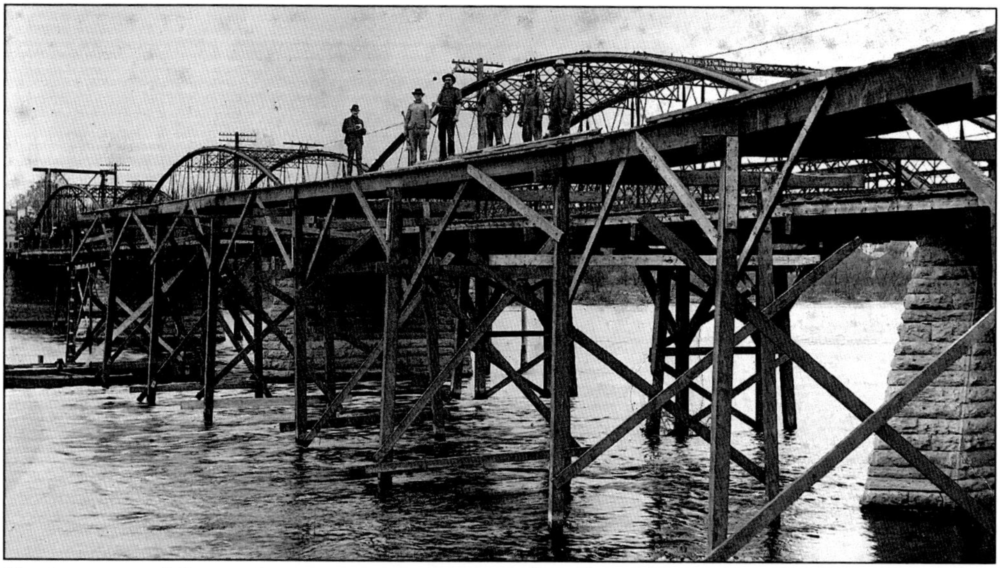

Having automobiles made it necessary to have roads to drive them on. By the late 19th century there were six railway bridges in Kankakee. A bridge for vehicles and pedestrians was built across the Kankakee River in 1874, but it had to be rebuilt after a flood in 1883 carried away two of the bridge's spans. This image shows high water at a second bridge over the Kankakee at Washington Avenue, *c.* 1890. (Kankakee County Museum Photographic Collection, P1179.)

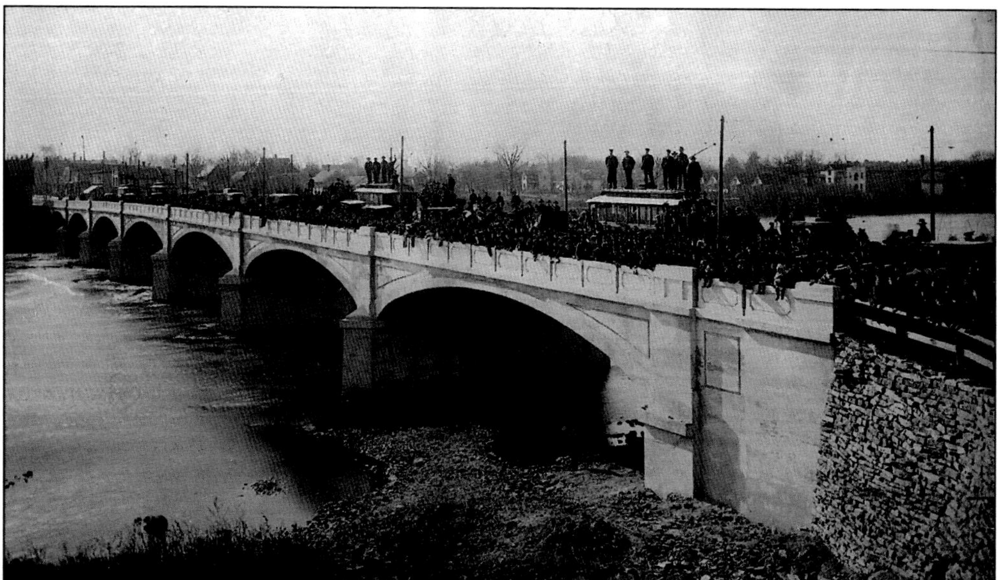

On April 15, 1904, work commenced on a new magnificent seven-span bridge over the Kankakee River at Washington Avenue. Constructed at a cost of $47,000, the bridge, meant for vehicular traffic, also had conduits built under the sidewalks for telephone and electric light wires, as well as lines from the city gas mains. The Washington Avenue Bridge was completed on October 15, 1904, and this photograph shows the crowd on the bridge during the dedication ceremonies held on November 14, 1904. Note the presence of four electric street cars on the bridge, along with several new-fangled automobiles. (Kankakee County Museum Photographic Collection, P1276.)

The airplane was a great symbol for the advance of the modern, characterized by the 20th century. On December 17, 1903, the Wright brothers made their first successful sustained controlled powered flight at Kill Devil Hill, near Kitty Hawk, North Carolina. Before long they had a competitor in the form of Glen Hammond Curtis, who by 1910 was selling his Curtis Pusher, which was shipped in crates and then assembled at home. Like the example in this photograph, showing Kankakee resident Art Smith sitting in the pilot's cage of his brand new Curtis in his Kankakee garage on September 5, 1910. (Kankakee County Museum Photographic Collection, P2595.)

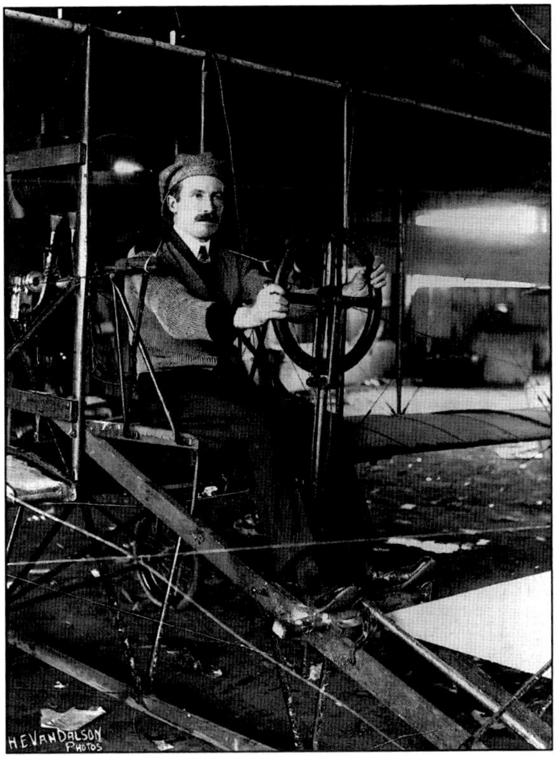

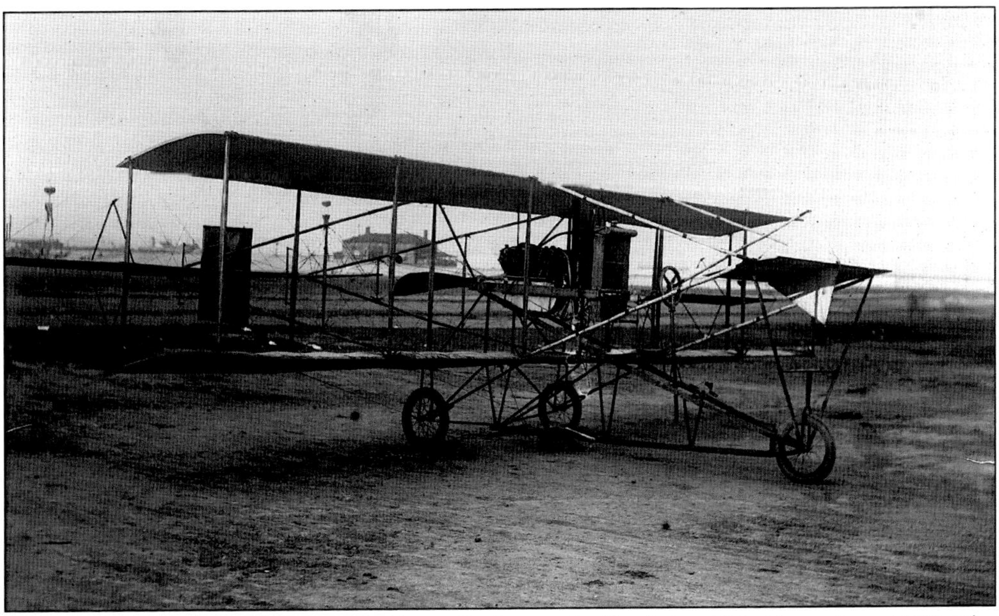

This photograph shows Art Smith's Curtis Pusher at the Kankakee Fair Grounds, c. 1910. The previous year, Glen Curtis had set the world speed record at Reims, France with a plane like this one, with the then astonishing air speed of 52.36 miles per hour. Curtis also held the record for the longest sustained flight, 141 miles from Albany, New York, to New York City. Powered flight was still a novelty that would have drawn crowds at the Kankakee Fair Grounds—aircrafts were indeed the future. (Kankakee County Museum Photographic Collection, P3569.)

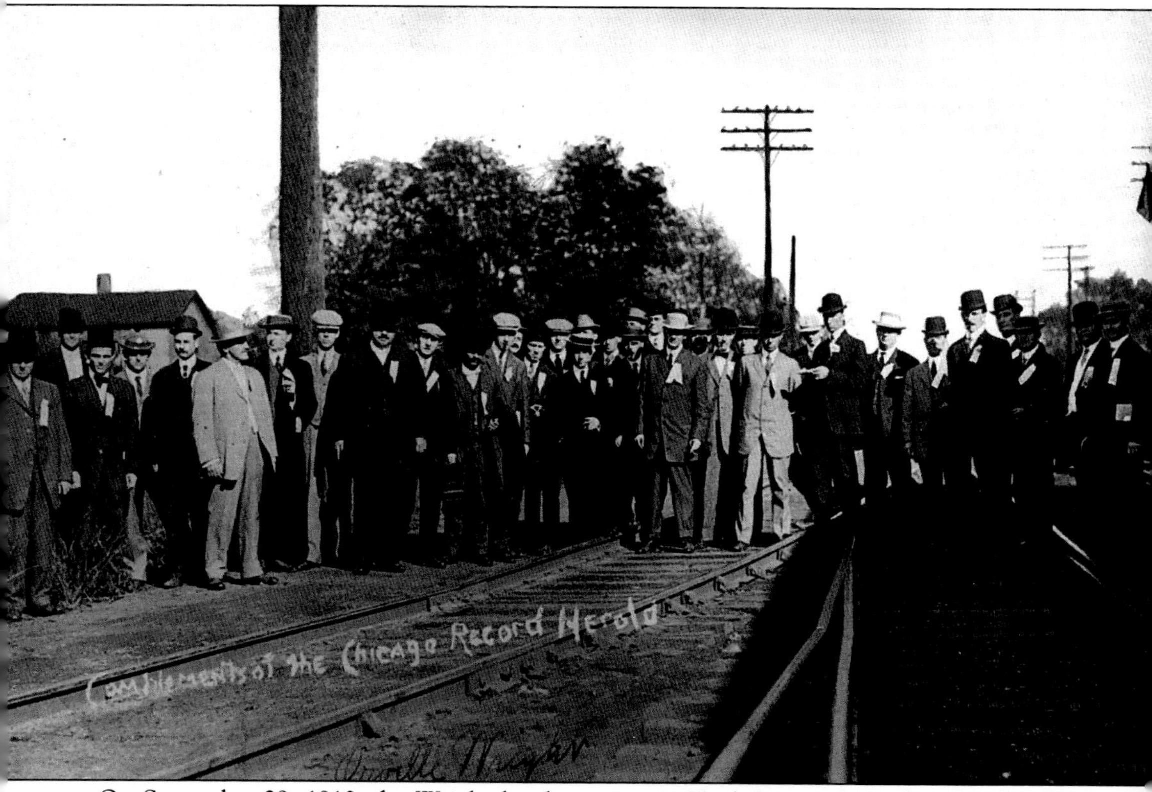

On September 29, 1910, the Wright brothers were in Kankakee, making their headquarters at the Kankakee Railroad Depot to monitor a race between one of their Flyers and the Illinois Central Railroad Daylight Special, running from Chicago to Springfield. The Wrights hoped to demonstrate the durability and practicality of their airplanes. The Flyer made Springfield in seven hours and twelve seconds, with two stops along the way, but Illinois Central's train won by 30 minutes. Wilbur Wright is the tall man wearing a derby, ninth from the right in the photograph and his brother Orville Wright appears 18th from the right with a check mark over his head. (Kankakee County Museum Photographic Collection, P5182.)

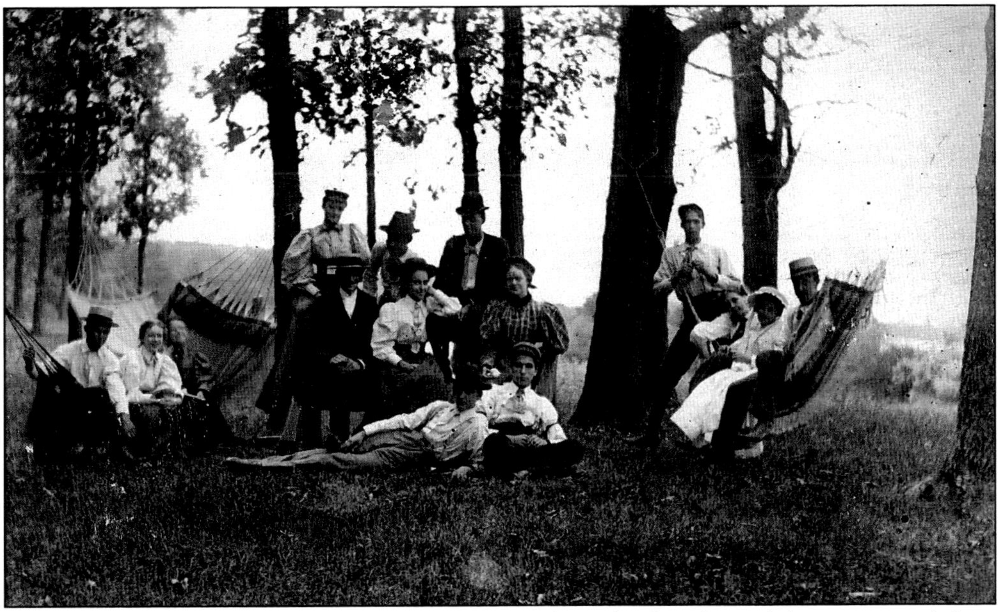

The City of Kankakee's citizens saw much change from the founding of the county and their community in the antebellum period, through the early beginnings of the 20th century. Several generations had passed and while life still flowed in the patterns common to most of them, as is illustrated in this image of a summer picnic party in Kankakee, c. 1890. Still, it was clear by 1900 that the character Kankakee was changing along with that of the nation, evolving amid ever greater mechanization and modernization. (Kankakee County Museum Photographic Collection, P8492.)

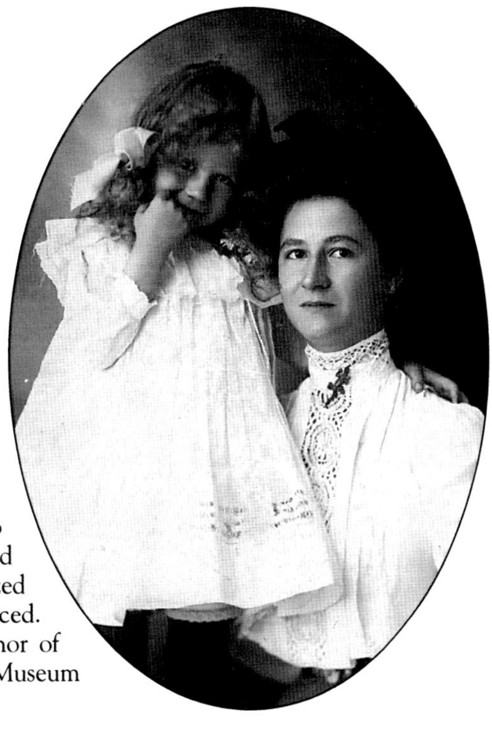

Kankakee's rich past would merge with the opportunities offered by the future. In this photograph, Claribel Nichols Small is shown with her adopted daughter, Sophroni, c. 1900. She had lost her two natural children in their infancy. Her husband Judge John Small was a prominent Kankakee lawyer and jurist, the son of Dr. Abram Lennington Small. Dr. Small came to Kankakee in 1850 to help fight a smallpox epidemic. Representing those who built Kankakee, Dr. Small had stayed to help mold his community. His son, Judge Small, symbolized equally well the future about to be embraced. His brother Len Small, would serve as governor of Illinois from 1921 to 1929. (Kankakee County Museum Photographic Collection, P5953.)

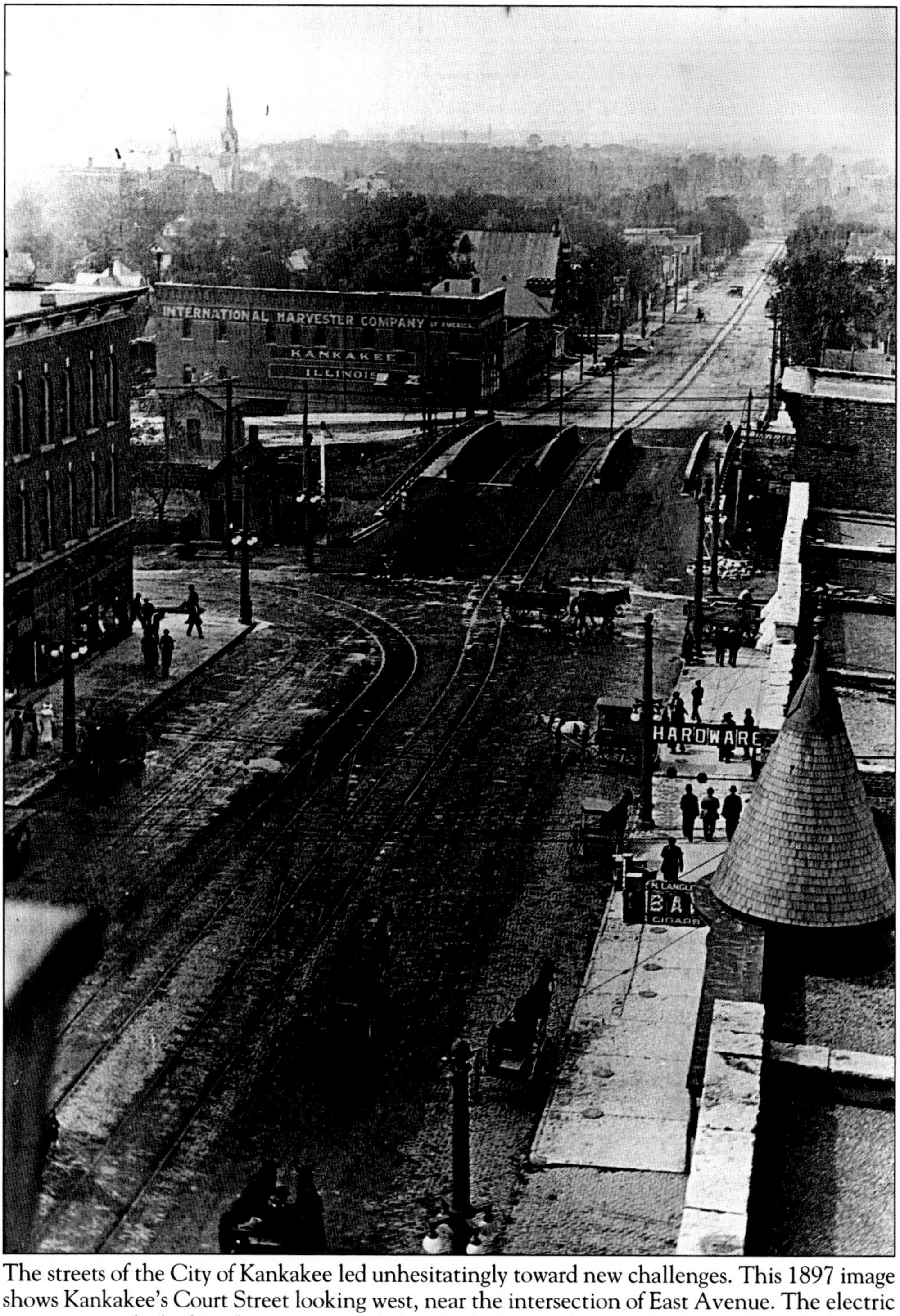

The streets of the City of Kankakee led unhesitatingly toward new challenges. This 1897 image shows Kankakee's Court Street looking west, near the intersection of East Avenue. The electric street car tracks laid in the street, coupled with the horse-drawn vehicles, well-symbolize the unity of Kankakee's rich past and promising future. (Kankakee County Museum Photographic Collection, P4031.)